85p

Greg Walters

D0061299

THE CAMBRIDGE BIBLE COMMENTARY

NEW ENGLISH BIBLE

GENERAL EDITORS
P. R. ACKROYD, A. R. C. LEANEY, J. W. PACKER

MATTHEW

THE
GOSPEL ACCORDING TO
MATTHEW

COMMENTARY BY

A. W. ARGYLE
Lecturer in Divinity, Regent's Park College, Oxford

CAMBRIDGE
AT THE UNIVERSITY PRESS
1963

PUBLISHED BY
THE SYNDICS OF THE CAMBRIDGE UNIVERSITY PRESS

Bentley House, 200 Euston Road, London, N.W.1
American Branch: 32 East 57th Street, New York 22, N.Y.
West African Office: P.O. Box 33, Ibadan, Nigeria

CAMBRIDGE UNIVERSITY PRESS

1963

Printed in the United States of America

CONTENTS

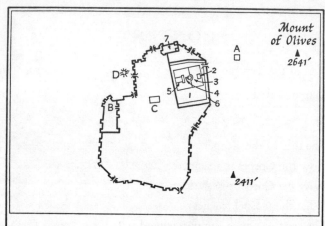

KEY

Jesus' arrest and trial

A Gethsemane
B Herod's Palace (the Praetorium)
C The Palace of the Hasmonaeans
D Calvary

0 ————————— 1 mile

⌐ Wall
)(Gateway

The Temple Area

1 The Court of the Gentiles
2 The Beautiful Gate
3 The Court of the Women
4 The Court of Israel (in the middle of which was the altar of sacrifice)
5 The Holy Place (enclosing the Holy of Holies)
6 Solomon's Portico
7 Antonia Fort

PLAN OF THE TEMPLE

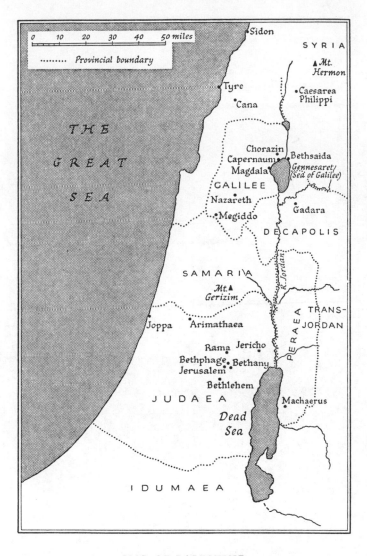

MAP OF PALESTINE

THE GOSPEL ACCORDING TO

MATTHEW

✳ ✳ ✳ ✳ ✳ ✳ ✳ ✳ ✳ ✳ ✳ ✳ ✳

THE TITLE OF THE GOSPEL

The titles of the books of the New Testament were not written by the authors themselves. This title is derived from Church lectionaries. In the oldest *codices* (i.e. manuscripts in book form) the four Gospels were bound together and called 'the Gospel', and the separate parts were headed 'according to Matthew', 'according to Mark' and so on. The English word 'Gospel' is the modern form of the Anglo-Saxon 'god-spell', which meant first 'good tidings' and afterwards 'God's story'. The Greek word *euangelion*, which it translates, meant originally 'a reward for good news', afterwards the 'good news' itself. This is the Christian usage, probably derived from Isaiah, especially 61: 1 ('The Spirit of the Lord God is upon me; because the Lord hath anointed me to preach good tidings unto the meek'), which, according to Luke 4: 18, was the prophetic reading for that Sabbath when Jesus preached in the synagogue at Nazareth. Matthew, Mark and Luke are known as the Synoptic Gospels, because they show marked similarity of viewpoint and treatment.

HOW THE GOSPEL IS ARRANGED

The Gospel according to Matthew was the one most highly regarded by the Fathers of the early Church, who quoted it or alluded to it more frequently than to any other. It is not the earliest Gospel. Mark's is earlier, and was extensively used both by Matthew, who reproduces ninety per cent of it, and by Luke who reproduces sixty per cent. The fact that Matthew

I

was placed first gave rise to the belief that it was the oldest Gospel, and that Mark's was an abridgement of it. This view is not held by any modern scholar outside the Roman Catholic Church. A comparison of parallel passages in Matthew and Mark shows that it is the former which abridges the latter. For instance, the healing of the paralytic is told by Mark in twelve verses (2: 1–12); in Matthew it occupies only eight (9: 1–8). The healing of the epileptic in Mark has sixteen verses (9: 14–29), in Matthew eight (17: 14–21).

But although Matthew was not the earliest Gospel, it has been in some ways the most influential. This is due to the full, clear and orderly way in which it describes events and records teaching. It begins with the genealogy and the nativity narratives (cc. 1 and 2). Then follow five clearly marked and well-defined sections, each consisting of events and of teaching relating to the events; and each ending with a formula which, literally translated, means: 'And it happened when Jesus had finished these sayings...' (7: 28; 11: 1; 13: 53; 19: 1; 26: 1). Possibly the author intentionally shaped his work like the 'Five Books of Moses' (the Pentateuch), Genesis, Exodus, Leviticus, Numbers, Deuteronomy, in the Old Testament.

The five sections, as outlined by B. W. Bacon (*Studies in Matthew*, 1930), are

3: 1 — 7: 29	Concerning Discipleship.
8: 1 — 11: 1	Concerning Apostleship.
11: 2 — 13: 53	Concerning the Hiding of the Revelation.
13: 54 — 19: 1 *a*	Concerning Church Administration.
19: 1 *b* — 26: 2	Concerning the Judgement.

Then follows the concluding climax: the Last Supper, the Arrest of Jesus, the Trial, the Crucifixion and the Resurrection (26: 3 — 28: 20).

From another point of view, however, a different pattern may be observed. Matthew used Mark's Gospel, and therefore largely reproduces his sequence of events and geographical outline. Thus we have in Matthew the following arrangement:

3: 1 — 4: 11	John the Baptist. The Baptism and Temptations of Jesus.
4: 12 — 13: 58	The Galilean Ministry.
14: 1 — 16: 28	Retirement from Galilee. Peter's confession. The first prediction of the Passion.
17: 1–27	The Transfiguration and its sequel.
18: 1–35	Teaching on humility, discipline and forgiveness.
19: 1 — 20: 34	The journey to Jerusalem.
21: 1 — 25: 46	The Ministry in Jerusalem.
26: 1 — 28: 20	The Passion and Resurrection.

The central point of the Gospel is the confession of Jesus' Messiahship by Peter at Caesarea Philippi (16: 13–20). Even in Mark this is clearly a turning-point; henceforth Jesus speaks openly to his disciples concerning his approaching suffering and death. But much more is made of this incident by Matthew, who adds a passage, found in this Gospel only, about Peter and the Church. Considerable prominence is given to Peter throughout the Gospel.

WHY THE GOSPEL WAS WRITTEN

The aim of the author is to show Jesus to be the Messiah of the Jews in fulfilment of Old Testament prophecy. He repeatedly stresses this fulfilment by quoting Old Testament passages, usually introducing each with some such words as 'this happened in order to fulfil what the Lord declared through a prophet'. These texts quoted to prove that Jesus was the foretold Messiah (and therefore called 'proof-texts') are to be found at 1: 23; 2: 6, 15, 18; 4: 15–16; 8: 17; 12: 18–21; 13: 35; 21: 4–5; 26: 56; 27: 9–10.

Jesus is further set forth as the proclaimer of the highest morality, the perfect Law. Hence much of his moral teaching is gathered together in the great collection of sayings called the Sermon on the Mount (5 — 7). As Moses received the old

Law on Mount Sinai, so Jesus delivers his perfect Law on the mount.

The author's outlook is essentially Jewish; his Gospel is designed to guide the thought and worship of a Jewish Christian Church on Palestinian or Syrian soil, possibly at Antioch. His interest in church affairs is illustrated by the fact that his is the only Gospel in which the Greek word *ecclesia*, 'church', 'congregation', occurs (16: 18; 18: 17). In the first passage he records the saying of Jesus: 'You are Peter, the Rock; and on this rock I will build my church'; in the second he records Jesus as teaching the disciples about discipline within the Church.

An interesting illustration of this concern with the Church is Matthew's treatment of the parable of the Lost Sheep. In Luke 15: 4-7 this parable is addressed by Jesus to the Pharisees and doctors of the law who had been criticizing him for eating with tax-gatherers and sinners. The story is there a defence of evangelism, the search for a lost sinner, and ends with the saying: 'there will be greater joy in heaven over one sinner who repents than over ninety-nine righteous people who do not need to repent'. But in Matt. 18: 12-14 the parable is addressed to the disciples, and its concern is with the restoration of the wanderer to the Church. The concluding saying is: 'It is not your heavenly Father's will that one of these little ones should be lost.'

The purpose of the Gospel, then, is to guide the life of the Church, and this in three respects: (*a*) worship; (*b*) discipline and ethical conduct; (*c*) missionary activity.

(*a*) Worship

This Gospel seems to be especially adapted for use in church worship. For instance, in the account of the Last Supper (Matt. 26: 26-9), whereas Mark (14: 22-5) gives the Lord's words about the bread as 'Take this; this is my body', Matthew has 'Take this and eat; this is my body'; and whereas, about the cup, Mark simply records 'They all drank of it',

Matthew represents Jesus as saying to his disciples 'Drink from it, all of you', thus changing the plain statement of fact into a 'rubric' (i.e. a direction for use) in a church communion service.

Matthew has moreover contrived to avoid doubts or questions which Mark's Gospel might arouse in a worshipper's mind. He makes it plain, for instance, that the baptism which Jesus received was not for him a baptism of personal repentance. Peter is praised for confessing Jesus to be the Messiah. Jesus does not say to the rich young man 'Why do you call me good?' (Mark 10: 18), but (literally translated) 'Why do you ask me about the good?' (Matt. 19: 17). It is made clear that the body of Jesus was not stolen from the tomb. The guards were bribed to spread that story (28: 12–15).

(b) *Discipline*

An important feature of the Gospel is its full and orderly presentation of moral instruction and regulations for church discipline. In the Sermon on the Mount there is clear teaching on such subjects as the ideal kind of Christian character, courtesy, reconciliation, sexual relationships, oaths, non-retaliation, love of enemies, avoidance of ostentation in alms-giving and prayer, and so on. Later there is instruction as to what is to be done if a member of the Christian Church wrongs another. If neither personal entreaty nor the judgement of the congregation can bring him to repentance, he is to be excommunicated (18: 15–17). The judgement of the community is ratified in heaven, for where the Church is gathered, there is Christ in the midst (18: 18–20). Nevertheless, if a man repents, there is to be unlimited mercy and forgiveness (18: 21–35).

In Matthew the moral teaching of Jesus is to some extent adapted to meet actual experience within the Church. For instance, our Lord's teaching on divorce according to Mark (10: 2–12), Luke (16: 18), and Paul (1 Cor. 7: 10–11) forbade absolutely both divorce and remarriage after divorce. For Matthew there is one condition on which divorce is permissible: in the case where the wife has been guilty of unchastity (5: 31–2; 19: 9). Here we see the beginning of the development of ecclesiastical law, based on the teaching of Jesus, but, under the guidance of the Holy Spirit, allowing for exceptions in hard cases.

(c) Missionary activity

Prominence is given in Matthew's Gospel to the missionary activity of the Church. In the great Mission charge to the Twelve in chapter 10, the Jews are given priority in the receiving of the Gospel message. 'Do not take the road to Gentile lands, and do not enter any Samaritan town; but go rather to the lost sheep of the house of Israel' (10: 5); 'before you have gone through all the towns of Israel the Son of Man will have come' (10: 23). But although there is much in Matthew which is Judaistic in interest and anti-Gentile in tone, the importance of the world-wide mission receives grand emphasis both at the opening and at the close of the Gospel. Nearer the beginning (2: 1–12), the first who come to the newly born Messiah are the Gentile astrologers. In the concluding verses Jesus bids his disciples: 'Go forth therefore and make all nations my disciples' (28: 19).

This discussion of the purpose of the Gospel naturally leads on to a consideration of its teaching about Jesus and the message which he proclaimed.

WHAT THE GOSPEL TEACHES

1. *Jesus, human and divine*

Jesus was manifestly a real human being. He was tempted, he hungered, he prayed, he confessed ignorance concerning some matters, on the cross he cried: 'My God, my God, why hast thou forsaken me?' Yet he was also divine. His birth was supernatural. He claimed a unique and intimate relationship with his Father and the divine right of the forgiveness of sins. He set his own authority above that of the Old Testament. He performed miracles of healing, and raised the dead, and bestowed the power to do the same upon his disciples. Other miracles which he performed were nature miracles: the stilling of the storm, feeding the multitudes, walking on the water. The centurion and his men at the cross declared, 'Truly this man was a son of God'. Indeed, Jesus was the Son of God in a unique and divine sense.

2. *Jesus the Messiah*

The word 'Messiah' is derived from the Hebrew *māshīach*, which means 'anointed one'. The Greek *Christos* and English 'Christ' have the same sense, 'anointed'. In the Old Testament the term 'messiah' was applied to Israel as the elect people (Hab. 3: 13), chosen by God to fulfil his purpose; and to the king (2 Sam. 1: 14). But gradually it came to denote particularly an ideal king, a descendant of David, who would come to deliver Israel and reign in righteousness (e.g. Zech. 9: 9–10). Jesus is set forth as this promised Messiah. He was born at Bethlehem, the city of David (2: 1, cf. Mic. 5: 2). Peter confessed him to be the Messiah, the Son of the living God (16: 16). The crowd acclaimed him Messiah by calling him 'Son of David' at his triumphal entry into Jerusalem (21: 9).

'Son of God' was in fact a messianic title. While Jesus was the Son of God in a deeper divine sense, he was also Son of God because he was the Messiah. Both at his Baptism and at his Transfiguration, the Divine Voice proclaimed 'this is my son' (3: 17; 17: 5). The reference is probably to Ps. 2: 7 ('Thou art my son'), and to be God's son meant being the Messiah. Jesus himself claimed Messiahship when, in fulfilment of the prophecy in Zech. 9: 9–10 he rode in triumph into Jerusalem (21: 1–9), and when challenged by the High Priest (26: 63–4, cf. Mark 14: 61–2).

But Jesus made no open claim to Messiahship in the earlier period of his ministry. He commanded his disciples (16: 20) and some whom he healed to be silent about it (e.g. 8: 4; miracles of healing were one of the expected signs of the

7

coming Messiah). The reason for these commands to keep the matter secret is probably that Jesus' conception of Messiahship was very different from that of popular expectation. The people looked for a political and military Messiah who would over-throw the Roman domination and establish an earthly king-dom. But Jesus came to seek and save lost sinners, to serve men in their need, and to establish a spiritual, heavenly kingdom.

3. *Jesus, the Son of Man*

The title that Jesus persistently and openly claimed was 'Son of Man'. It occurs only on the lips of Jesus himself in the Gospels. It is an extremely difficult title to interpret. Behind the phrase lies the Aramaic *bar nasha* which means simply 'man', but which could also be used as a special title. In the Old Testament 'son of man' (Hebrew: *ben adam*) is often a poetical synonym for man, e.g. Ps. 8: 4

> What is man that thou art mindful of him?
> And the son of man that thou visitest him?

In Ezekiel, where it occurs more than ninety times, the phrase describes the prophet himself as the lowly, insignificant person whom God nevertheless condescends to address. Some scholars believe that Jesus took the title from the book of Ezekiel. But it is more likely that he derived it from the book of Daniel (7: 13-14). This chapter describes Daniel's vision of the four beasts, and then adds: 'I saw in the night visions, and, behold, there came with the clouds of heaven one like unto a son of man, and he came even to the ancient of days, and they brought him near before him. And there was given him dominion, and glory, and a kingdom....' The interpretation explains that the four beasts signify four kings, the heads of four empires. The 'one like unto a son of man' represents 'the saints of the Most High', that is, the people of God. Thus, in the book of Daniel (written about 165 B.C. in the time of the Maccabaean revolt against Antiochus Epiphanes) the 'one like unto a son of man' represents the community of the faithful.

The book of Daniel is the only one which Jesus actually alludes to when speaking of himself as the Son of Man (Matt. 24: 30, cf. Mark 13: 26; Matt. 26: 64, cf. Mark 14: 62). It is reasonable therefore to infer that it was the book of Daniel that he had in mind when he used the title. The title occurs also in a messianic sense in a work called *The Similitudes of Enoch*, but it is doubtful whether this was pre-christian. T. W. Manson believed that Jesus used the title at first in the community sense which we find in Daniel, and meant by it not only himself, but also the community of his disciples. But Jesus seems always to use it to mean himself. For instance, in Matt. 9: 6, Mark 2: 10 ('the Son of Man has the right on earth to forgive sins'), he is claiming for himself the divine authority to forgive sins. In Matt. 12: 8, Mark 2: 28 ('the Son of Man is sovereign over the Sabbath'), he again appears to mean himself. Jesus uses the term again in the predictions of his suffering and cross, where it clearly means himself.

Yet there is an element of truth in Manson's contention. Jesus seems in all the above instances to associate his disciples with himself. Although only God and Jesus can forgive sins in an absolute sense, Jesus teaches his disciples that they must forgive one another (Matt. 6: 14–15; 18: 21–2). When Jesus declared the Son of Man to be sovereign over the Sabbath, it was his disciples' action in plucking corn on the Sabbath that he was defending. Jesus not only predicted his own sufferings as Son of Man, he also taught that if a man would be his disciple, he must suffer and take up his cross (Matt. 16: 24; Mark 8: 34). Nevertheless, the direct reference of the title Son of Man is to Jesus himself.

Jesus uses the title in three ways: (1) to refer to himself as he is at the time of speaking, e.g. 8: 20; (2) to predict his coming Passion, e.g. 17: 12; (3) to predict his coming in glory and triumph and judgement, e.g. 16: 28. This coming (Greek *parousia*) would bring to an end 'this present evil age' and establish the kingdom of God completely.

4. The kingdom of Heaven

(a) Jewish background

The central theme of the preaching and teaching of Jesus was 'the kingdom of God', or, as Matthew prefers to say 'the kingdom of Heaven'. 'Heaven' in this phrase is a reverent synonym for God, in accordance with the Jewish habit of not mentioning God directly. The Greek word for 'kingdom' is *basileia* which is used in the Gospels as a translation of the Hebrew *malkūth* (Aramaic *malkūtha*) meaning 'sovereignty', 'kingly rule'. It does not denote a territory, though it does of course imply a community of subjects over whom God reigns.

From the Old Testament the Jews of Jesus' time derived a threefold conception of the kingdom of God.

(1) *It is eternal*: e.g. Ps. 145: 13

Thy kingdom is an everlasting kingdom,
And thy dominion endureth throughout all generations.

and universal: e.g. Ps. 103: 19

The Lord hath established his throne in the heavens;
And his kingdom ruleth over all.

(2) *It is, however, only partially recognized on earth.* Since God reigns eternally and universally, he is by right king of the whole world, but much of the world does not recognize nor obey his sovereignty; so that his kingdom is not yet realized in fact. Israel is the special people of God, and among them his rule is realized in so far as they obey his commandments revealed in the Law. According to the rabbis, if a man daily recites Deut. 6: 4, 'Hear, O Israel, the Lord our God is one Lord', known as the *Shema* ('hear'), he is said to 'take upon himself the yoke of the divine sovereignty'.

(3) *Its full consummation is in the future.* While the Jews believed that God was already king *by right*, they acknowledged that his reign was not yet universal *in fact*. The full consummation of the kingdom lay in the future. It would be established at the end of this present evil age and usher in the blessed

messianic age to come. This conception of the kingdom is called 'eschatological', meaning 'relating to the last age' (from the Greek *eschatos*, 'last'). The unknown writer of Isa. 40 — 55 looked forward to this future kingdom: 'How beautiful upon the mountains are the feet of him that bringeth good tidings, that publisheth peace, that bringeth good tidings of good, that publisheth salvation; that saith unto Zion, "Thy God reigneth!"' (52: 7).

(b) *The teaching of Jesus*

Jesus' preaching of the Gospel began, according to Mark 1: 15, with the pronouncement: 'The time has come; the kingdom of God is upon you; repent, and believe the Gospel.' That is, 'the season foretold by the prophets has been fulfilled; the kingdom of God has drawn near; repent and believe the good tidings'. Matthew's version (4: 17) is 'Repent; for the kingdom of Heaven is upon you'. According to Matt. 3: 2, John the Baptist had proclaimed the same message. It is disputed by scholars whether the Greek word translated 'is upon you' (lit. 'has drawn near') means 'is approaching and will soon be here' or 'has arrived and is here'. From another saying it seems clear that Jesus did teach that the kingdom had already arrived: 'If it is by the Spirit of God that I drive out the devils, then be sure the kingdom of God has already come upon you' (Matt. 12: 28; Luke 11: 20). Not only did Jesus himself preach the arrival of the kingdom: he taught his disciples to do the same (Matt. 10: 7; Luke 10: 9).

The kingdom of God was also the kingdom of Christ (Matt. 16: 28; John 18: 36). Indeed in the person of Jesus the kingdom is manifested; for in him the divine rule was perfectly obeyed. To identify oneself with Christ by becoming his disciple is to enter the kingdom and receive eternal life (Mark 10: 17–31; Matt. 19: 16–30). The connexion between being a subject of God's reign and enjoying eternal life (i.e. full, abundant and everlasting life, the life of the blessed messianic age) is so close that in the Fourth Gospel the phrase 'eternal life' is virtually substituted for the kingdom, which is alluded to in only two passages (John 3: 3; 18: 36).

Whereas from one point of view the kingdom had already broken into the world with the coming of Christ, from another point of view its complete fulfilment was still in the future. It was expected to come with power at the end of history with Christ's final coming. The early Church expected this to happen in the near future. Indeed Jesus is represented as predicting that it would happen in the lifetime of some of his disciples: 'I tell you this: there are some standing here who will not taste death before they have seen the Son of Man coming in his kingdom' (Matt. 16: 28). The technical term which Matthew alone of the Gospels uses for this final coming of the Son of Man is *parousia*, 'coming', 'arrival' (Matt. 24: 3, 27, 37, 39).

Much of the teaching of Jesus about the kingdom is given in parables. A parable is a word-picture or story designed to illustrate a single point. In Matthew ten parables are introduced with the formula: 'the kingdom of Heaven is like': 13: 25 (the darnel), 31 (the mustard-seed), 33 (yeast), 44 (treasure), 45 (the pearl of very special value), 47 (the drag-net), 18: 23 (the unmerciful servant), 20: 1 (the labourers in the vineyard), 22: 2 (the wedding-feast), 25: 1 (the ten girls). Other parables of the kingdom are 'the sower' (13: 4), 'a man going abroad' (25: 14), 'the last judgement' (25: 31).

The most probable explanation of the parables in chapter 13 is that the kingdom is a present reality which is sure finally to reach its full consummation. In some parables, especially those in chapter 25, the emphasis seems to lie chiefly upon the coming *parousia* and the future judgement.

THE SOURCES WHICH THE WRITER USED

(1) The principal source used by our author was the Gospel according to Mark, which was also used by Luke. Ninety per cent of the subject-matter of Mark is reproduced in Matthew in language very largely identical with that of Mark. Luke

reproduces more than half of Mark. Where either Matthew or Luke departs from Mark's order, the other keeps to it.

Both Matthew and Luke improve the roughness of Mark's Greek style, replacing his present tenses in narration by past tenses, omitting many of his uses of 'immediately' (a word which Mark uses forty-two times), substituting classical words for rough words used in conversation, and removing phrases likely to cause offence. For instance, in his account of Jesus' ministry at Capernaum Mark writes: 'IIe could work no miracle there, except that he put his hands on a few sick people and healed them; and he was taken aback by their want of faith.' Matthew 13: 58 has 'And he did not work many miracles there: such was their want of faith.' Mark suggests that Jesus *could not* work miracles there, Matthew that he *chose* not to do so because of their lack of faith. Luke omits it altogether. In Mark 10: 18 Jesus says to the questioner: 'Why do you call me good? No one is good except God alone.' Matthew 19: 17 has: 'Good?' said Jesus. 'Why do you ask me about that? One alone is good.' Both Matthew and Luke omit Mark's references to Jesus' embracing little children (Mark 9: 36; 10: 16). Matthew softens Jesus' rebuke of the disciples in the storm on the lake. Mark 4: 40 has 'Have you no faith even now?' Matthew 8: 26 has 'How little faith you have', and alters the rude cry of the disciples 'Master, we are sinking. Do you not care?' (Mark 4: 38) to 'Save us, Lord; we are sinking'.

Both Matthew and Luke abridge many sections of Mark (cf. p. 2) in order to make room on their scrolls for their other material. (The Gospels were originally written on papyrus scrolls, perhaps about 30 feet long.) Matthew and Luke also reduce Mark's duplicate expressions: for instance Mark (1: 32) writes 'that evening after sunset'. Matthew (8: 16) has simply: 'when evening fell', Luke (4: 40) 'at sunset'.

(2) In addition to their Marcan material both Matthew and Luke have other matter in common, some of it in identical or largely identical Greek words, the rest in different Greek

words. Of this non-Marcan matter common to Matthew and Luke there are three possible explanations: (*a*) use of Luke by Matthew; (*b*) use of Matthew by Luke; (*c*) use by Matthew and Luke of a common source, which scholars call Q, possibly because this is the first letter of the German *Quelle*, 'source'.

(*a*) The first explanation has found little support.

(*b*) The second is upheld by some modern scholars.

(*c*) Most scholars adopt the third explanation, that Matthew and Luke used a common source other than Mark. This is known as 'the Q hypothesis'. Where the Greek of Matthew and Luke in the Q passages is identical, or virtually so, the source must have been a Greek document. Where the Greek of the two Gospels is very different, though the subject-matter is similar, we must suppose that either the one author or the other or both have rewritten the source. Some scholars suppose that variant translations of the Aramaic tradition may account for some of the differences. No two reconstructions of Q agree entirely, but all the champions of the Q hypothesis agree that it contained no Passion narrative. This is a damaging admission. The Passion was the principal part of the Gospel, and it is difficult to imagine anyone in the early days of the Church constructing a document without a Passion narrative. Most scholars, however, prefer to adhere to the Q hypothesis rather than adopt either of the alternative explanations. The two Gospels seem so independent of one another in so many respects (e.g. the nativity narratives and the accounts of the Resurrection appearances) that it is difficult to believe that the one was in any way dependent upon the other. Nevertheless the Q hypothesis is very far from having been proved.

(3) In addition to the Marcan and the non-Marcan matter which he has in common with Luke, there is much that is found only in Matthew. This consists roughly of 221 verses. It is not all material of the same kind, but is made up of several distinct strands.

(*a*) *Narrative*: nativity stories; stories about Peter; Passion and Resurrection stories; also miscellaneous narratives.

14

(*b*) *Discourses*, some with a Judaistic bias, some with an anti-Pharisaic strain, some urging restriction of the mission to Jews, some advocating extension of the mission to Gentiles.

(*c*) *Quotations from the Old Testament*, often introduced with the formula to stress fulfilment (see above p. 3).

(*d*) *Editorial matter*. The evangelists were not mere 'scissors and paste' compilers; they could write introductory or interpretative sentences of their own. For instance, Matthew introduces a summary statement at 4: 23, 'He went round the whole of Galilee, teaching in the synagogues, preaching the Gospel of the Kingdom, and curing whatever illness or infirmity there was among the people'; and a very similar one at 9: 35.

BEFORE THE WRITTEN GOSPELS

Behind the literary sources lies oral tradition. The Gospel was originally proclaimed by word of mouth in the preaching and missionary activity of the early Church. When proclaiming the essence of the Gospel (Greek *kerygma*), preachers stressed the fulfilment of Old Testament prophecy in the death, burial and resurrection of Jesus Christ (e.g. Paul emphasizes 'in accordance with the scriptures' in 1 Cor. 15: 1–6). Hence the large amount of space devoted in the Gospels to the Passion and Crucifixion of Jesus, and the events immediately leading up to them. As converts were made and churches founded, there was an additional need for teaching (Greek *didachē*) to guide the life and conduct of the new communities.

Both the preaching and the teaching in the early Church played a decisive part in shaping the oral tradition which eventually came to be written down.

WHO WROTE THE GOSPEL?

Our knowledge that the Gospel according to Mark is one of the sources of this Gospel helps us in considering the problems of the authorship of the Gospel.

The words 'according to Matthew' which we find in the heading of the Gospel were not written by the author, but became its title by the middle of the second century A.D. The work itself is anonymous. It cannot have been written by the apostle Matthew, because it is based upon the Gospel of Mark. An apostle would not have needed to depend upon the writing of one who was not an apostle.

How did this work come to be ascribed to Matthew? In cases where the author of a Gospel was unknown, it was natural for his book to be attributed to an apostle. The fact that this Gospel substitutes the name Matthew (9: 9) for that of Levi in Mark 2: 14 may have suggested this ascription of authorship. Or does the Gospel at least incorporate work by Matthew?

Papias, bishop of Hierapolis, who wrote about A.D. 130, states: 'Matthew composed the *logia* in the Hebrew [i.e. probably Aramaic] language, and each person interpreted them as he was able.' What did Papias mean by the *logia*? It is a Greek word meaning 'oracles'. Some scholars have suggested that he referred to the 'proof-texts' from the Old Testament which are introduced in the Gospel by the formula 'that it might be fulfilled' or the like. These do seem to have been translated from Aramaic, for they correspond neither to the Hebrew nor to the Greek Old Testament (Septuagint, LXX) exactly, but are probably based on Aramaic Targums, that is, paraphrase translations of the Old Testament books for use in the synagogues. (In other places the writer sometimes follows the Hebrew, sometimes the LXX.) Others have suggested that Papias meant the document known as Q. But it is impossible to be sure what Papias meant or even whether his information is reliable. The fourth-century historian Eusebius, who records Papias' statement, says that Papias was of very limited intelligence.

Whoever the author of Matthew was, he wrote for a church of Jewish Christians probably at Syrian Antioch. He must have been a Jewish Christian, for he uses Jewish phrases like 'kingdom of heaven', and the tone of his Gospel is Judaistic and, at times, anti-Gentile. As we have seen, he is interested in setting Jesus forth as the Jewish Messiah, the fulfilment of the Jewish scriptures, a greater Moses bringing forth the perfect Law. Jesus is the true Rabbi, the true Teacher, and no one else is worthy of the name (Matt. 23: 8–10). This reflects a time when the Christian Church which had at first thought of itself as part of the historical Israel, or as privileged to be joined to it, began to claim to be the true Israel or people of God by itself. It now believed that Israel (or the Jews) in the historical sense had ceased to be God's people by rejecting his Messiah.

WHEN DID HE WRITE?

The date of the Gospel must be later than that of Mark, which it uses. Mark's Gospel is usually dated shortly after the outbreak of the Neronian persecution in A.D. 64, say about A.D. 65–7. According to the tradition of Irenaeus and most of the ancient writers, it was composed after the deaths of Peter and Paul in Rome, where Mark was a companion of Peter (1 Peter 5: 13). We have to allow time for Mark's Gospel to acquire authority, to be copied, to reach Palestine and Syria, and to be digested by the author of Matthew. This could hardly have been accomplished until after A.D. 70, the date of the fall of Jerusalem, which is clearly presupposed in Matt. 22: 7, 'The king was furious; he sent troops to kill those murderers and set their town on fire'. We must remember also Matthew's interest in church order, which reflects a time when the Christian Church had developed a separate organization and order of worship. Matthew seems to follow the rabbinical method of codifying church law as a practical guide. We conclude that the Gospel was written towards the end of the first century, probably not earlier than A.D. 80.

THE TIMES IN WHICH JESUS LIVED

At this time Palestine was firmly under the domination of Rome. It was divided into three parts: (1) Samaria, Judaea, and Idumaea constituted the province of Judaea, governed by a Roman official called a procurator, resident in the land, with headquarters at Caesarea. The procurator from A.D. 26 to 36 was Pontius Pilate, an unprincipled and ruthless governor. (2) Galilee, and a strip of land east of the River Jordan known as Peraea, constituted the tetrarchy (the fourth part of a province) of Antipas, a son of Herod the Great. (3) The district to the north and east of the Sea of Galilee constituted the tetrarchy of Philip, another of Herod's sons. Over all these districts Rome was ruler, though the control differed somewhat in the three sections, and Rome always showed marked deference to the Jewish religion and to local customs. (See map, p. ix.)

Space will not permit us to follow the history further, except to say that discontent with the rule of Rome among the Zealot party (see p. 20) eventually led to the rebellion which ended in the destruction of Jerusalem prophesied by Jesus (Mark 13: 2, cf. Matt. 24: 2; Matt. 22: 7; Luke 21: 20). In A.D. 70 Titus entered Jerusalem. The temple and the city itself were burned. Many thousands were taken prisoner and afterwards sold into slavery. Only a remnant of the Jews remained in Palestine.

The Pharisees

These were the religious leaders of Israel, strict observers of the Mosaic law, to which they had made additions derived from the traditions of their forefathers. They exalted the letter of the law, and especially their oral traditions, above the claims of mercy and love. The best of them, however, were not hypocrites, but sincerely pious. The genuine Pharisee hated hypocrisy. 'Whatever good a man does, he should do it for the glory of God', was one of their sayings. The opposition of the Pharisees to Jesus and his disciples was bitter and coupled with that of the Sadducees eventually led to the Crucifixion.

The Scribes

These were the lawyers, teachers and exponents of the law, whose business it was to hand on and define by fresh decisions the legal tradition. Their decisions in particular cases themselves became law. There were Scribes who were not Pharisees, and whose decisions the Pharisees rejected; but in the main the Scribes were themselves Pharisees, whose decisions the Pharisaic party accepted as binding.

The Sadducees

This name is derived either from a Hebrew word meaning 'righteous' or from the proper name 'Zadok' ('Sons of Zadok'). Zadok was a priest in the reign of King David. They were comparatively few in number. Connected with the best priestly families (Acts 5: 17), their aims were political rather than religious. They were aristocrats whose following included only the wealthy. They were sympathetic to Greek thought and despised the legalism of the patriotic Pharisees and their ardent hopes of deliverance from foreign rule. They adhered to the Mosaic law, but rejected the legal tradition which the Pharisees had added to it. They frowned upon apocalyptic literature and eschatological expectations, and denied that there was any resurrection (Acts 23: 8). They were more responsible than any other group for the Crucifixion of Jesus.

The Qumran Community

Among hundreds of scrolls found in the caves of Qumran in 1947 and since then, some have proved invaluable in throwing light upon the background of the origins of Christianity.

These Dead Sea Scrolls contain the scriptures of a sect which flourished in the ravine of Qumran and the vicinity at the north-west end of the Dead Sea, probably during the first two centuries B.C. and the first century A.D. The flight of the community from Qumran probably took place by A.D. 68 and the date of the flight was probably also the date when the scrolls were deposited in the caves where they were found. The sect seems to have been very like the Essenes who are known to have dwelt in the locality.

According to most authorities the Qumran Sect expected three deliverers: a prophet like Moses (cf. Deut. 18: 18) and two Messiahs, one a high priest, the other a king. See further *The Scriptures of the Dead Sea Sect*, translated by G. Vermes (Penguin Books, 1962) and *From Judaean Caves* by Robert Leaney (1961).

The Zealots

The Zealots, or Cananaeans, were the revolutionary political party, whose activities frequently issued in open rioting. One of the twelve disciples, named Simon, was a Zealot (Matt. 10:4; Mark 3:18). Judas, the Galilean, sometimes called Judas the Gaulonite of Gamala, who opposed the census of A.D. 6, indeed founded a religious sect sworn to 'invincible liberty and to God as their only leader and Lord' (Josephus, *Antiquities*, XVIII, 1, 6). Their rebellion failed, as Gamaliel reminds the Council in Acts 5: 37. A violent group of Zealots, called *Sicarii* (assassins), arose after the middle of the century, and they held out for three years after the fall of Jerusalem in A.D. 70 (cf. Acts 21: 38).

The Samaritans

These were the members of a religious community found in the central part of the country—Samaria—where Mount Gerizim by Shechem was their sacred place. The exact origin of this religious group is obscure, and the indications in the Old and New Testaments present a picture which is clearly in part governed by Jewish opposition to a community whose religious ancestry was the same as their own and who claimed greater antiquity.

The point in history at which a sharp division appeared between Jews and Samaritans cannot be stated exactly. Nehemiah had to face difficulties from Sanballat, the Governor of Samaria; but it appears clear that the difficulties were not of a religious kind. The writer of the books of Chronicles, Ezra and Nehemiah seems to be aware of a division which he never-theless would like to see healed. A separate temple on Mount Gerizim probably dates from the time of Alexander the Great, but there is evidence of later contacts between Jews and Samaritans, and this suggests that a complete hardening of the breach did not come until a later date. Anti-Samaritan military action by John Hyrcanus in the latter half of the second century B.C. may well have aggravated this.

In the Old Testament a number of passages (e.g. 2 Kings 17: 34; Ezra 4: 1–3) have been interpreted as anti-Samaritan propaganda, suggesting that the Samaritans were really of alien origin. But there is little internal evidence in the life and theology of the Samaritan community to suggest that this is so—at any rate, if there was foreign blood, there was accept-ance of the full obligations of Israelite religion (cf. 2 Kings 17: 28; Ezra 4: 2). They accepted the five Books of Moses as the authoritative Scripture.

In the time of Herod, the Samaritans generally sided with the enemies of the Jews. When the country passed into the hands of the Romans, Samaria was rebuilt and beautified by Herod, whose wife Malthace was a Samaritan, and was named by him Sebastē, the Greek equivalent of *Augusta*, in honour of Augustus Caesar. Herod made the city the capital of the whole district which was also called Samaria.

The dogmas which the Samaritans held were as follows:

(1) *The unity of God.* They offered prayers to him through the merits of the patriarchs and Moses.

(2) *Moses as his only prophet.* Hence they rejected all the Jewish books except the Pentateuch.

(3) *Mount Gerizim as the house of God*, the true place of worship.

(4) *The Messiah doctrine.* They expected the Messiah, whom they called *Taheb* ('restorer' or 'he who returns', the exact meaning is uncertain) to come and establish the true religion, destroy its foes, live 110 years on earth and then die.

(5) *The Resurrection.* They believed that this would take place after the death of the Messiah, and would be accompanied by the final judgement, when the righteous would go into the Garden of Eden and the wicked be burned with fire.

The Synagogue

The origin of the synagogue, in which the congregation gathered to worship, is uncertain. By the time of Jesus synagogues were to be found throughout the ancient world, wherever Jews had settled.

Of the synagogues of Palestine, the Gospels name Nazareth (Matt. 13: 54; Mark 6: 2; Luke 4: 16) and Capernaum (Mark 1: 21; Luke 7: 5; John 6: 59) as those in which Jesus taught. For the holding of public worship in the synagogue the presence of at least ten adult males was required. Women were not counted as members of the synagogue congregation. Yet even a woman could take part in the reading of the Sabbath lesson. Women were zealous attenders of the synagogue, and in the Dispersion they played an important part in synagogue life. Paul found in the 'place of prayer' at Philippi a gathering of women (Acts 16: 13).

The 'president of the synagogue' was responsible for maintaining order there (see Luke 13: 14). It was his task to decide who was to conduct public worship (Acts 13: 15). If he himself wished to take part in the reading of the Scriptures, he had to be invited by others to do so.

The reading from the Scriptures by members of the congregation was a principal part of synagogue worship. Passages first from the Pentateuch, then from the prophets, would be read. The one who read from the prophets might also lead in prayer. If he were competent to do so, he might preach a sermon which was an exposition of the lesson, as Jesus did in Nazareth (Luke 4: 20 f.). In the synagogue at Pisidian Antioch, after the readings from the Law and the prophets, Paul responded to an invitation to deliver an address of exhortation (Acts 13: 15–16).

Proselyte Baptism

According to the teaching of later Judaism, a Gentile who was converted to the Jewish religion was required to be circumcised and baptized and then offer a sacrifice. The baptism was by immersion and signified purification or consecration. In the case of women, baptism and sacrifice only were required; but for both male and female proselytes sacrifice was abolished after the destruction of the temple.

The baptism of the proselyte had for its purpose his cleansing from the impurity of idolatry and the restoration of the purity of a new-born man. Like John's baptism, it was one of repentance. John's baptism, however, differed from proselyte baptism in two respects: (1) it was administered to Jews; (2) John prophesied that the one who would come after him would baptize not with water, but with the Holy Spirit and with fire. The Essenes and the Qumran community also practised baptism; but for them it was a repeatable act; proselyte baptism, like that of John the Baptist and of the Christians, is once for all, unique and unrepeatable.

✻   ✻   ✻   ✻   ✻   ✻   ✻   ✻   ✻   ✻   ✻   ✻   ✻

The Coming of Christ

THE TABLE OF DESCENT

A TABLE of the descent of Jesus Christ, son of David, **1** son of Abraham.

Abraham was the father of Isaac, Isaac of Jacob, Jacob **2** of Judah and his brothers, Judah of Perez and Zarah (their **3** mother was Tamar), Perez of Hezron, Hezron of Ram, Ram of Amminadab, Amminadab of Nahshon, Nahshon **4** of Salma, Salma of Boaz (his mother was Rahab), Boaz

6 of Obed (his mother was Ruth), Obed of Jesse; and Jesse
was the father of King David.

    David was the father of Solomon (his mother had been
7 the wife of Uriah), Solomon of Rehoboam, Rehoboam of
8 Abijah, Abijah of Asa, Asa of Jehoshaphat, Jehoshaphat of
9 Joram, Joram of Azariah, Azariah of Jotham, Jotham of
10 Ahaz, Ahaz of Hezekiah, Hezekiah of Manasseh, Manas-
11 seh of Amon, Amon of Josiah; and Josiah was the father
of Jeconiah and his brothers at the time of the deportation
to Babylon.

12   After the deportation Jeconiah was the father of Sheal-
13 tiel, Shealtiel of Zerubbabel, Zerubbabel of Abiud, Abiud
14 of Eliakim, Eliakim of Azor, Azor of Zadok, Zadok of
15 Achim, Achim of Eliud, Eliud of Eleazar, Eleazar of
16 Matthan, Matthan of Jacob, Jacob of Joseph, the husband
of Mary, who gave birth to Jesus called Messiah.

17   There were thus fourteen generations in all from
Abraham to David, fourteen from David until the
deportation to Babylon, and fourteen from the deportation until the Messiah.

☆ The genealogy of Jesus in Matthew is divided into three
sub-sections, each containing fourteen names (verse 17). This
arrangement was probably suggested by the numerical value
of the three Hebrew letters which make up the consonants
of the name David (D V D = 4+6+4). The threefold
division is 2-6ᵃ (Abraham to David), 6ᵇ-11 (David to the
deportation to Babylon), 12-16 (the deportation to Babylon
to Christ).

    Matthew's list of names in the first section is probably
derived from 1 Chron. 1 — 2 (cf. Ruth 4: 18-21), in the
second section from 1 Chron. 3: 5, 10-15 (LXX), in the
third from an unknown source.

The actual number of names in the third section is not fourteen but thirteen, unless Mary is counted in the series as virgin mother.

In both Matthew and Luke 3: 23–38 the descent is traced through Joseph, not Mary. Matthew traces the descent through the direct royal line (David and Solomon), and Luke by a side line through David's son Nathan (2 Sam. 5: 14). The two lists coincide again at the names of Zerubbabel, the founder of the second temple, and his father Shealtiel, and then again part company until they reach Mary's husband, Joseph.

1. *Jesus Christ.* 'Christ' means 'anointed one', 'messiah', but is here used as a proper name.

Son of David. A messianic title. To a Jewish Christian the Messiahship of Jesus would need to be guaranteed by his Davidic descent.

Son of Abraham, probably also a messianic title. The descent of the Messiah from Abraham is dwelt upon in a Jewish Pharisaic work called *The Testaments of the Twelve Patriarchs, Levi,* VIII, 15. God's special promises to Israel had started with Abraham (Gen. 12).

2. *Judah.* All-important as the tribe providing the king, as in Gen. 49: 10.

3. *Tamar.* It was unusual to mention women in a Jewish genealogy. Tamar was first the wife of Er, then of Onan, then of Judah, by whom she bore Perez and Zarah. The way in which this happened was a disgrace to Judah. It is told in Gen. 38. Tamar herself is something of a heroine in Ruth 4: 12.

5. *Salma, Boaz, Rahab.* Cf. Ruth 4: 20 f.; 1 Chron. 2: 11. It is nowhere said in the Old Testament that Rahab the harlot was the mother of Boaz. She hid Joshua's spies, and sent them out in safety (Josh. 2). The story of *Ruth,* a Moabitess (a nation hated by the Jews), is told in the book of that name.

6. *King David.* 'King' stresses the importance of David in the table of descent.

wife of Uriah, i.e. Bathsheba (2 Sam. 11—12), cf. 1 Chron. 3: 5. David fell in love with her and arranged for Uriah to be placed in the forefront of the battle so that he was killed. David then married Bathsheba.

7. *Asa*, i.e. King Asa.

8. *Joram* (the father) of Azariah, another name for Uzziah.

9. Three kings are omitted after Joram (Ahaziah, Joash, Amaziah), and one (Jehoiakim) after Josiah. The purpose of this artificial device is to secure the three groupings of fourteen.

In verse 16 some Greek manuscripts and the old Latin read: 'Joseph to whom was betrothed Mary, a virgin, who gave birth to Jesus.' One early Syriac witness has: 'Joseph, and Joseph, to whom Mary, a virgin, was betrothed, was the father of Jesus.' The former variant stresses the virgin birth, the latter apparently denies it. The reading of our text has the support of the greatest authorities. *

THE BIRTH OF JESUS

18 This is the story of the birth of the Messiah. Mary his mother was betrothed to Joseph; before their marriage she found that she was with child by the Holy Spirit.
19 Being a man of principle, and at the same time wanting to save her from exposure, Joseph desired to have the
20 marriage contract set aside quietly. He had resolved on this, when an angel of the Lord appeared to him in a dream. 'Joseph son of David,' said the angel, 'do not be afraid to take Mary home with you as your wife. It is
21 by the Holy Spirit that she has conceived this child. She will bear a son; and you shall give him the name Jesus
22 (Saviour), for he will save his people from their sins.' All this happened in order to fulfil what the Lord declared
23 through the prophet: 'The virgin will conceive and bear a son, and he shall be called Emmanuel', a name which

means 'God is with us'. Rising from sleep Joseph did as 24
the angel had directed him; he took Mary home to be his
wife, but had no intercourse with her until her son was 25
born. And he named the child Jesus.

* The nativity narratives of Matthew and Luke have little in
common except the persons of Joseph and Mary and the fact
of the virgin birth in Bethlehem towards the end of the reign
of Herod the Great. Matthew's story is told from the point of
view of Joseph, Luke's from that of Mary. There is no adequate
reason to doubt that the virgin birth is historical. No con-
vincing motive has yet been suggested for inventing the story.
Many would urge that a supernatural birth of Jesus' body best
accords with the miracles of the resurrection and ascension.
Others, noticing that it is apparently unknown to the rest of
the New Testament (including the early writers Paul and
Mark), believe that the idea grew up to account for the
miracle of Jesus and that it was suggested by the Old Testament
passages such as Matthew quotes, especially 'The virgin will
conceive and bear a son' from Isa. 7: 14 which he quotes at
1: 23.

18. *the Messiah* (Greek *Christos*). Some MSS have 'Jesus
Christ'. But our text probably has the right reading.

betrothed. Betrothal was almost equivalent to marriage in
Jewish law. A Jewish betrothal could be dissolved only if the
man gave the woman a writ of divorce. A betrothed girl was
a widow if her fiancé died. Mary having been betrothed to
Joseph, Joseph was legally her husband even before marriage.
Yet betrothal was distinguished from marriage which took
place only when the bridegroom took the bride to his home
and the marriage was consummated.

Holy Spirit. The phrase, as in the Old Testament, suggests
the all-creative power of God. Jesus had no human father.
His birth was supernatural. Only Matthew and Luke mention
the virgin birth.

19. *a man of principle.* The Greek (*dikaios*) means 'just', i.e. a loyal and conscientious observer of the Jewish Law.

at the same time is not in the Greek, but is implied by the sense. Instead of involving Mary in publicity and scandal (the law strictly required stoning for a betrothed woman who was convicted of infidelity, cf. Deut. 22: 23–4), he wished to avail himself of a provision whereby a divorce could, if the husband so desired, be effected privately in the presence of two witnesses.

20. *dream.* Matthew frequently tells of revelation through dreams (cf. 2: 12, 13, 19, 22; 27: 19). The belief in dreams as means of divine communication and also in angelic appearances was widespread in the ancient world.

21. *Jesus* is the Greek form of Joshua, which means 'Yahweh is salvation'.

will save his people from their sins alludes to Ps. 130: 8

> 'And he shall redeem Israel
> From all his iniquities'.

22. *in order to fulfil.* On this formula see p. 3. Similar formulae are found in the rabbinic writings.

23. The citation from Isa. 7: 14 agrees in the main with the LXX, where *parthenos* 'maiden' is an inexact translation of a Hebrew word '*almāh*', which means simply a young woman of marriageable age, whether married or not. What Isaiah meant was that the approaching deliverance of Israel would be so notable that a young woman would give her child this name Emmanuel, 'God with us' (cf. Isa. 8: 8). Isa. 7: 14 had no place in Jewish messianic expectation. Matthew seized upon the LXX rendering of it to confirm the virgin birth story which was already established in the Christian tradition.

25. Jesus had brothers and sisters (Matt. 13: 55–6; Mark 6: 3). There is no reason to suppose that they were Joseph's children by a former wife. ✷

THE VISIT OF THE MAGI

Jesus was born at Bethlehem in Judaea during the reign of **2** Herod. After his birth astrologers from the east arrived in 2 Jerusalem, asking, 'Where is the child who is born to be king of the Jews? We observed the rising of his star, and we have come to pay him homage.' King Herod was 3 greatly perturbed when he heard this; and so was the whole of Jerusalem. He called a meeting of the chief 4 priests and lawyers of the Jewish people, and put before them the question: 'Where is it that the Messiah is to be born?' 'At Bethlehem in Judaea', they replied; and they 5 referred him to the prophecy which reads: 'Bethlehem 6 in the land of Judah, you are far from least in the eyes of the rulers of Judah; for out of you shall come a leader to be the shepherd of my people Israel.'

Herod next called the astrologers to meet him in private, 7 and ascertained from them the time when the star had appeared. He then sent them on to Bethlehem, and said, 8 'Go and make a careful inquiry for the child. When you have found him, report to me, so that I may go myself and pay him homage.'

They set out at the king's bidding; and the star which 9 they had seen at its rising went ahead of them until it stopped above the place where the child lay. At the sight 10 of the star they were overjoyed. Entering the house, they 11 saw the child with Mary his mother, and bowed to the ground in homage to him; then they opened their treasures and offered him gifts: gold, frankincense, and myrrh. And being warned in a dream not to go back to 12 Herod, they returned home another way.

✻ Although Matthew's Gospel has at times a strong Jewish bias, it both begins and ends with reference to the Gentiles. Here the world-wide mission of the Church is pre-figured. The Son of God was revealed first to Jews (Mary and Joseph), then to the Gentiles (the foreign astrologers).

1. *Bethlehem* means 'the house of bread'. It was the birth-place of David, 5 miles south of Jerusalem.

Herod, i.e. Herod the Great. He became Governor of Galilee in 47 B.C. and was given the title 'King of Judaea' by Antony and Octavius in 40 B.C. According to Matthew's dating, Jesus must have been born some weeks or months before Herod's death in the spring of 4 B.C.

astrologers. Greek *magoi*, Latin *magi*. The word has two senses, a good and a bad. (*a*) According to Herodotus (I, 101) the Magi were originally a tribe of the Medes who became a priestly caste among the Persians (I, 132), as the Chaldaeans did in Babylon (Dan. 1: 4, etc.). In this sense, the *magi* were wise men, observers of the stars, astrologers. (*b*) The word later acquired the sinister sense of magician or sorcerer, e.g. 'Simon who was a practising *magus*' (as Acts 8: 9 means literally) and Bar-Jesus or Elymas the *magus* (translated 'sorcerer' at Acts 13: 6, 8). It is unlikely that Matthew intended this bad sense of 'sorcerer'. The word is therefore correctly rendered here 'astrologers'. Matthew does not tell us how many there were nor what their names were.

from the east. The Greek for 'east' is *anatolai* in the plural. In the singular the word means 'rising' as in the next verse.

2. *the rising of his star*. Greek: 'the star at its rising' (*anatolé* in the singular). The association of the birth of great men and great events with the appearance of stars was a common feature in the ancient world, e.g. the fall of Troy and the birth of Alexander the Great.

4. *chief priests*. Probably members of the families from whom the high priests were at that time appointed.

lawyers. Greek: 'scribes', experts in the Jewish Law. See p. 19.

5. *the prophecy.* Micah 5: 2. The quotation differs both from the Hebrew and from the LXX. Like the other 'proof-texts' peculiar to Matthew, it is probably taken from a collection of testimonies based on a Targum, i.e. an Aramaic paraphrase translation of the Old Testament for use in the synagogues. The passage was understood to mean that the Messiah would be born at Bethlehem.

6. *to be the shepherd* echoes 2 Sam. 5: 2.

7. *ascertained.* Greek: 'inquired carefully' (cf. verse 8).

when the star had appeared. This would be important for astrology, and also to enable Herod to estimate the age of the child.

8. *pay him homage.* A false reason, as the sequel shows.

9. *went ahead of them.* It seems to be implied that the star had been guiding them in their journey from east to west. Now it guides them in their journey from Jerusalem south-westward to Bethlehem.

11. *house.* According to Luke (2: 7, 13) Jesus was born in a manger. The *magi* arrived at a later stage, by which time the holy family may have been lodged in the house. According to an early tradition the birth-place was a cave (Justin Martyr, Origen, Jerome). A cave beneath the house could well serve as a manger. The *treasures* were the containers in which the gifts were carried (cf. Deut. 28: 12). The gifts were products of Arabia, but gold was found also in Babylonia and elsewhere. There are echoes of Isa. 60: 6 ('they shall bring gold and frankincense, and shall proclaim the praises of the Lord') and Ps. 72: 10 ('the kings of Tarshish and of the isles shall bring presents: the kings of Sheba and Seba shall offer gifts'). Probably no symbolism is intended. The gifts are such as could be used in worship and were suitable presents for a king.

12. *warned.* The Greek word means 'instructed by an oracle'. *

THE FLIGHT INTO EGYPT

13 After they had gone, an angel of the Lord appeared to Joseph in a dream, and said to him, 'Rise up, take the child and his mother and escape with them to Egypt, and stay there until I tell you; for Herod is going to search for the
14 child to do away with him.' So Joseph rose from sleep, and taking mother and child by night he went away with
15 them to Egypt, and there he stayed till Herod's death. This was to fulfil what the Lord had declared through the prophet: 'I called my son out of Egypt.'

✻ 13. The nearest part of Egypt was not far from Bethlehem. Herod's reasons for seeking to kill Jesus were presumably fear, jealousy and political expediency (see verse 3).

  15. The quotation is from Hos. 11: 1 where 'my son' refers to Israel, whom in the Exodus God called out of Egypt. ✻

THE MASSACRE OF THE INNOCENTS

16 When Herod saw how the astrologers had tricked him he fell into a passion, and gave orders for the massacre of all children in Bethlehem and its neighbourhood, of the age of two years or less, corresponding with the time he had
17 ascertained from the astrologers. So the words spoken
18 through Jeremiah the prophet were fulfilled: 'A voice was heard in Rama, wailing and loud laments; it was Rachel weeping for her children, and refusing all consolation, because they were no more.'

✻ 16. The murder of the children and the failure to kill Israel's Redeemer recall the story of Pharaoh and Moses (Exod. 1: 15 — 2: 10).

age of two years or less. This shows that Jesus was not yet two years old.

17. The quotation is from Jer. 31: 15. *Rachel* was ancestress of Benjamin and Ephraim. *Rama* was an Ephraimite town 8 miles north of Jerusalem. Jeremiah's words concern the Ephraimites going into exile in Babylon. ✶

REMOVAL FROM EGYPT TO NAZARETH

The time came that Herod died; and an angel of the Lord 19 appeared in a dream to Joseph in Egypt and said to him, 'Rise up, take the child and his mother, and go with them 20 to the land of Israel, for the men who threatened the child's life are dead.' So he rose, took mother and child with 21 him, and came to the land of Israel. Hearing, however, 22 that Archelaus had succeeded his father Herod as king of Judaea, he was afraid to go there. And being warned by a dream, he withdrew to the region of Galilee; there he 23 settled in a town called Nazareth. This was to fulfil the words spoken through the prophets: 'He shall be called a Nazarene.'

✶ Herod died in 4 B.C. The language of verse 20 has been coloured by the story of Moses (Exod. 4: 19).

Herod bequeathed to *Archelaus* Judaea, Samaria and Idumaea, with the title 'king'. Augustus soon after refused Archelaus the title 'king', until he should have won it by good behaviour; but at the time referred to 'king' is correct. The title Augustus later gave him was 'ethnarch'. He was removed for brutality in A.D. 6 and banished.

22. *he was afraid.* Joseph feared that Archelaus would continue his father's attempt to kill Jesus.

Galilee. The name means a circle. Its inhabitants were largely Gentile (Isa. 9: 1; Matt. 4: 15, 'heathen Galilee'). In Galilee

Archelaus could not harm the child; Herod Antipas ruled Galilee and Peraea, and he was evidently not likely to be a threat to the life of Jesus.

23. *Nazareth*. The village of Nazareth is not mentioned in any ancient records outside the New Testament. It was evidently a very insignificant place (cf. John 1: 46, 'can anything good come from Nazareth?'). The prophecy said to be fulfilled by his settling there is not found in the Old Testament. Yet the prophets referred to must be Old Testament Scriptures. Suggested passages are Num. 6; Judg. 13: 5; Isa. 11: 1, where the Hebrew word for 'branch' is *nēzĕr*.

Nazarene. Greek *Nazōraios*. Matthew evidently understands the name to mean 'an inhabitant of Nazareth'. The Christians were later known as a sect of the same name (Acts 24: 5). But there is also an intended allusion to the manner of the birth of Samson (Judg. 13: 24) as analogous to that of Christ, and more particularly to Samson's vocation as a *Nazir* (LXX *Naziraios*). A Nazirite was one, whether man or woman, who undertook either for life or for a shorter time a vow to observe certain rules, involving various abstinences, e.g. from all intoxicants and from cutting the hair (see Num. 6). ✻

THE MINISTRY OF JOHN THE BAPTIST

3 About that time John the Baptist appeared as a preacher
2 in the Judaean wilderness; his theme was: 'Repent; for
3 the kingdom of Heaven is upon you!' It is of him that the prophet Isaiah spoke when he said, 'A voice crying aloud in the wilderness, "Prepare a way for the Lord; clear a straight path for him."'
4 John's clothing was a rough coat of camel's hair, with a leather belt round his waist, and his food was locusts and
5 wild honey. They flocked to him from Jerusalem, from

all Judaea, and the whole Jordan valley, and were baptized 6
by him in the River Jordan, confessing their sins.

When he saw many of the Pharisees and Sadducees 7
coming for baptism he said to them: 'You vipers' brood!
Who warned you to escape from the coming retribution?
Then prove your repentance by the fruit it bears; and do 8, 9
not presume to say to yourselves, "We have Abraham
for our father." I tell you that God can make children
for Abraham out of these stones here. Already the axe is 10
laid to the roots of the trees; and every tree that fails to
produce good fruit is cut down and thrown on the fire.
I baptize you with water, for repentance; but the one who 11
comes after me is mightier than I, and I am not fit to take
off his shoes; he will baptize you with the Holy Spirit and
with fire. His shovel is ready in his hand and he will 12
winnow his threshing-floor; the wheat he will gather into
his granary, but he will burn the chaff on a fire that can
never go out.'

* John the Baptist marks the beginning of the Christian
message of salvation. Matthew gives him the title 'the
Baptist'. John was truly a great man, as Jesus said (11: 11,
'never has there appeared on earth a mother's son greater than
John the Baptist'), yet his message of repentance and judgement, resembling that of the Old Testament prophets, falls
short of the Christian Gospel of grace (i.e. God's unmerited
love for sinners which takes the initiative in seeking and saving
the lost), so that John was outside the Kingdom that Jesus
came to preach, so far as its earthly manifestation is concerned:
'the least in the kingdom of Heaven is greater than he' (11: 11).

1. *the Judaean wilderness* is the mountainous region west
of the Dead Sea. The Dead Sea Scroll, the *Manual of Discipline*
(VIII, 13–16), refers to the clearing of the way of the Lord in the

wilderness as the preparation of the messianic age, quoting
Isa. 40: 3, as Matthew does in verse 3.

2. *Repent*. The Greek word means 'change your mind'.
The corresponding Hebrew and Aramaic words mean 'change
direction', 'turn back'. *kingdom of Heaven*. See pp. 10-12.

3. The quotation is from Isa. 40: 3 where 'the Lord' is
'Yahweh'. Matthew no doubt thought of Jesus. The Hebrew
and LXX say 'the paths of our God'. All three Synoptists
have 'his paths', the paths of Jesus, for whom John prepares
the way.

John is here compared to Elijah (cf. 2 Kings 1: 8), who
was similarly dressed.

4. *locusts*. Several kinds of locusts (insects like grasshoppers)
are still eaten by Arabs and are allowed by Jewish food laws.

6. *baptized*. The Greek verb *baptizo* means 'dip', 'im-
merse'. On the relation between John's baptism and proselyte
baptism, see p. 23.

7. *Pharisees and Sadducees*. See pp. 18, 19.

vipers, poisonous serpents, type of evil cunning. 'That ser-
pent of old' is a description of Satan (Rev. 12: 9).

9. In the Aramaic saying of John there would be a pun.
'God can make children (*bānîm*) for Abraham out of these
stones (*'abhānîm*).'

11. *the one who comes after me* is the Messiah, to whom
'might' (power) was to belong (Isa. 9: 6).

he will baptize you. The coming baptism is described by
both Matthew and Luke as a baptism 'with the Holy Spirit
and with fire'. In Mark 1: 8, John 1: 33, Acts 1: 5, it is a
baptism 'with [the] Holy Spirit'. 'Fire' means the fire of
judgement, as in the next verse. *

THE BAPTISM OF JESUS

13 Then Jesus arrived at the Jordan from Galilee, and came
14 to John to be baptized by him. John tried to dissuade him.
'Do you come to me?' he said; 'I need rather to be

baptized by you.' Jesus replied, 'Let it be so for the 15
present; we do well to conform in this way with all that
God requires.' John then allowed him to come. After 16
baptism Jesus came up out of the water at once, and at
that moment heaven opened; he saw the Spirit of God
descending like a dove to alight upon him; and a voice 17
from heaven was heard saying, 'This is my Son, my
Beloved, on whom my favour rests.'

* Unlike Mark, Matthew states that it was the purpose of
Jesus to be baptized that made him leave Galilee.

Verses 14 and 15 are peculiar to Matthew. They are an early
attempt to explain why Jesus was baptized and to assure
Christians that his was not a baptism of personal repentance.
Jesus was sinless (2 Cor. 5: 21, 'Christ was innocent of sin';
Heb. 4: 15, 'tested every way, only without sin'; 7: 26,
'guileless . . . separated from sinners'; 1 Pet. 1: 19, 'without
mark or blemish'; 1 John 3: 5, 'there is no sin in him'; John
8: 46, 'which of you can prove me in the wrong?'). The
Gospel according to the Ebionites (*c.* A.D. 117) quotes John
the Baptist, after the heavenly voice has spoken, as asking Jesus
to baptize him. In the Gospel according to the Nazarenes,
belonging to the early second century A.D., and used by a
Jewish Christian sect in Beroea in Coele-Syria, we read:
'Behold the Lord's mother and his brothers said to him:
"John the Baptist baptizes for the remission of sins; let us go
and be baptized by him." But he said to them: "In what have
I sinned, that I should go and be baptized by him? Unless
perchance this very word that I have spoken is [a sin of ?]
ignorance."' Probably the motive of Jesus in being baptized
was to identify himself with the sinners whom he came to
save ('he was numbered with the transgressors', Isa. 53: 12;
Mark 15: 28; Luke 22: 37) and with the mission of John the
Baptist.

16. *he saw.* In Mark 1: 10 this experience is a 'vision' of

Jesus, an inward experience. In Luke 3: 22 it is an outward event. In Matthew it is both.

Spirit. Greek *pneuma*, which means literally 'wind', 'breath'. The Holy Spirit descended upon Jesus to inspire and empower him for his ministry. 'Perpetual inspiration is as necessary to the life of goodness, holiness and happiness as perpetual respiration is necessary to animal life' (William Law).

dove. This was for the rabbis a symbol of Israel and, less often, of the Spirit. In Gen. 1: 2 the Spirit is said to 'brood' over the waters at the first creation—the metaphor of a bird.

17. Jesus was declared to be the Son of God by a Voice from Heaven. The rabbis taught that sometimes the heavens opened and an echo of the Divine Voice (*Bath Qōl*, 'the daughter of the Voice') was heard. Matthew has *This is my Son* (i.e. a public declaration to the bystanders). Mark has 'Thou art my Son' (i.e. a private declaration to Jesus), a quotation from Ps. 2: 7, which was interpreted as referring to the Messiah. *my Beloved, on whom my favour rests* recalls passages which describe the Servant of the Lord (Isa. 42: 1; 44: 2). Jesus was convinced at his baptism that he was called to be Messiah, not in the sense of popular expectation, a political leader and military deliverer, but a Messiah who came in lowliness to serve and save men from their sins, and to usher in not an earthly, but a heavenly kingdom. The Greek word translated 'Beloved' can mean 'only', especially in the phrase 'an only son'. ✶

THE TEMPTATIONS OF JESUS

4 Jesus was then led away by the Spirit into the wilderness, to be tempted by the devil.

2   For forty days and nights he fasted, and at the end of
3 them he was famished. The tempter approached him and said, 'If you are the Son of God, tell these stones to become
4 bread.' Jesus answered, 'Scripture says, "Man cannot live on bread alone; he lives on every word that God utters."'

The devil then took him to the Holy City and set him 5
on the parapet of the temple. 'If you are the Son of God,' 6
he said, 'throw yourself down; for Scripture says, "He
will put his angels in charge of you, and they will support
you in their arms, for fear you should strike your foot
against a stone."' Jesus answered him, 'Scripture says 7
again, "You are not to put the Lord your God to the
test."'

Once again, the devil took him to a very high mountain, 8
and showed him all the kingdoms of the world in their
glory. 'All these', he said, 'I will give you, if you will 9
only fall down and do me homage.' But Jesus said, 10
'Begone, Satan; Scripture says, "You shall do homage to
the Lord your God and worship him alone."'

Then the devil left him, and angels appeared and waited 11
on him.

* Mark (1: 12–13) records the fact that Jesus was tempted, but
gives no details about the temptations. The three temptations
are described by Matthew and Luke, but in Luke the last two
occur in reverse order.

1. It was the Divine will that Jesus should experience
the testing of his vocation to be Messiah. He was led by
the Spirit to the wilderness heights to be tempted by the
devil.

2. *forty days.* Cf. Exod. 24: 18, Moses in the mount forty
days and forty nights; 1 Kings 19: 8, Elijah fasted forty days
and forty nights; Num. 14: 33–4, Israel wandered in the
wilderness forty years.

at the end of them. In Mark the temptations go on *during* the
forty days, in Luke both during and *at the end.*

3. First temptation. *If you are the Son of God*, echoing the
words of the Voice at the baptism. The challenge to the
Messiah to turn stones into bread probably refers to the current

belief that the messianic age would bring a miraculous abundance of material goods. Jesus replies by quoting Deut. 8: 3 (LXX).

5. Second temptation. *the Holy City*, Jerusalem, so described only in Matthew and in Revelation in the New Testament.

parapet. Greek: 'little wing'; R.V. 'pinnacle'.

6. The devil quotes Ps. 91: 11–12, which is evidently intended to be understood to refer to the Messiah.

7. Jesus replies by quoting Deut. 6: 16 where the reference to putting God to the test is explained by Exod. 17: 1–7: 'To test God's good faith is to show one's own lack of faith' (T. W. Manson, *Sayings of Jesus*, p. 45). It is wrong to presume upon God's providence.

8. Third temptation. From no mountain could Jesus see all the kingdoms of the world. It is an imaginary experience. Jesus sees in a vision or in his imagination the whole world. If he would obtain an earthly rule over the world, he must yield to the tempter and worship him. But Christ's true mission was very different. His kingdom is not of this world (John 18: 36). It is a spiritual kingdom of obedience to God's sovereignty.

10. Jesus replies by quoting Deut. 6: 13.

11. *the devil left him*. Jesus faces temptation again when he says to Peter 'Away with you, Satan' (16: 23) just as here he says 'Begone, Satan'; he faces it again in Gethsemane (26: 36–46). But already the devil has been decisively beaten (cf. Luke 10: 18, 'I watched how Satan fell, like lightning, out of the sky'). ✻

THE MINISTRY IN GALILEE; THE CALLING OF THE DISCIPLES

12 When he heard that John had been arrested, Jesus with-
13 drew to Galilee; and leaving Nazareth he went and settled at Capernaum on the Sea of Galilee, in the district of

Zebulun and Naphtali. This was in fulfilment of the 14
passage in the prophet Isaiah which tells of 'the land of 15
Zebulun, the land of Naphtali, the road by the sea, the
land beyond Jordan, heathen Galilee', and says:

> 'The people that lived in darkness saw a great light; 16
> Light dawned on the dwellers in the land of death's
>   dark shadow.'

From that day Jesus began to proclaim the message: 17
'Repent; for the kingdom of Heaven is upon you.'

Jesus was walking by the Sea of Galilee when he saw 18
two brothers, Simon called Peter and his brother Andrew,
casting a net into the lake; for they were fishermen. Jesus 19
said to them, 'Come with me, and I will make you fishers
of men.' They left their nets at once and followed him. 20

He went on, and saw another pair of brothers, James 21
son of Zebedee and his brother John; they were in the
boat with their father Zebedee, overhauling their nets.
He called them, and at once they left the boat and their 22
father, and followed him.

He went round the whole of Galilee, teaching in the 23
synagogues, preaching the gospel of the Kingdom, and
curing whatever illness or infirmity there was among the
people. His fame reached the whole of Syria; and sufferers 24
from every kind of illness, racked with pain, possessed by
devils, epileptic, or paralysed, were all brought to him,
and he cured them. Great crowds also followed him, 25
from Galilee and the Ten Towns, from Jerusalem and
Judaea, and from Transjordan.

✳ 12. *John had been arrested.* The circumstances of his arrest
are described in 14: 3–12 (Mark 6: 17–18; Luke 3: 19–20).

He rebuked Herod for marrying his brother's wife, and incurred the enmity of the latter. Josephus adds the further explanation that John was imprisoned at Machaerus because Herod feared that his power over the people might result in a political rising (*Antiquities*, XVIII, 52). John 3: 24 implies that the ministry of Jesus began before John's imprisonment, but in Judaea. Matthew (following Mark) is describing the beginning of the ministry in Galilee.

13. *Capernaum* probably occupied the site of the modern Tell Hūm on the N.W. shore of the Sea of Galilee. The remains of a later synagogue are still to be seen among other ruins.

15. The quotation is from Isa. 9: 1-2, agreeing neither with the Hebrew nor with the LXX, but rather a mixture of both, probably based on an Aramaic Targum.

heathen Galilee, i.e. Galilee of the Gentiles, to whom was promised a share in the coming blessing.

sea. In Isaiah this probably meant the Mediterranean, here probably the Sea of Galilee, the road running from Damascus past the Sea of Galilee to the Mediterranean.

17. *Repent.* See on 3: 2.

kingdom of Heaven. See pp. 10-12.

is upon you. It is disputed whether the Greek verb here means simply 'has drawn near' or 'has arrived'. If the different Greek verb used at Matt. 12: 28; Luke 11: 20 ('the kingdom of God has already come upon you') can be regarded as an equivalent, then the second meaning is right. The Reign of God is in any case present in the person of Jesus, for in him God's sovereignty over human nature is complete, and all who receive Jesus in faith become God's subjects. Nevertheless, as we shall see, there are passages where the kingdom is clearly thought of as future (e.g. 8: 11; 16: 28; 25: 34; 26: 29).

18. *Peter.* A Greek name meaning 'Rock' (see 16: 18). The Aramaic equivalent is *Cephas* (John 1: 42; 1 Cor. 1: 12, etc.).

Andrew. A Greek name, meaning 'brave'.

19. *fishers of men.* Catching others for Christ, winning them for the kingdom, bringing them to salvation.

21. *James.* Greek *Jacōbos*, Jacob.

24. *epileptic.* The rare Greek word here means 'moon-struck' ('lunatic'), but it came to be applied to epileptics (cf. 17: 15). It does not necessarily indicate insanity as 'lunatic' does.

25. *the Ten Towns.* Greek *Decapolis*, a confederation of ten Greek towns. The region included all Bashan and Gilead. ✷

The Sermon on the Mount

THE BEATITUDES

WHEN HE SAW the crowds he went up the hill. There 5 he took his seat, and when his disciples had gathered round him he began to address them. And this is the 2 teaching he gave:

'How blest are those who know that they are poor; 3
    the kingdom of Heaven is theirs.

How blest are the sorrowful; 4
    they shall find consolation.

How blest are those of a gentle spirit; 5
    they shall have the earth for their possession.

How blest are those who hunger and thirst to see right 6
        prevail;
    they shall be satisfied.

How blest are those who show mercy; 7
    mercy shall be shown to them.

How blest are those whose hearts are pure; 8
    they shall see God.

43

9   How blest are the peacemakers;
        God shall call them his sons.
10   How blest are those who have suffered persecution for
        the cause of right;
        the kingdom of Heaven is theirs.

11   'How blest you are, when you suffer insults and persecu-
12   tion and every kind of calumny for my sake. Accept it
with gladness and exultation, for you have a rich reward
in heaven; in the same way they persecuted the prophets
before you.

✻ Matthew states that Jesus withdrew from the crowd by
going up the hillside, and thus addressed his disciples on the
hill. As Moses received the Law on Mount Sinai, so Jesus
delivered his perfect Law on the mount. The Sermon is much
longer in Matthew than in Luke, and no doubt includes many
sayings which Jesus uttered on different occasions, and which
Matthew has gathered together into one sermon.

1. *took his seat.* It was customary for rabbis to sit when
teaching.

3–12. Beatitudes are common in the Old Testament,
especially in the Psalms: e.g. Psalm 1: 1, 'Blessed is the man
that walketh not in the counsel of the wicked'. They are found
also in Greek literature, but there the blessings promised are
materialistic. The beatitudes of Jesus contain spiritual promise
and challenge.

Matthew has nine, Luke (6: 20–3) has four. They are more
briefly expressed in Luke than in Matthew, and all in the
second person plural. The form of the beatitudes in Matthew
emphasizes the 'blessedness' of the inner disposition of a man
rather than something which outward circumstances may
have caused in him. For example, in Matthew we read *How
blest are those who know that they are poor* (the Greek says
literally 'Blest the poor in spirit!'); Luke has 'How blest are

44

you who are poor'. *Blest* means something like 'enjoying God's favour and destined to enter his eternal Kingdom'.

those who know that they are poor are like the 'poor' of the Psalms: e.g. Ps. 69: 29, 'But I am poor and sorrowful: Let thy salvation, O God, set me up on high'. These poor were the saintly people who in the days of foreign rule remained faithful to their religion. In contrast, the people of Laodicea, the luke-warm church, are condemned because they say 'how rich I am', and do not know that they are really poor spiritually (Rev. 3: 17). Those who know that they are poor, and so rely on God and not on themselves, are truly *blest*.

4. The second beatitude brings out one important meaning of *blest* by contrasting present sorrow with future bliss.

5. The third, which has no parallel in Luke, seems to be an adaptation of Ps. 37: 11, 'the meek shall inherit the land'.

6. In Luke the blessing is pronounced upon the hungry, in Matthew upon *those who hunger and thirst to see right prevail*. The contrast between present and future is that between a famine and a feast. In Jewish and Christian imagery, the happy messianic age to come is likened to a great feast. The next four beatitudes have no parallel in Luke.

8. The sixth beatitude is the one which most captured the attention of the early Fathers. 'The thought of the *Vision of God* as the goal of human life, and the determinant, therefore, of Christian conduct, came rapidly to its own' (K. E. Kirk, *The Vision of God*, p. 1). Irenaeus (*c.* A.D. 175) declared: 'The glory of God is a living man; and the life of man is the vision of God' (*Against Heresies*, IV, 34, 7). Only the pure in heart can attain to this spiritual vision of God.

9. The seventh beatitude means by 'peacemakers', not appeasers, but those who actively overcome evil with good.

11. *calumny*, i.e. false accusation and slander. Those who suffer for their loyalty to the Messiah will be blest in his Kingdom. *

SALT AND LIGHT

13 'You are salt to the world. And if salt becomes tasteless, how is its saltness to be restored? It is now good for nothing but to be thrown away and trodden underfoot.

14 'You are light for all the world. A town that stands
15 on a hill cannot be hidden. When a lamp is lit, it is not put under the meal-tub, but on the lamp-stand, where it
16 gives light to everyone in the house. And you, like the lamp, must shed light among your fellows, so that, when they see the good you do, they may give praise to your Father in heaven.

* 13. Salt is very important in hot countries for the preservation of food which it keeps pure and to which it gives flavour. Like salt, a disciple of Jesus is of use only so long as he retains his distinctive quality of discipleship. If he loses his zeal and devotion, he is like salt that has become insipid and therefore, useless, incapable of keeping that which it touches pure and pleasant.

14. The disciples are also the light of the world. Compare the saying in the Dead Sea Scrolls: 'All the sons of justice tread in the ways of light' (*Manual of Discipline*, III, 20). In Isa. 42: 6, the servant of the Lord is said to be the light of the Gentiles (cf. Isa. 49: 6). In the rabbinic literature God, Adam, Israel, the Law, the Temple, are all in turn said to be the light of the world. In John 8: 12 Jesus says, 'I am the light of the world'.

The teaching in verses 14–16 seems at first sight inconsistent with the command to do good in secret (6: 1–4). But Jesus commends the setting of a good public example when the motive is the glory of God, not when the motive is self-glorification.

15. *the meal-tub*. A measure holding about a peck. *

JESUS FULFILS THE LAW AND THE PROPHETS

'Do not suppose that I have come to abolish the Law and 17
the prophets; I did not come to abolish, but to complete. 18
I tell you this: so long as heaven and earth endure, not a
letter, not a stroke, will disappear from the Law until all
that must happen has happened. If any man therefore sets 19
aside even the least of the Law's demands, and teaches
others to do the same, he will have the lowest place in the
kingdom of Heaven, whereas anyone who keeps the Law
and teaches others so will stand high in the kingdom of
Heaven. I tell you, unless you show yourselves far better 20
men than the Pharisees and the doctors of the law, you can
never enter the kingdom of Heaven.

* 17. In the teaching of Jesus, as in that of Paul, there is a
double attitude to the Law. On the one hand Jesus praised the
Law, as here. He taught that in its inner meaning and divine
purpose the Law had its full place in the eternal will of God.
On the other hand, as he came to remove the priestly perversions of worship, so he came to remove the lawyer's
perversions of the Law; and he refused to accept their doctrine
of salvation by the mere works of the Law. He declared that
a new heart of love was better than sacrifice.

18. *I tell you this.* Greek: 'Amen [i.e. truly] I tell you': a
favourite formula of Jesus.

a letter. The Greek is 'iota', i.e. the smallest letter of the
Greek alphabet, corresponding to *yōdh*, the smallest letter of
the Hebrew alphabet.

a stroke. The Greek word means literally a 'horn', a corner
or stroke of a letter, or perhaps a mark of punctuation.

20. The righteousness which exceeds that of the Pharisees
and the doctors of the Law, and which is required for entrance
into the kingdom of Heaven, is about to be explained in the

antitheses which follow. It is not mere mechanical obedience to rules. Jesus penetrates below the surface to the fundamental principles, and shows the spirit behind the Law. ✳

MURDER AND ANGER; ADULTERY; DIVORCE; VOWS AND OATHS; RETALIATION; LOVE OF ONE'S NEIGHBOUR

21 'You have learned that our forefathers were told, "Do not commit murder; anyone who commits murder must
22 be brought to judgement." But what I tell you is this: Anyone who nurses anger against his brother must be brought to judgement. If he abuses his brother he must answer for it to the court; if he sneers at him he will have to answer for it in the fires of hell.

23   'If, when you are bringing your gift to the altar, you suddenly remember that your brother has a grievance
24 against you, leave your gift where it is before the altar. First go and make your peace with your brother, and only then come back and offer your gift.

25   'If someone sues you, come to terms with him promptly while you are both on your way to court; otherwise he may hand you over to the judge, and the judge to the
26 constable, and you will be put in jail. I tell you, once you are there you will not be let out till you have paid the last farthing.

27   'You have learned that they were told, "Do not commit
28 adultery." But what I tell you is this: If a man looks on a woman with a lustful eye, he has already committed adultery with her in his heart.

29   'If your right eye leads you astray, tear it out and fling it away; it is better for you to lose one part of your body

than for the whole of it to be thrown into hell. And if 30
your right hand is your undoing, cut it off and fling it
away; it is better for you to lose one part of your body
than for the whole of it to go to hell.

'They were told, "A man who divorces his wife must 31
give her a note of dismissal." But what I tell you is this: 32
If a man divorces his wife for any cause other than unchastity he involves her in adultery; and anyone who
marries a woman so divorced commits adultery.

'Again, you have learned that they were told, "Do not 33
break your oath", and, "Oaths sworn to the Lord must
be kept." But what I tell you is this: You are not to swear 34
at all—not by heaven, for it is God's throne, nor by earth, 35
for it is his footstool, nor by Jerusalem, for it is the city of
the great King, nor by your own head, because you can- 36
not turn one hair of it white or black. Plain "Yes" or 37
"No" is all you need to say; anything beyond that comes
from the devil.

'You have learned that they were told, "An eye for an 38
eye, and a tooth for a tooth." But what I tell you is this: 39
Do not set yourself against the man who wrongs you. If
someone slaps you on the right cheek, turn and offer him
your left. If a man wants to sue you for your shirt, let 40
him have your coat as well. If a man in authority makes 41
you go one mile, go with him two. Give when you are 42
asked to give; and do not turn your back on a man who
wants to borrow.

'You have learned that they were told, "Love your 43
neighbour, hate your enemy." But what I tell you is this: 44
Love your enemies and pray for your persecutors; only 45
so can you be children of your heavenly Father, who

makes his sun rise on good and bad alike, and sends the
46 rain on the honest and the dishonest. If you love only
those who love you, what reward can you expect? Surely
47 the tax-gatherers do as much as that. And if you greet
only your brothers, what is there extraordinary about
48 that? Even the heathen do as much. You must therefore be all goodness, just as your heavenly Father is all
good.

✽ 21. The *forefathers* are the generation who were alive when
the Law was given from Sinai. '*Do not commit murder*' (Exod.
20: 13; Deut. 5: 17) is the sixth commandment of the
Decalogue. The following words are based on Exod. 21: 12,
Lev. 24: 17, Deut. 17: 8–13. The penalty for murder was death.
Jesus distinguished between the outward act and the inward
disposition which produces the act and says that the inward
disposition is as evil as the act it produces. Jesus sets his own
authority above that of the Mosaic law, thus making a tre-
mendous claim for himself. Whereas the prophets had said:
'Thus saith the Lord', Jesus says, 'I tell you'.

22. *brother* would suggest to Jewish ears a fellow Jew, but
in the intention of Jesus it refers to any fellow human being.

abuses his brother. lit. 'says to his brother, Raca'. The meaning
of this word is uncertain. It is probably based on an Aramaic
word meaning 'empty', and so 'empty-headed', 'stupid'.

court, i.e. the Sanhedrin, the supreme Jewish legal court.

sneers. lit. 'says, Fool'.

fires of hell. lit. Gehenna of fire. 'Gehenna' means 'the
valley of Hinnom', a ravine outside Jerusalem, where human
sacrifices had once been offered. In Jesus' day it was used for
burning the refuse of Jerusalem, and so became the symbol of
the future punishment of the wicked.

23. The lay Jew who offered a sacrifice brought his gift to
the inner court of the temple. Before he could enter this court
he had to bathe and change his clothes. Jesus says: 'You cannot

enter into right relationship with God if you are not in right relationship with your brother.'

25–6. The parallel passage in Luke (12: 57–9) is in a context which concerns the end of the age. In Matthew's context it seems to mean: 'The present may be your last chance to be reconciled; if you fail to take it, you will be in danger of Gehenna.'

26. *farthing*. The Latin *quadrans* = 2 mites. Luke has 'the last *lepton*', a Greek word meaning a very small coin, about a fourth of a farthing.

27. *Do not commit adultery* is the seventh commandment (Exod. 20: 14; Deut. 5: 18). Jesus distinguishes between the act and the inward disposition that produces the act. The inward disposition is as sinful as the act which springs from it.

29. The hyperbole (exaggeration) which follows vividly brings out the urgency of taming the natural desires and passions at all costs.

31. The quotation is from Deut. 24: 1.

32. The exception in our Lord's declaration, *for any cause other than unchastity*, is an addition to the teaching of Jesus as found in Mark 10: 11–12; Luke 16: 18; 1 Cor. 7: 10–11, where Jesus is said to forbid divorce and remarriage after divorce without any exception. His reasons are given in Mark 10: 6–9, and are based upon the purpose of God in instituting marriage according to the Creation story (Gen. 2: 24, 'Therefore shall a man leave his father and mother, and shall cleave unto his wife; and they shall be one flesh'). The question on what grounds a man might divorce his wife was discussed in the time of our Lord by the rival Pharisaic Schools of Hillel and Shammai. The debate between them related to the interpretation of the Mosaic permission of divorce in Deut. 24: 1–3. The School of Hillel held that the Law allowed a man to divorce his wife practically 'on any and every ground' (cf. Matt. 19: 3). That of Shammai maintained that the only legitimate cause was the wife's infidelity. The Matthaean addition of the excepting clause would bring Jesus' teaching into agreement

with that of Shammai. But according to Mark, Luke and
1 Corinthians, Jesus agreed with neither side: he discounte-
nanced divorce altogether, and especially forbade marriage
after divorce. But there is another possible interpretation of
Matthew's adding *for any cause other than unchastity* here and at
19: 9. He may be putting into words what Mark and the
others took for granted, being accepted by all, Jesus included—
that unchastity was the only possible ground for divorce
because it destroyed the unity between man and wife.

33. *Do not break your oath.* This is not an exact quotation
of any Old Testament passage. The prohibition of perjury is
found in Lev. 19: 12. Like it is the third commandment of
the Decalogue in Exod. 20: 7 and Deut. 5: 11. 'Thou shalt not
take the name of the Lord thy God in vain.' The Law does
not forbid oaths, but it does forbid false oaths which are
regarded as taking God's name in vain. Jesus would abolish
oaths altogether as unnecessary for those who habitually tell
the truth as his disciples are expected to do. This radical rejection of oaths is paralleled in the *Damascus Document* of the
Dead Sea Scrolls (XIX, 1).

34. *Oaths* by the name of God were regarded as binding.
Swearing by heaven or earth was not binding. But Jesus
prohibits idle swearing together with religious oaths. He
alludes to Isa. 66: 1, 'The heaven is my throne and the earth
is my footstool'.

38–9. Jesus rejects the law of exact retaliation or 'tit-for-tat'
(Exod. 21: 22–5), which had been designed to check un-
bridled vengeance. Jesus commends non-retaliation, returning
active love for active enmity.

40. The *shirt* (Greek *chitōn*) was a long undergarment with
sleeves; the *coat* (Greek *himation*) was a sort of blanket worn
over it, and used by the poor as a coverlet at night. A plaintiff
could sue for the former, but not for the latter (Exod. 22: 26;
Deut. 24: 12–13).

41. *makes you go.* The Greek verb means to compel a person
to do some public service. The system seems to have begun

in the Persian empire which authorized State couriers to commandeer service or property for public use. Under the Roman empire the same word was used for the requisition of similar services by the Army. A civilian could be compelled to carry a soldier's luggage. The same word is used in Matt. 27: 32; Mark 15: 21, where the Roman soldiers in charge of the crucifixion compelled Simon of Cyrene to carry the cross.

43. The command *Love your neighbour* comes from Lev. 19: 18, where by 'neighbour' is meant 'fellow Israelite'. The rabbis extended its meaning to include Gentile converts to Judaism. Nowhere in the Old Testament is there a command to hate one's enemies. But in the Dead Sea Scrolls we read the command to love everyone whom God has elected and to hate everyone whom he has rejected...to hate all sons of darkness (*Manual of Discipline*, 1, 4, 10).

44. Jesus commands his disciples to love their enemies even as God loves sinners who, in so far as they are sinners, are at enmity with God.

45. The goal of the disciple is to be like God.

48. *all goodness.* The Greek says 'Be perfect', that is, not a stained-glass window saint but 'complete', 'comprehensive', 'good towards everyone, not only those you like'—just as God is good towards the wicked as well as towards the good, sending sun and rain on both (verse 45). ✲

ALMSGIVING; PRAYER; THE LORD'S PRAYER; FORGIVENESS AND FASTING

'Be careful not to make a show of your religion before **6**
men; if you do, no reward awaits you in your Father's
house in heaven.

'Thus, when you do some act of charity, do not 2
announce it with a flourish of trumpets, as the hypocrites
do in synagogue and in the streets to win admiration from
men. I tell you this: they have their reward already. No; 3

when you do some act of charity, do not let your left
4 hand know what your right is doing; your good deed
must be secret, and your Father who sees what is done in
secret will reward you.

5 'Again, when you pray, do not be like the hypocrites;
they love to say their prayers standing up in synagogue
and at the street-corners, for everyone to see them. I tell
6 you this: they have their reward already. But when you
pray, go into a room by yourself, shut the door, and pray
to your Father who is there in the secret place; and your
Father who sees what is secret will reward you.

7 'In your prayers do not go babbling on like the heathen,
who imagine that the more they say the more likely they
8 are to be heard. Do not imitate them. Your Father knows
what your needs are before you ask him.

9 'This is how you should pray:

"Our Father in heaven,
Thy name be hallowed;
10 Thy kingdom come,
Thy will be done,
On earth as in heaven.
11 Give us today our daily bread.
12 Forgive us the wrong we have done,
As we have forgiven those who have wronged us.
13 And do not bring us to the test,
But save us from the evil one."

14 For if you forgive others the wrongs they have done, your
15 heavenly Father will also forgive you; but if you do not
forgive others, then the wrongs you have done will not
be forgiven by your Father.

'So too when you fast, do not look gloomy like the 16 hypocrites: they make their faces unsightly so that other people may see that they are fasting. I tell you this: they have their reward already. But when you fast, anoint 17 your head and wash your face, so that men may not see 18 that you are fasting, but only your Father who is in the secret place; and your Father who sees what is secret will give you your reward.

✻ 1. There is no real contradiction between verse 1 and 5: 16. The motive in the show of religion is self-glory, not the glory of God.

2. The almsgiving of the disciples is to be a strictly private affair. To make it a spectacle for an admiring audience is to be a 'hypocrite' (lit. 'actor').

3. The *left hand's* ignorance of what the right hand is doing is a metaphor of extreme secrecy. The relation of the right hand to the left is used by the Arabs as a type of closest fellowship. So probably the verse means 'do not let even your closest friend know about your generosity'. The generosity which is unknown to man is known to God.

5–6. Prayer, like almsgiving must be exercised in private, not with a view to parade. The saying does not discourage public worship, but here too prayer must be genuine communion with God, not outward show.

7. Prayer also must not be mere *babbling* like that of *the heathen*. Their prayers are long because they think they must address the right god and so all the gods are mentioned by name to ensure including the right one; and the right epithet must be used, so many epithets are used to ensure including the right one. The Christian has to address only one God, the heavenly Father who already knows what we need, so that there is no necessity for a long list of requests either.

9–13. In Luke 11: 2–4, the Lord's Prayer exists in a shorter, simpler form, probably nearer to the original. In prayer Jesus

3   55   A B C

himself addressed God simply as Father (Mark 14: 36, 'Abba, Father'; cf. Matt. 11: 25–6; Luke 10: 21). The addition of 'my' or 'our' was required in Jewish usage from motives of reverence, though it was seldom in pre-Christian times, and only in late writings, that the individual Jew spoke of God as his Father.

9. Matthew's *Our Father* probably, therefore, reflects usage in the synagogue services of Jewish Christians on Palestinian soil. The prayer begins with adoration of God; the first requests are for the hallowing of his name and the coming of his Reign and the doing of his will.

Thy name be hallowed. Both this and the following petition resemble the old Aramaic prayer of the synagogue worship known as Kaddish: 'Magnified and sanctified be his great name in the world which he has created according to his will. May he establish his kingdom during your life and during your days and during the life of all the House of Israel, and say ye, Amen.' The hallowing of God's name means the acknowledgement and worship of the true God throughout the world, which depends upon the coming of his Reign in visible triumph.

11. *our daily bread.* The word translated 'daily' is so rare that no one knows what it means. It may mean 'for the following day', 'our bread for the morrow'.

12. *the wrong we have done.* Greek: 'debts', a Jewish way of describing sins.

13. *do not bring us to the test.* The Greek word for 'test' may mean either 'temptation' or 'trial', 'tribulation'. The petition asks that the disciples may not be exposed to trials so severe that their loyalty to God may be undermined. Some Latin Fathers add: 'which we cannot bear'. Others read: 'do not allow us to be led into temptation'. These various alternatives show how difficult to understand the early Church found this petition.

the evil one. Greek: 'the evil', but probably 'the evil one', i.e. the Devil is meant. Some inferior MSS add the doxology

'For thine is the kingdom, the power and the glory', but this is a later attempt to give a still more liturgical form to a prayer which is already more liturgical, that is, more in the form in which it would be used in public divine service, in Matthew than in Luke.

14–15. This makes more explicit what has already been said about forgiveness in the Lord's Prayer. While only God can forgive sins in the sense of giving an absolute and final pardon, it is the duty of disciples to forgive others the wrongs that they have done to them. Failure to do this means that the disciples themselves will not be forgiven by God.

16. The Jews observed many fasts, e.g. on the Day of Atonement and at the New Year, as well as those undertaken by individuals as a special means of self-discipline. The Pharisees *make their faces unsightly* by not washing and by putting ashes on the head so that men might know that they were fasting, and admire their piety.

17. If the disciples observe fasts, they must see to it that men do not know about it. They must not act like the 'hypocrites' (actors). *

EARTHLY AND HEAVENLY TREASURE

'Do not store up for yourselves treasure on earth, where 19 it grows rusty and moth-eaten, and thieves break in to steal it. Store up treasure in heaven, where there is no 20 moth and no rust to spoil it, no thieves to break in and steal. For where your wealth is, there will your heart be also. 21

'The lamp of the body is the eye. If your eyes are 22 sound, you will have light for your whole body; if the 23 eyes are bad, your whole body will be in darkness. If then the only light you have is darkness, the darkness is doubly dark.

'No servant can be slave to two masters; for either he 24 will hate the first and love the second, or he will be devoted to the first and think nothing of the second. You cannot serve God and Money.

25 'Therefore I bid you put away anxious thoughts about food and drink to keep you alive, and clothes to cover your body. Surely life is more than food, the body more

26 than clothes. Look at the birds of the air; they do not sow and reap and store in barns, yet your heavenly Father

27 feeds them. You are worth more than the birds! Is there a man of you who by anxious thought can add a foot to

28 his height? And why be anxious about clothes? Consider how the lilies grow in the fields; they do not work,

29 they do not spin; and yet, I tell you, even Solomon in all

30 his splendour was not attired like one of these. But if that is how God clothes the grass in the fields, which is there today, and tomorrow is thrown on the stove, will he not

31 all the more clothe you? How little faith you have! No, do not ask anxiously, "What are we to eat? What are we

32 to drink? What shall we wear?" All these are things for the heathen to run after, not for you, because your heavenly

33 Father knows that you need them all. Set your mind on God's kingdom and his justice before everything else, and

34 all the rest will come to you as well. So do not be anxious about tomorrow; tomorrow will look after itself. Each day has troubles enough of its own.

✵ 20. Heavenly wealth (fellowship with God and the service of God) is incorruptible, and very different from the amassing of earthly riches, which so far from decreasing worry about the future, actually increase worry lest they be stolen or perish.

treasure in heaven is a Jewish idea. In Jewish literature the good deeds of a religious man are often described as treasures stored up in heaven.

22. *sound*, i.e. healthy.

23. *bad*, i.e. diseased.

in darkness, i.e. blind.

your whole body is an Aramaic way of saying 'you yourself'. The language is figurative, meaning 'if what you imagine to be vision and insight is really blindness and stupidity, your blindness is complete and disastrous'.

24. *Money.* The word in the original is *Mammon,* Aramaic for 'wealth'. The service of God and the service of money are incompatible, for God asks for self-sacrifice, money urges selfishness and self-advancement. 'The love of money is the root of all evil things' (1 Tim. 6: 10).

25–33. Jesus is calling for absolute faith and trust in the providence of God's love, and the putting of his will and purpose before all else. God provides for birds and flowers; how much more will he provide for men, his children. It is noteworthy that Jesus did not give as the reason for not worrying about the future a belief that the end of the world was imminent. Instead he gave as the reason the fact of God's providence and the trustworthiness of his love.

34. This verse, which brings in a different and rather discordant note, can be paralleled in Jewish literature. The Greek word here translated 'troubles' means 'evil' (*kakia*), i.e. material evil or calamities, a sense which the word never has elsewhere in the New Testament. Elsewhere it always means 'moral evil'. Perhaps verse 34 was added by Matthew from a Jewish source. ✽

'JUDGE NOT', AND OTHER TEACHING

'Pass no judgement, and you will not be judged. For 7 1,2 as you judge others, so you will yourselves be judged, and whatever measure you deal out to others will be dealt back to you. Why do you look at the speck of sawdust in your 3 brother's eye, with never a thought for the great plank

4 in your own? Or how can you say to your brother, "Let
me take the speck out of your eye", when all the time
5 there is that plank in your own? You hypocrite! First
take the plank out of your own eye, and then you will see
clearly to take the speck out of your brother's.

6   'Do not give dogs what is holy; do not feed your pearls
to pigs: they will only trample on them, and turn and
tear you to pieces.

7   'Ask, and you will receive; seek, and you will find;
·8 knock, and the door will be opened. For everyone who
asks receives, he who seeks finds, and to him who knocks,
the door will be opened.

9   'Is there a man among you who will offer his son a
10 stone when he asks for bread, or a snake when he asks for
11 fish? If you, then, bad as you are, know how to give your
children what is good for them, how much more will
your heavenly Father give good things to those who ask
him!

12   'Always treat others as you would like them to treat
you: that is the Law and the prophets.

13   'Enter by the narrow gate. The gate is wide that leads
to perdition, there is plenty of room on the road, and
14 many go that way; but the gate that leads to life is small
and the road is narrow, and those who find it are few.

* 1. Judgement belongs to God. Of course the disciples
must discriminate between right and wrong, good and bad;
but it is not their business to sit in judgement upon their
neighbours or to presume to allocate to them their status as
before God. God alone can do that.

    3. The saying of the *speck* and the *plank* continues the same
theme. Self-judgement is the first necessity. A reformed

character is the best means of securing the reformation of another.

6. In rabbinic literature the dog is considered to be among the wild beasts, and the pig to be unclean. The Gentiles were called 'dogs' or 'swine', because they were the enemies of Israel. This verse, therefore, looks like a bit of Jewish exclusiveness and may be ascribed to the Judaistic and anti-Gentile tone of much of the matter peculiar to Matthew. The early Fathers interpreted *what is holy* to mean the Eucharist. The *Didachē* (Teaching of the Twelve Apostles) interprets the command as one to withhold the Eucharist from the unbaptized and the heathen. The text does not refer to the Eucharist.

7. The giver and discloser and opener is God. This saying encourages petitionary prayer (i.e. the kind of prayer which is a request).

12. The Golden Rule. Matthew differs from Luke 6: 31 only in adding 'that is the Law and the prophets'. The Golden Rule is found in a negative form in Jewish literature: 'What thou thyself hatest, do to no man' (Tobit 4: 15).

13–14. The figure of the two ways is common in the Old Testament (e.g. Jer. 21: 8, 'Behold I set before you the way of life and the way of death'). Vice is the easier way, the way of least resistance. The way of goodness and self-sacrifice requires concentration and effort, and a good leader, the Good Shepherd who goes before and shows the way. ✶

FALSE PROPHETS; CHARACTER AND LIFE; FALSE
DISCIPLES; WISE AND FOOLISH BUILDING

'Beware of false prophets, men who come to you dressed 15 up as sheep while underneath they are savage wolves. You 16 will recognize them by the fruits they bear. Can grapes be picked from briars, or figs from thistles? In the same 17 way, a good tree always yields good fruit, and a poor tree bad fruit. A good tree cannot bear bad fruit, or a poor 18

19 tree good fruit. And when a tree does not yield good
20 fruit it is cut down and burnt. That is why I say you will
recognize them by their fruits.

21   'Not everyone who calls me "Lord, Lord" will enter
the kingdom of Heaven, but only those who do the will
22 of my heavenly Father. When that day comes, many will
say to me, "Lord, Lord, did we not prophesy in your
name, cast out devils in your name, and in your name
23 perform many miracles?" Then I will tell them to their
face, "I never knew you: out of my sight, you and your
wicked ways!"

24   'What then of the man who hears these words of mine
and acts upon them? He is like a man who had the sense
25 to build his house on rock. The rain came down, the
floods rose, the wind blew, and beat upon that house;
but it did not fall, because its foundations were on rock.
26 But what of the man who hears these words of mine and
does not act upon them? He is like a man who was foolish
27 enough to build his house on sand. The rain came down,
the floods rose, the wind blew, and beat upon that house;
down it fell with a great crash.'

28   When Jesus had finished this discourse the people were
29 astounded at his teaching; unlike their own teachers he
taught with a note of authority.

✻ 15–16. The criterion for distinguishing the characters of
men is the fruit they bear. From the man who is good at heart,
good action and good influence will flow. If the fruit is evil,
the tree is evil, and the only hope is to remove the old tree and
get a new one. If a man's deeds are evil, a new man, a new
character, a new life are required. The proof of the regenerate
man will be manifested in obedience to the will of God

revealed in Christ. The *Didachē*, meaning 'Teaching of the Twelve Apostles', says 'by their behaviour shall the false and true prophets be known'.

16. *Can grapes be picked* etc. Jas. 3: 12 has 'Can a fig-tree, my brothers, yield olives or a vine figs? No more does salt water yield fresh.'

19. Repeated from 3: 10 (the teaching of John the Baptist). Of course it must be borne in mind that Jesus himself was able to see good even in bad people, and he came to save, not to destroy. In actual life men are a mixture of good and evil. It is still true that the evil that is in man must be utterly destroyed if it is to be replaced by good.

21. In Luke 6: 46 the reference is to present discipleship. In Matthew the saying is made eschatological, i.e. it is made to relate to the day of judgement and the future kingdom.

22. *that day*, i.e. the day of judgement; it is derived from the Old Testament prophets, and is frequent in apocalyptic literature.

prophesy, not merely to tell the future, but to interpret the Scriptures and preach the gospel of the Kingdom.

in your name. To invoke the name of Jesus was to summon his power to one's aid.

23. Jesus openly claims to be the Judge at the last day (cf. 25: 31–46).

out of my sight, you and your wicked ways! is a quotation from Ps. 6: 8.

24–7. This parable is found also in Luke 6: 47–9, with slight differences. In Matthew the two builders choose different sites, the wise man rock, the foolish sand. In Luke the two came to the same place, but the wise man 'dug deep and laid the foundations on rock', while the foolish man built on the soil without foundations. Matthew speaks of rains, floods and wind. Luke mentions only the river. Matthew ascribes the security of the wise man to his having built on rock; Luke to the fact that the house was 'soundly built'.

24. *these words of mine*, i.e. the words of the Sermon on the

Mount. Whereas the prophets had declared that wisdom lay in doing the will of God, Jesus asserts that the wise man is he who does the will of Jesus, thereby making a high claim for the significance of his own Person. The rock is hearing and doing. The sand is hearing without doing. In the day of crisis (i.e. probably, the Day of Judgement), the one man stands firm, the other goes under. Therefore do not merely hear the teaching; act on it. 'It is not by hearing the law, but by doing it, that men will be justified before God' (Rom. 2: 13). 'Be sure that you act on the message and do not merely listen; for that would be to mislead yourselves' (Jas. 1: 22).

28. Here comes the regularly recurring editorial formula which marks the close of each of the five great discourses in Matthew (see p. 2).

Note that whereas the Sermon began by being addressed to the disciples (verse 2), it ended by being addressed to the people. Exactly the same change is found in Luke (compare 6: 20 with 7: 1). ✵

Teaching and Healing

THREE HEALINGS

8
2 AFTER HE HAD come down from the hill he was fol-
lowed by a great crowd. And now a leper approached him, bowed low, and said, 'Sir, if only you will, you can
3 cleanse me.' Jesus stretched out his hand, touched him, and said, 'Indeed I will; be clean again.' And his leprosy
4 was cured immediately. Then Jesus said to him, 'Be sure you tell nobody; but go and show yourself to the priest, and make the offering laid down by Moses for your cleansing; that will certify the cure.'

5   When he had entered Capernaum a centurion came up

to ask his help. 'Sir,' he said, 'a boy of mine lies at home 6
paralysed and racked with pain.' Jesus said, 'I will come 7
and cure him.' But the centurion replied, 'Sir, who am I 8
to have you under my roof? You need only say the word
and the boy will be cured. I know, for I am myself under 9
orders, with soldiers under me. I say to one, "Go", and
he goes; to another, "Come here", and he comes; and
to my servant, "Do this", and he does it.' Jesus heard him 10
with astonishment, and said to the people who were
following him, 'I tell you this: nowhere, even in Israel,
have I found such faith.

'Many, I tell you, will come from east and west to feast 11
with Abraham, Isaac, and Jacob in the kingdom of
Heaven. But those who were born to the kingdom will 12
be driven out into the dark, the place of wailing and
grinding of teeth.'

Then Jesus said to the centurion, 'Go home now; 13
because of your faith, so let it be.' At that moment the
boy recovered.

Jesus then went to Peter's house and found Peter's 14
mother-in-law in bed with fever. So he took her by the 15
hand; the fever left her, and she got up and waited on him.

When evening fell, they brought to him many who 16
were possessed by devils; and he drove the spirits out with
a word and healed all who were ill, to make good the 17
prophecy of Isaiah: 'He took away our illnesses and lifted
our diseases from us.'

* 2. The Hebrew word translated 'leprosy' in the Old
Testament comprises various skin-diseases, some of which were
curable. People suffering from 'leprosy' in any of its forms
were commanded by the Law not to associate with other

people, and were forbidden to enter a house. If approached, they had to cry out in warning: 'Unclean, unclean' (Lev. 13: 45–6). If they believed themselves to be cured, they had to go to a priest to be certified clean. If so certified, they had to go through a ritual of purification and offer the sacrifices prescribed in Lev. 14.

a leper approached him, thus violating the Law.

4. The reason for the command to tell nobody was Jesus' desire to keep his Messiahship a secret for the time being. Miraculous cures were expected to be accompaniments of Messiahship. Jesus did not want to be surrounded by crowds looking for these miraculous displays; his conception of Messiahship was different from theirs. See pp. 7–8.

the priest, i.e. the one officiating. The purification ceremony could be carried out only in Jerusalem.

the offering laid down by Moses included two live clean birds, one of which was killed and the other set free as part of the disinfection ritual (Lev. 14: 4–7).

5–13. The word translated 'boy' (Greek: *pais*) can mean either 'son' or 'servant'. Luke 7: 1–10 makes it clear that he understands the boy to have been a servant (Greek: *doulos*). There is a somewhat similar incident of the healing of a nobleman's son at Capernaum in John 4: 46–53. In Matthew the centurion himself comes to Jesus, in Luke he sends first elders of the Jews and then friends. Hence in Luke, the words of the centurion are added: 'I did not presume to come in person.' Otherwise the dialogue in Matthew and Luke is largely the same.

5. *centurion*. In the Roman Army a centurion commanded 100 men. According to Luke 7: 5, this centurion had built a synagogue for the Jews, though himself a Gentile. Because the centurion knows how to give and receive commands, he believes that Jesus can just command a cure from a distance and it will take place. This is indeed a great faith in the power of Jesus.

11–12. These verses are found in a different context in Luke (13: 28–9). The picture is that of a great banquet in the days of the Messiah. The belief that many Gentiles will be accepted is found in Isa. 45: 6, 'that they may know from the rising of the sun and from the west that there is none beside me', and 49: 12, 'lo, these shall come from far: and lo, these from the north and from the west'.

12. *those who were born to the kingdom* (lit. 'the sons of the kingdom') are Jews. John the Baptist gave the same warning (3: 9–10).

the dark, the place of wailing and grinding of teeth. An expression characteristic of Matthew. These were formerly characteristics of Sheol (i.e. the underworld, Hades, the grave), but, in our Lord's time, part of the usual description of Gehenna, the place where the wicked were punished. See note on 5: 22. Cf. Ps. 112: 10, 'The wicked...shall gnash with his teeth'.

13. The centurion's faith was rewarded. The boy recovered *at that moment.* In the Synoptic Gospels (except in the case of the demoniacs) Jesus always requires faith as the pre-condition of a healing miracle being performed. In the Fourth Gospel, on the other hand, healing miracles are 'signs' designed to evoke faith.

14. Mark tells us that Simon and Andrew lived in the same house at Capernaum. Jesus entered it along with Simon and Andrew, James and John.

16. *When evening fell.* Matthew has taken the first clause of Mark's double expression 'at evening, after sunset' (1: 32). Luke took the second clause (4: 40) (see p. 13).

17. *prophecy of Isaiah.* The 'proof text' (Isa. 53: 4) is added by Matthew with the usual introductory formula. The quotation follows the Hebrew, and is independent of the LXX. ✶

TEACHING ABOUT DISCIPLESHIP; CALMING THE
STORM; HEALING DEMONIACS

At the sight of the crowds surrounding him Jesus gave 18
word to cross to the other shore. A doctor of the law 19
came up, and said, 'Master, I will follow you wherever
you go.' Jesus replied, 'Foxes have their holes, the birds 20

their roosts; but the Son of Man has nowhere to lay his
21 head.' Another man, one of his disciples, said to him,
22 'Lord, let me go and bury my father first.' Jesus replied,
'Follow me, and leave the dead to bury their dead.'

23   Jesus then got into the boat, and his disciples followed.
24 All at once a great storm arose on the lake, till the waves
were breaking right over the boat; but he went on
25 sleeping. So they came and woke him up, crying: 'Save
26 us, Lord; we are sinking!' 'Why are you such cowards?'
he said; 'how little faith you have!' Then he stood up and
rebuked the wind and the sea, and there was a dead calm.
27 The men were astonished at what had happened, and
exclaimed, 'What sort of man is this, that even the wind
and the sea obey him?'

28   When he reached the other side, in the country of the
Gadarenes, he was met by two men who came out from
the tombs; they were possessed by devils, and so violent
29 that no one dared pass that way. 'You son of God,' they
shouted, 'what do you want with us? Have you come
30 here to torment us before our time?' In the distance a
31 large herd of pigs was feeding; and the devils begged
him: 'If you drive us out, send us into that herd of pigs.'
32 'Begone', he said. Then they came out and went into the
pigs; the whole herd rushed over the edge into the lake,
and perished in the water.

33   The men in charge of them took to their heels, and
made for the town, where they told the whole story, and
34 what had happened to the madmen. Thereupon the whole
town came out to meet Jesus; and when they saw him
9 they begged him to leave the district and go. So he got
into the boat and crossed over, and came to his own town.

✻ 18–22. This section follows awkwardly upon the last. In verse 16 it is late evening, as in Mark 1: 32. The incident of healing is followed in Mark by a period of night and the dawn of a new day, as one would expect. But Matthew appears to ignore the fact that it was evening. An interview takes place to which a parallel occurs in Luke 9: 57–60, at the close of the Galilean ministry. In Matthew this interview takes place when Jesus is about to embark on a boat.

19. The *doctor of the law* offers to follow Jesus, and Jesus replies in effect: 'Count the cost.'

20. By *Son of Man* here cannot be meant 'man', 'mankind' in general; for the saying would then not be true. It may be here, like its Aramaic equivalent (*barnasha*), a roundabout way of saying 'I', or it may signify Jesus in his present humility and poverty, in which the disciples too are involved (see pp. 8–9). Thus a corporate sense, like that in Dan. 7:9–14, is not impossible here; but the primary reference is probably to Jesus himself.

21. A disciple asks leave to go first and bury his father. The duty of giving decent burial to the dead, especially near relatives, was placed very high among the Jews. But the claims of the kingdom have a first priority.

22. *leave the dead to bury their dead* is a difficult saying, the meaning of which is uncertain. Perhaps it means that those who do not recognize the prior claims of the kingdom, which have precedence even over family obligations, are spiritually dead, and may be left to bury their (physically) dead.

23–7. Mark (4: 35) says it was evening. Matthew omits this as irrelevant for teaching purposes. For the same reason Matthew omits Mark's statement that there were other boats accompanying him, and that Jesus was in the stern and that he lay on a cushion. Matthew also avoids setting the disciples in so bad a light as Mark does. Thus while they say in Mark: 'Master, we are sinking! Do you not care?', in Matthew they say: *Save us, Lord; we are sinking!* In Mark Jesus says to the disciples: 'Have you no faith even now?', in Matthew he says, *how little faith you have!*

26. By *faith* is meant here 'trust in God'. In Mark Jesus says to the sea, 'Hush! Be still!'

27. *What sort of man is this...?* Power over nature must mean that he has divine power and authority.

28. *Gadarenes*, inhabitants of Gadara. Three readings are found in the MSS of all three Gospels: Gadarenes, Gergesenes, Gerasenes. It is difficult to be sure of the precise locality. Gadara is too far south. There was a Gerasa on the confines of Arabia, which is too far away. Gergesenes may suggest the modern Khersa, on the east coast of the sea. The territory of Gadara may have extended to the coast. Whereas in Mark there is one demoniac, in Matthew there are two. Matthew considerably abridges Mark's account.

29. *before our time*, i.e. before the final judgement. The demons were afraid of being prematurely condemned to the 'torment' which was to be their ultimate fate.

34. *begged him to leave the district.* It is not suggested that they were annoyed at the financial loss. They were uneasy at the mysterious power that was in Jesus.

9: 1. *his own town.* Capernaum. In Mark and Luke the following scene is set in a house. Matthew implies that men came bringing the paralytic to Jesus as he came to land. ✻

THE HEALING OF THE PARALYTIC;
THE CALL OF MATTHEW; FASTING

2 And now some men brought him a paralytic lying on a bed. Seeing their faith Jesus said to the man, 'Take heart,
3 my son; your sins are forgiven.' At this some of the lawyers said to themselves, 'This is blasphemous talk.'
4 Jesus read their thoughts, and said, 'Why do you harbour
5 these evil thoughts? Is it easier to say, "Your sins are for-
6 given", or to say, "Stand up and walk"? But to convince you that the Son of Man has the right on earth to forgive sins'—he now addressed the paralytic—'stand up,

take your bed, and go home.' Thereupon the man got up, 7
and went off home. The people were filled with awe at the 8
sight, and praised God for granting such authority to men.

As he passed on from there Jesus saw a man named 9
Matthew at his seat in the custom-house; and he said
to him, 'Follow me.' And Matthew rose and followed
him.

When Jesus was at table in the house, many bad 10
characters—tax-gatherers and others—were seated with
him and his disciples. The Pharisees noticed this, and said 11
to his disciples, 'Why is it that your master eats with tax-
gatherers and sinners?' Jesus heard them and said, 'It is 12
not the healthy that need a doctor, but the sick. Go and 13
learn what that text means, "I require mercy, not sacrifice." I did not come to invite virtuous people, but sinners.'

Then John's disciples came to him with the question: 14
'Why do we and the Pharisees fast, but your disciples do
not?' Jesus replied, 'Can you expect the bridegroom's 15
friends to go mourning while the bridegroom is with
them? The time will come when the bridegroom will be
taken away from them; that will be the time for them to
fast.

'No one sews a patch of unshrunk cloth on to an old 16
coat; for then the patch tears away from the coat, and
leaves a bigger hole. No more do you put new wine into 17
old wine-skins; if you do, the skins burst, and then the
wine runs out and the skins are spoilt. No, you put new
wine into fresh skins; then both are preserved.'

* 2. *bed*, probably a rug or light pallet.
  their faith, including, no doubt, that of the sick man.

3. *blasphemous.* Only God can forgive sins. 'I, even I, am he that blotteth out thy transgressions for mine own sake' (Isa. 43: 25). Jesus was claiming God's right and power. He saw that forgiveness of the man's sin was a necessary condition of his healing.

6. *Son of Man.* Jesus himself, who has the right on earth to forgive sins. But, on a lower plane, his disciples also are called upon to forgive sins (Matt. 6: 14–15). It is easier to say *your sins are forgiven* than to say *stand up and walk*, because the latter can be immediately tested by the event. By doing the harder task, i.e. healing the paralytic, Jesus proves the validity of his claim to forgive sins.

8. *The people were filled with awe* at the cure because they sensed the divine power in Jesus.

for granting such authority to men. This is Matthew's addition, implying that the disciples share in Christ's right and power to forgive sins, though in a lower and less absolute sense, suggesting the communal aspect of the term 'Son of Man' here more strongly than at 8: 20.

9. Cf. Mark 2: 13–17; Luke 5: 27–32, where the tax-gatherer's name is Levi. Only Matthew substitutes the name Matthew for that of Levi, thus identifying Matthew with the tax-gatherer as in the list of disciples in 10: 3. See p. 16.

custom-house, the tax office, or toll-house.

10. *in the house.* Luke says 'of Levi'. This would explain the presence of many tax-gatherers. In Mark and Matthew Jesus is himself the host.

11. *sinners,* i.e. persons who do not observe the Mosaic law, and people of lax morals. Tax-gatherers, since they dealt with all sorts of people, including Gentiles, were probably careless in regard to the Mosaic law. People hated them because they exacted more money than was strictly due.

12. When criticized for eating with such people, Jesus argues in effect: Who need a doctor? Sick people. Who need spiritual healing? People who are spiritually sick, sinners.

13. *Go and learn.* Jesus implies that the Pharisees do not

understand the Scriptures. He quotes to them Hos. 6: 6, which is quoted in the Gospels only here and at 12: 7.

14–17. Fasting was compulsory only on the day of Atonement, 10th Tishri (seventh month, September–October), and on publicly proclaimed fast days. The reference is to private, voluntary fasting, which the disciples of Jesus did not keep. The Pharisees fasted on two days a week.

15. *the bridegroom* in the Old Testament is a title of God, as the husband of Israel (Isa. 62: 5). Jesus is the bridegroom of the disciples, the new Israel (cf. Matt. 25: 1; John 3: 29; Rev. 18: 23). Probably therefore by *the bridegroom* Jesus here means himself. If so, the statement about *the bridegroom* being *taken away* is his first prediction of his death. In his repudiation of fasting for his disciples so long as he is with them in the flesh, Jesus rejects the scribal traditions which had been added to the Law; the Law itself did not require frequent fasting. The religion of Jesus is the religion of joy. On the other hand, the practice of fasting in the early Church, after Jesus had been *taken away*, is envisaged.

16–17. Jesus adds the sayings about the new patch on an old coat, and the new wine in old wine skins. His meaning is that the new teaching of the Gospel cannot be fitted into the old teaching of Judaism. It is bound to destroy the latter. The new teaching of Jesus requires a new religion and a new Church. Jesus did not reject the Old Testament (see 5: 17), but the current religious practice as fostered by the Scribes and Pharisees. *

MIRACLES OF HEALING

Even as he spoke, there came a president of the synagogue, 18
who bowed low before him and said, 'My daughter has just died; but come and lay your hand on her, and she will live.' Jesus rose and went with him, and so did his 19
disciples.

Then a woman who had suffered from haemorrhages 20

for twelve years came up from behind, and touched the
21 edge of his cloak; for she said to herself, 'If I can only
22 touch his cloak, I shall be cured.' But Jesus turned and
saw her, and said, 'Take heart, my daughter; your faith
has cured you.' And from that moment she recovered.

23   When Jesus arrived at the president's house and saw the
24 flute-players and the general commotion, he said, 'Be off!
The girl is not dead: she is asleep'; but they only laughed
25 at him. But, when everyone had been turned out, he
went into the room and took the girl by the hand, and she
26 got up. This story became the talk of all the country
round.

27   As he passed on Jesus was followed by two blind men,
28 who cried out, 'Son of David, have pity on us!' And
when he had gone indoors they came to him. Jesus asked,
'Do you believe that I have the power to do what you
29 want?' 'Yes, sir', they said. Then he touched their eyes,
30 and said, 'As you have believed, so let it be'; and their
sight was restored. Jesus said to them sternly, 'See that
31 no one hears about this.' But as soon as they had gone
out they talked about him all over the country-side.

32   They were on their way out when a man was brought
33 to him, who was dumb and possessed by a devil; the devil
was cast out and the patient recovered his speech. Filled
with amazement the onlookers said, 'Nothing like this
34 has ever been seen in Israel.' But the Pharisees said, 'He
casts out devils by the prince of devils.'

✻ 18. *president of the synagogue*. In the Greek, Matthew has
'ruler' simply. Mark has 'the president of one of the synagogues came up, Jairus by name', who says that his daughter
is at the point of death. Messengers come later to tell Jairus

that his daughter is dead. In Matthew the *president of the synagogue* tells Jesus straightway that his daughter is dead. Matthew has thus considerably abridged Mark's story. On the synagogue and its officials, see p. 22.

20. *a woman who had suffered from haemorrhages* would be unclean, according to the Law. Perhaps that is why she *came up from behind*.

touched the edge of his cloak, probably the tassel which every Jew wore (Num. 15: 38–41; Deut. 22: 12). Her act was one of faith, and because of it she was cured.

23. At the president's house the mourning ceremonies were filling the house with noise. For a funeral even the poorest Jew was expected to hire not less than two flutes and one wailing woman.

24. *asleep.* 'Sleep' is a common way of referring to death both among Jews and among Christians; but here there is a contrast with death, because the death of this girl is only temporary. Mark tells us she was twelve years old, and that when she recovered, she rose up and walked: and Jesus ordered the affair to be kept a secret, and that she should be given something to eat.

27–34. Just as in 8: 28 Matthew speaks of two demoniacs, where Mark speaks of only one, so here Matthew speaks of two blind men, where Mark (10: 46–52; cf. Luke 18: 35–43) speaks of only one, Bartimaeus. In Matthew the event is part of a busy day in Capernaum. In Mark it is at Jericho.

27. *Son of David*, i.e. Messiah. Jesus does not comment on the title, but asks whether they have faith in his power to heal them, which again is the precondition of a cure. Jesus sternly commands them to keep the cure a secret. It is difficult to see how they could have done this, and in fact they *talked about him all over the country-side* (verse 31).

32. *They were on their way out.* Probably Jesus and his disciples. The group bringing the dumb demoniac met Jesus as he left the house.

34. This verse is omitted by Codex Bezae (D), the Western Text, also by two old Latin MSS and the Sinaitic Syriac. The weight of other MSS is in favour of retaining it. *The prince of devils* is Satan. ✻

SENDING OUT THE DISCIPLES

35 So Jesus went round all the towns and villages teaching in their synagogues, announcing the good news of the Kingdom, and curing every kind of ailment and disease.
36 The sight of the people moved him to pity: they were
37 like sheep without a shepherd, harassed and helpless; and he said to his disciples, 'The crop is heavy, but labourers
38 are scarce; you must therefore beg the owner to send labourers to harvest his crop.'

10   Then he called his twelve disciples to him and gave them authority to cast out unclean spirits and to cure every kind of ailment and disease.

2   These are the names of the twelve apostles: first Simon, also called Peter, and his brother Andrew; James son of
3 Zebedee, and his brother John; Philip and Bartholomew, Thomas and Matthew the tax-gatherer, James son of
4 Alphaeus, Lebbaeus, Simon, a member of the Zealot party, and Judas Iscariot, the man who betrayed him.

5   These twelve Jesus sent out with the following instructions: 'Do not take the road to gentile lands, and do not
6 enter any Samaritan town; but go rather to the lost sheep
7 of the house of Israel. And as you go proclaim the
8 message: "The kingdom of Heaven is upon you." Heal the sick, raise the dead, cleanse lepers, cast out devils. You received without cost; give without charge.
9   'Provide no gold, silver, or copper to fill your purse,

no pack for the road, no second coat, no shoes, no stick; 10
the worker earns his keep.

'When you come to any town or village, look for some 11
worthy person in it, and make your home there until you
leave. Wish the house peace as you enter it, so that, if 12,13
it is worthy, your peace may descend on it; if it is not
worthy, your peace can come back to you. If anyone 14
will not receive you or listen to what you say, then as
you leave that house or that town shake the dust of it off
your feet. I tell you this: on the day of judgement it will 15
be more bearable for the land of Sodom and Gomorrah
than for that town.

'Look, I send you out like sheep among wolves; be 16
wary as serpents, innocent as doves.

* Verses 35–8 give an editorial report of the widespread
activity of Jesus and the need for more workers in view of the
urgency of the task.

36. *like sheep without a shepherd* alludes to Num. 27: 17,
'that the congregation of the Lord be not as sheep which have
no shepherd', and 1 Kings 22: 17, 'I saw all Israel scattered upon
the mountains, as sheep that have no shepherd.'

10: 2–4. Similar lists are given in Mark 3: 16–19; Luke
6: 14–16; and Acts 1: 13.

2. Only here does Matthew use the word 'apostles'. The
word means 'those sent'. It is applied in the New Testament
not only to the twelve, but to Paul, Barnabas, Matthias, James
Jesus' brother, the other brothers of Jesus, and others. The
Christian apostle is one sent with a commission to proclaim
salvation through Christ. The twelve were sent out by Jesus
who bestowed upon them his authority to preach and to
heal.

Simon or Simeon is almost always thought of as first in
importance among the disciples. His surname Peter (Greek

Petros) translates his Aramaic nickname *Kepha*' 'rock' (Greek *petra*). *Andrew* is a Greek name meaning 'manly', 'brave'. *James* is in Greek *Jacōbos* (Jacob).

3. *Philip* is a Greek name meaning 'lover of horses'.

The *bar* in *Bartholomew* ought to mean 'son of', but the derivation of the remainder of the word is uncertain. Perhaps the name means 'son of Tolmai or Tolomai'.

Thomas means 'twin' (cf. 'the Twin', John 11: 16).

Matthew is called the tax-gatherer to recall 9: 9.

James is called the *son of Alphaeus* to distinguish him from James the son of Zebedee. Mark 2: 14 (parallel to Matt. 9: 9) calls Levi, the tax-gatherer, the son of Alphaeus, but it may not be the same Alphaeus.

Lebbaeus. Many manuscripts read Thaddaeus as in Mark 3: 18.

4. *Simon, a member of the Zealot party* (see p. 20). The R.V. has Simon the Cananaean, a word which comes from the Aramaic, meaning *zealot*.

Judas. Always named last in the synoptic lists of the twelve, and always with mention of his betrayal of Jesus.

Iscariot may mean 'man of Kerioth', a place in Judaea; or it may come from an Aramaic word meaning 'the false', i.e. practically 'the traitor'.

5. Matthew has 'conflated' Jesus' *instructions* by bringing together matter derived from the charge to the twelve in Mark 6: 7–13, non-Marcan matter which he has in common with Luke, and matter peculiar to himself. He has included in his account of the mission-charge sayings which look beyond the missionary tour of the twelve to the wider mission of the Church. The disciples' first mission is to Israel alone (5–6). This instruction occurs only in Matthew. Jesus generally worked in Jewish territory, though Mark (7: 24–31; 8: 27 — 9: 1) recounts his travels on Gentile soil, and Luke tells us that he was once in the neighbourhood of Samaria (Luke 9: 52 f.). But Jesus rarely ministered to Gentiles, and then without entering their homes.

6. *lost*, i.e. in spiritual need, sinful.

7. The twelve are to proclaim the message which Jesus himself had proclaimed, '*the kingdom of Heaven is upon you*', i.e. is very near, or actually present. See on 4: 17. The call to repentance is presumably implied.

8. The healing acts which they are commissioned to do are such as Jesus has been doing (chapters 8 and 9).

raise the dead. Many MSS, including important early versions, omit these words. Those which include them vary in the place where they put them (this is usually a sign of interpolation). The most reliable MSS, however, have the words placed as in the N.E.B. The disciples have received, without deserving it or paying for it, the power to heal, so they must give without charge the free gift of which they are only the stewards.

9–10. They are to take no money (this was usually carried in belts), no extra equipment, and *no stick* which was allowed in Mark's account. They are to travel light to ensure speed, and let their hearers supply their needs.

10. *the worker earns his keep* (Greek: 'food'). Luke has 'pay' (10: 7, cf. 1 Tim. 5: 18, 'the workman earns his pay').

12. *Wish the house peace*, i.e. give the inmates the Jewish greeting 'Peace be unto you'. This greeting was believed to rest upon the house if it was worthy and gave a welcome to the apostles and their message; otherwise it would return to the apostles, and they must leave, shaking the dust off their feet as a sign that the apostles have discharged their responsibility and that the inhospitable household or town will suffer judgement for their churlish rejection of the message of salvation.

15. *Sodom and Gomorrah* were proverbial examples of great wickedness (Gen. 19). But their punishment in the Day of Judgement will be less severe than that of those who reject the Gospel.

16. *I send you out like sheep among wolves* is found also in Luke 10: 3, except that Luke has 'lambs'. But the proverb which follows is peculiar to Matthew. *

DO NOT BE AFRAID

17 'And be on your guard, for men will hand you over to
18 their courts, they will flog you in the synagogues, and you
will be brought before governors and kings, for my sake,
19 to testify before them and the heathen. But when you are
arrested, do not worry about what you are to say; when
the time comes, the words you need will be given you;
20 for it is not you who will be speaking: it will be the Spirit
of your Father speaking in you.

21 'Brother will betray brother to death, and the father
his child; children will turn against their parents and send
22 them to their death. All will hate you for your allegiance
to me; but the man who holds out to the end will be
23 saved. When you are persecuted in one town, take refuge
in another; I tell you this: before you have gone through
all the towns of Israel the Son of Man will have come.

24 'A pupil does not rank above his teacher, or a servant
25 above his master. The pupil should be content to share his
teacher's lot, the servant to share his master's. If the
master has been called Beelzebub, how much more his
household!

26 'So do not be afraid of them. There is nothing covered
up that will not be uncovered, nothing hidden that will
27 not be made known. What I say to you in the dark you
must repeat in broad daylight; what you hear whispered
28 you must shout from the house-tops. Do not fear those
who kill the body, but cannot kill the soul. Fear him
rather who is able to destroy both soul and body in hell.

29 'Are not sparrows two a penny? Yet without your
30 Father's leave not one of them can fall to the ground. As

for you, even the hairs of your head have all been counted. So have no fear; you are worth more than any number of 31 sparrows.

'Whoever then will acknowledge me before men, 32 I will acknowledge him before my Father in heaven; and 33 whoever disowns me before men, I will disown him before my Father in heaven.

✻ This section is addressed to the Christian Church rather than to the missionaries whom Jesus sent out.

17. The following verses anticipate active persecution such as confronted the Church after Pentecost. Similar verses occur in Mark 13: 9–13. The *courts* are probably the local sanhedrins, composed of twenty-three members each, which were held in Jewish cities other than Jerusalem. They probably met in the *synagogues*. Flogging was usually done by the synagogue attendant. Rabbinical law limited the strokes to thirty-nine.

18. The *governors* may be Roman officials, like Pontius Pilate.

The *kings* would include puppet kings like Herod the Great and Herod Antipas.

20. *the Spirit of your Father*, i.e. the Holy Spirit, to whom as in Mark 13: 11 is assigned here the task of teaching and prompting. Cf. John 14: 26, 'the Holy Spirit whom the Father will send in my name, will teach you everything, and will call to mind all that I have told you'.

23. This verse predicts the coming of the Son of Man before all the towns of Israel have been visited by the missionaries. Jesus can hardly have predicted that his own *parousia* (return from heaven in glory) would take place during the present missionary tour! It must be a post-resurrection saying of the early Church.

24–5. This saying is found in a different form in Luke 6: 40, 'A pupil is not superior to his teacher; but everyone, when his training is complete, will reach his teacher's level.' Even when fully educated, the pupil is no greater than his teacher, so must be content with his teacher's lot. As Jesus has been persecuted, so will Christians. As Jesus has been called Beelzebub, so will Christians.

25. *Beelzebub.* The name means 'lord of flies'. It is applied to the prince of demons, Satan, at 12: 24, where a full explanation is given.

26. *do not be afraid of them*; fear God. In the Day of Judgement all truth will be revealed and will determine man's eternal destiny. Augustine was inspired by these words to declare that whatever the fate of the Christian's body, he would not lose the resurrection, since Christ has exhorted us not to fear those who kill the body but cannot kill the soul (*On the City of God*, I, 12).

28. *soul* here means the real self.

hell, i.e. Gehenna (see 5: 22).

29. *sparrows* were sold to be eaten, and still are eaten in Mediterranean countries today. The Roman coin here referred to (the *As*) was in value 1/15th of a denarius (= a labourer's daily wage. See 20: 13). Sparrows were so cheap that an extra one was thrown in if two of these Roman coins were paid. Yet God is concerned about them. How much more for men and women, his children (cf. Matt. 6: 26, 30). ✴

THE COST OF DISCIPLESHIP

34 'You must not think that I have come to bring peace to the earth; I have not come to bring peace, but a sword.
35 I have come to set a man against his father, a daughter against her mother, a young wife against her mother-in-
36 law; and a man will find his enemies under his own roof.
37   'No man is worthy of me who cares more for father or mother than for me; no man is worthy of me who
38 cares more for son or daughter; no man is worthy of me

who does not take up his cross and walk in my footsteps.
By gaining his life a man will lose it; by losing his life 39
for my sake, he will gain it.

'To receive you is to receive me, and to receive me is 40
to receive the One who sent me. Whoever receives a 41
prophet as a prophet will be given a prophet's reward,
and whoever receives a good man because he is a good
man will be given a good man's reward. And if anyone 42
gives so much as a cup of cold water to one of these little
ones, because he is a disciple of mine, I tell you this: that
man will assuredly not go unrewarded.'

When Jesus had finished giving his twelve disciples **11**
their instructions, he left that place and went to teach and
preach in the neighbouring towns.

* 34–6. Cf. Luke 12: 51–3. A *sword* divides; so does the
truth which Jesus came to bring. It is more important than
family unity. While Christ's ultimate purpose is to reconcile
men to God and to one another, in the battle for the truths of
his Kingdom men will take sides, and even families will be
divided.

37–9. Christ must come first. The disciple's love of Christ
must exceed his love even of his nearest relatives and lead him
to brave self-denial and even crucifixion itself for Christ's sake.
The Roman use of crucifixion was well known in Palestine,
and Jesus could use it as symbolic of extreme self-sacrifice.
Self-sacrifice, says Jesus, is the only true life.

39. This saying occurs in six different forms, cf. Luke
17: 33; Matt. 16: 25 = Mark 8: 35 = Luke 9: 24; John 12: 25.
The word translated 'life' here is the same as that translated
'soul' in verse 28 (*psychē*). Both meanings are included here.
By gaining his (physical) life, a man will lose his real self; by
losing his (physical) life, a man will gain his real self.

40. The one sent out represents the one who sent him, so

that to receive a disciple of Christ is to receive Christ, and to receive Christ is to receive God. This high claim is made by Jesus in all four Gospels.

41. He who welcomes a prophet as a prophet (such as John the Baptist was; there were also Christian prophets later) will receive a prophet's reward (God's blessing). He who gives only a cup of cold water (typical of a minor service) to one of these little ones (i.e. outwardly insignificant disciples) because they follow Christ, will receive a reward, because the service was in effect rendered to Jesus himself.

11: 1. Note the regular formula at the end of a long discourse. This ends the section on apostleship. Matthew makes no mention of the departure of the disciples, or their work, or their return. Mark on the other hand summarizes the course of the mission (6: 12–13) and their report (6: 30). So does Luke in regard to the twelve (9: 6, 10) and in regard to the seventy-two (10: 17). Perhaps Matthew thought of the mission as actually taking place after the resurrection. ✶

JOHN THE BAPTIST AND JESUS

2 John, who was in prison, heard what Christ was doing,
3 and sent his own disciples to him with this message: 'Are you the one who is to come, or are we to expect some
4 other?' Jesus answered, 'Go and tell John what you hear
5 and see: the blind recover their sight, the lame walk, the lepers are clean, the deaf hear, the dead are raised to life,
6 the poor are hearing the good news—and happy is the man who does not find me a stumbling-block.'

7 When the messengers were on their way back, Jesus began to speak to the people about John: 'What was the spectacle that drew you to the wilderness? A reed-bed
8 swept by the wind? No? Then what did you go out to see? A man dressed in silks and satins? Surely you must

84

look in palaces for that. But why did you go out? To see ⁹
a prophet? Yes indeed, and far more than a prophet. He is ¹⁰
the man of whom Scripture says,

> "Here is my herald, whom I send on ahead of you,
> And he will prepare your way before you."

I tell you this: never has there appeared on earth a mother's ¹¹
son greater than John the Baptist, and yet the least in the
kingdom of Heaven is greater than he.

'Ever since the coming of John the Baptist the kingdom ¹²
of Heaven has been subjected to violence and violent men
are seizing it. For all the prophets and the Law foretold ¹³
things to come until John appeared, and John is the ¹⁴
destined Elijah, if you will but accept it. If you have ears ¹⁵
that can hear, then hear.

'How can I describe this generation? They are like the ¹⁶
children sitting in the market-place and shouting at each
other,

> "We piped for you and you would not dance."   ¹⁷
> "We wept and wailed, and you would not mourn."

For John came, neither eating nor drinking, and they say, ¹⁸
"He is possessed." The Son of Man came eating and ¹⁹
drinking, and they say, "Look at him! a glutton and a
drinker, a friend of tax-gatherers and sinners!" And yet
God's wisdom is proved right by its results.'

✵ 2. Jesus himself continued his active ministry in the Jewish
cities of the region.

3. John's question, brought by his disciples, recalls his
own preaching (3: 11)—'the one who comes after me',
etc. The question implies that John had believed that Jesus'
ministry was the fulfilment of his own preaching, but what

he had since heard had led him to doubt. The kind of Messiah whom John had expected would not act as Jesus did.

4-6. Jesus in reply tells the messengers of John to report to their master what he had accomplished, in words reminiscent of some prophecies in Isaiah (29: 18-19; 35: 5-6; 61: 1). The point of Christ's answer lies in the deliberate contrast between the picture Jesus draws and the preaching of John. John looked for judgement issuing in the destruction of the wicked. Jesus declares that he has not come to destroy them, but to restore, heal and save them. The powers of the age to come have already arrived. He who understands this will not find Jesus *a stumbling-block* to faith, but become his disciple and receive God's blessing.

7. As *the messengers* return, Jesus proceeds to praise John the Baptist to the crowd and to identify him as the forerunner, a greater than a prophet, the one foretold by Mal. 3: 1, 'Behold, I send my messenger, and he shall prepare the way before me'. In the quotation 'the way before me' has been changed to 'your way' to make it refer to Jesus. In Malachi the messenger or herald (= Elijah) is the forerunner of God himself, and there is no suggestion of a Messiah.

11. *a mother's son*, i.e. a human being. *John the Baptist* is one of the greatest men; yet he is outside the *kingdom of Heaven* in its present manifestation as God's reign in the ministry of Jesus, because he had no gospel of the unmerited love of God which takes the initiative in seeking and saving the lost. So that *the least in the kingdom . . . is greater than he.*

12. This difficult saying can be interpreted in three different ways: (1) *The kingdom* is violently treated; its members are oppressed. This would make the kingdom equivalent to the Church, a meaning it has nowhere else. (2) *The kingdom* is violently snatched at by those who misunderstand it as a political kingdom, such as the Zealots. (3) *The kingdom* is violently stormed by enthusiastic people who are eager to enter it. This last meaning seems to make the best sense. The whole saying will then mean—'From John's time until now

men of spiritual force lay hold of the reign of God; for the law and the prophets were until John, but now the new age has come'. (The parallel saying in Luke 16: 16 is like this last explanation.)

14. *John is the destined Elijah*, foretold by Mal. 4: 5. People in the days of Jesus were looking for the return of Elijah. Some thought Jesus himself was Elijah returned (Mark 8: 28; Matt. 16: 14; Luke 9: 19). The identification of John with Elijah is specially stressed in Matthew; and Jesus himself makes the identification both here and in the descent from the Mount of Transfiguration (Mark 9: 11-13; Matt. 17: 10-13). But in the Fourth Gospel John the Baptist himself is made to reject the identification (John 1: 20). Matthew emphasizes that John is Elijah returned, because the Jews held that the true Messiah must be anointed and proclaimed as such by Elijah.

16-19 (cf. Luke 7: 31-2). This parable illustrates the unresponsiveness of men to any sort of religious appeal. The way of John was too stern for them, that of Jesus was too lax.

The people are like *children..in the market-place* who will play neither at weddings nor at funerals.

The *Son of Man* here clearly refers to Jesus himself. His wisdom in associating socially with tax-gatherers and sinners proves *God's wisdom* to be *right by its results* (lit. 'deeds'). Some MSS have 'children'. ✻

LAMENTS OVER THE CITIES OF GALILEE AND GREAT THANKSGIVING

Then he spoke of the towns in which most of his miracles 20 had been performed, and denounced them for their impenitence. 'Alas for you, Chorazin!' he said; 'alas for 21 you, Bethsaida! If the miracles that were performed in you had been performed in Tyre and Sidon, they would long ago have repented in sackcloth and ashes. But it will 22 be more bearable, I tell you, for Tyre and Sidon on the day

23 of judgement than for you. And as for you, Capernaum, will you be exalted to the skies? No, brought down to the depths ! For if the miracles had been performed in Sodom which were performed in you, Sodom would be standing
24 to this day. But it will be more bearable, I tell you, for the land of Sodom on the day of judgement than for you.'

25 　　At that time Jesus spoke these words: 'I thank thee, Father, Lord of heaven and earth, for hiding these things from the learned and wise, and revealing them to the
26,27 simple. Yes, Father, such was thy choice. Everything is entrusted to me by my Father; and no one knows the Son but the Father, and no one knows the Father but the Son and those to whom the Son may choose to reveal him.

28 　　'Come to me, all whose work is hard, whose load is
29 heavy; and I will give you relief. Bend your necks to my yoke, and learn from me, for I am gentle and humble-
30 hearted; and your souls will find relief. For my yoke is good to bear, my load is light.'

* 21. *Chorazin* is not mentioned elsewhere in the Bible nor in Josephus. It is probably to be identified with Chirbet Kerāze, about 3 miles north of Tell Hūm (Capernaum). There is no account in the Gospels of any visit of Jesus to Chorazin, yet clearly he had exercised an important ministry there. This shows the big gaps in the story of his ministry in the Gospels.

Bethsaida was on the east side of Jordan, near its entry into the Sea of Galilee.

Tyre and Sidon were heathen cities. They will be judged more leniently on the Day of Judgement because they have not had the opportunity which Chorazin and Bethsaida have had and rejected.

23. *Capernaum* was a centre of the Galilean ministry of Jesus, but its people's arrogance led them to reject Jesus. Retribution

in its case will be more severe than that on *Sodom* which would have repented if it had had Capernaum's privilege.

depths. Greek: 'Hades', i.e. Sheol, the grave. The saying is based on Isa. 14: 13, 15 (Hebrew, not LXX): 'And thou shalt be brought down to Sheol, to the uttermost parts of the pit.' Sheol expresses the lowest shame, as heaven expresses the highest glory.

25-30. The great thanksgiving, self-revelation, and invitation.

25. *for hiding.* Jesus thanks the Father because, although he hid these things (i.e. the truths of the kingdom) from the learned and wise (such as the doctors of the law), he revealed them to the simple (the disciples).

26. This could be translated: 'Yes, I thank thee, Father, that such was thy choice.'

27. *Everything.* Either all knowledge or all power or both. This self-revelation of Jesus occurs in a slightly different form in Luke who writes 'knows who the Son is' and 'knows who the Father is', instead of simply 'knows the Son' and 'knows the Father'. The saying as a whole makes high divine claims for the Person of Jesus and his intimate relationship to the Father. It resembles many sayings in the Fourth Gospel.

28-9. In this invitation Jesus appears to identify himself with the Wisdom of God who is represented as saying in Ecclus. 51: 23: 'Draw near unto me, ye unlearned, and lodge in the house of instruction.' The author of Ecclesiasticus is appealing for the study of the Law in which he sees the wisdom of God. Rabbis often spoke of the *yoke* of the Law, but always in praise. To accept this yoke, they claimed, was to put off the yoke of earthly kingdoms and worldly care. This claim is made good in Jesus' higher interpretation of the Law and his gift to his followers of the power to obey it. The metaphor of the yoke suggests 'sharing' the burden. The yoke was made for two. As a carpenter Jesus must often have made yokes, and have made them as smooth and easy to bear as possible.

The whole section 25-30 is in rhythmical prose and may

have its origins in Aramaic poetry uttered by Jesus. Its background is thoroughly Jewish, and may be compared to hymns of thanksgiving in the Dead Sea Scrolls. The Old Testament too contains the idea that man knows God because God first knows him. There is no need to doubt that this passage is a genuine utterance of Jesus. *

Controversy

PLUCKING CORN AND HEALING ON THE SABBATH

12 ONCE ABOUT that time Jesus took a walk on the Sabbath through the cornfields; and his disciples, feeling hungry, began to pluck some ears of corn and eat
2 them. The Pharisees noticed this, and said to him, 'Look, your disciples are doing something which is forbidden on
3 the Sabbath.' He answered, 'Have you not read what
4 David did when he and his men were hungry? He went into the House of God and ate the consecrated loaves, though neither he nor his men had a right to eat them, but
5 only the priests. Or have you not read in the Law that on the Sabbath the priests in the temple break the Sabbath
6 and it is not held against them? I tell you, there is some-
7 thing greater than the temple here. If you had known what that text means, "I require mercy, not sacrifice",
8 you would not have condemned the innocent. For the Son of Man is sovereign over the Sabbath.'
9 He went on to another place, and entered their syna-
10 gogue. A man was there with a withered arm, and they asked Jesus, 'Is it permitted to heal on the Sabbath?'
11 (Their aim was to frame a charge against him.) But he

said to them, 'Suppose you had one sheep, which fell into
a ditch on the Sabbath; is there one of you who would
not catch hold of it and lift it out? And surely a man is 12
worth far more than a sheep! It is therefore permitted
to do good on the Sabbath.' Turning to the man he said, 13
'Stretch out your arm.' He stretched it out, and it was
made sound again like the other. But the Pharisees, on 14
leaving the synagogue, laid a plot to do away with him.

Jesus was aware of it and withdrew. Many followed, 15
and he cured all who were ill; and he gave strict injunc- 16
tions that they were not to make him known. This was in 17
fulfilment of Isaiah's prophecy:

'Here is my servant, whom I have chosen,   18
 My beloved, on whom my favour rests;
 I will put my Spirit upon him,
 And he will proclaim judgement among the nations.
 He will not strive, he will not shout,   19
 Nor will his voice be heard in the streets.
 He will not snap off the broken reed,   20
 Nor snuff out the smouldering wick,
 Until he leads justice on to victory.
 In him the nations shall place their hope.'   21

* 1–8. This incident is what scholars of the Form-critical
school call a 'paradigm' or 'pronouncement story'. That is,
it is a short account of a conversation of Jesus with his
opponents, ending in a terse saying, and is suitable for an
illustration in a sermon. Matthew has taken it from Mark 2:
23–8 (cf. Luke 6: 1–5).

1–2. When the Gospels were written, the Sabbath was not
observed by Gentile Christians, and no doubt this 'paradigm',
and the incident that follows it, were used as examples to

justify this freedom. In the story itself the duty to keep the Sabbath is acknowledged both by Jesus and the disciples' critics. The question was whether the Law allowed exceptions. Deut. 23: 25 permits the plucking and eating of a neighbour's corn, provided it was not reaped with a sickle. To pluck corn was equivalent to harvesting which was forbidden on the Sabbath not by the Law but by the oral traditions of the Scribes. Jesus, for the sake of argument, assumes that his disciples have broken the Law, but argues that the disciples' hunger justified their action, just as David when he was hungry broke the Law which said that only the priests might eat the shewbread (1 Sam. 21: 1–6).

to pluck some ears of corn was technically to reap. Luke 6: 1 adds that they rubbed them in their hands (as they would have to before eating): this was equivalent to threshing. These are two of the thirty-nine chief kinds of work forbidden by the Scribal tradition, as we learn from the Mishnah (see Index).

4. The House of God into which David went was at Nob.

the consecrated loaves were the loaves placed in the presence of God, the bread of the presence, the shewbread, prescribed in Exod. 25: 30, 'And thou shalt set upon the table shewbread before me alway'. Josephus tells us that this was baked on Friday and brought and laid upon the holy table early on the Sabbath. It stayed there until the next Sabbath, when the priests were allowed to eat it, but no one else.

5–7. These verses are added by Matthew to Mark's account. Technically *the priests in the temple break the Sabbath* for they labour in offering sacrifices on that day (as prescribed by Num. 28: 9–10), but the requirements of the temple justify the break. The authority of Jesus is *greater than the temple*. The text quoted in verse 7 is from Hos. 6: 6, where the meaning is 'Mercy is more important than sacrifice'. Jesus did not forbid sacrifice. This text has been quoted before in 9: 13.

8. *Son of Man* here refers to Jesus himself, but as it is his disciples' action that he is justifying there is also a community reference (see pp. 8–9).

9-10. The Pharisees regarded healing on the Sabbath as lawful only when life was in danger. Jesus asserted the right to do any helpful action on the Sabbath, and to heal even when life was not in danger.

12. *It is...permitted to do good on the Sabbath.* The School of Hillel allowed one to comfort a mourner or visit a sick man and pray for him, for this was to do good. Jesus goes further and claims that to heal a man is also an example of doing good, and no violation of the Sabbath. It is noteworthy that the opponents of Jesus take his ability to heal for granted. When Jesus had effected the cure, the Pharisees plotted to destroy him. Mark 3: 6 says that they made their plots with the party of Herod Antipas. It does not follow that the whole of the Pharisaic party was against Jesus.

15-16. In these verses Matthew sums up Mark 3: 7-12. Jesus departed because further controversy might lead to his arrest or bring him the kind of publicity that would hinder his work. He ordered silence about his healing work to prevent the growth of popular excitement. It was part of the messianic secret, for the Messiah was expected to work healing miracles. Jesus did not intend to fulfil the role of the Messiah of popular expectation, an earthly king and deliverer, but a humble servant who would save men from their sins.

18-19. The quotation is from Isa. 42: 1-4. It does not agree entirely either with the Hebrew or with the LXX, but probably follows an Aramaic Targum. It is the longest Old Testament quotation in Matthew and suggests that Matthew understood Jesus' motive, in commanding silence, to be humility and gentleness. He identified the *servant* of the quotation with Jesus. In the Old Testament passage the servant of God is Israel. It was through the bestowal of the Spirit of the Lord that individuals and nations were enabled to achieve great aims. Jesus is to fulfil the destiny which God appointed for Israel, but which Israel as a whole failed to fulfil. By *judgement* is meant God's requirements both ceremonial and moral.

19. The Old Testament passage means that Israel in her

effort to convert the Gentiles must use gentle, patient and unobtrusive methods as befitted her lowly estate amongst her powerful heathen neighbours. The knowledge of God was to penetrate the world quietly.

20. The *broken reed* and the *smouldering wick* signify the faint and almost extinct elements of faith and goodness in those to whom the message is preached.

21. *In him*. lit. 'in his name'. *the nations shall place their hope*. The Hebrew has: 'And for his law shall the isles hope.' *

HEALING A BLIND AND DUMB MAN; THE BEELZEBUB CONTROVERSY; SAYINGS ABOUT GOOD AND EVIL

22 Then they brought him a man who was possessed; he was blind and dumb; and Jesus cured him, restoring both
23 speech and sight. The bystanders were all amazed, and the word went round: 'Can this be the Son of David?'
24 But when the Pharisees heard it they said, 'It is only by Beelzebub prince of devils that this man drives the devils out.'

25 He knew what was in their minds; so he said to them, 'Every kingdom divided against itself goes to ruin; and no town, no household, that is divided against itself can
26 stand. And if it is Satan who casts out Satan, Satan is divided against himself; how then can his kingdom stand?
27 And if it is by Beelzebub that I cast out devils, by whom do your own people drive them out? If this is your
28 argument, they themselves will refute you. But if it is by the Spirit of God that I drive out the devils, then be sure the kingdom of God has already come upon you.

29 'Or again, how can anyone break into a strong man's house and make off with his goods unless he has first tied the strong man up before ransacking the house?

'He who is not with me is against me, and he who does 30 not gather with me scatters.

'And so I tell you this: no sin, no slander, is beyond 31 forgiveness for men, except slander spoken against the Spirit, and that will not be forgiven. Any man who speaks 32 a word against the Son of Man will be forgiven; but if anyone speaks against the Holy Spirit, for him there is no forgiveness, either in this age or in the age to come.

'Either make the tree good and its fruit good, or make 33 the tree bad and its fruit bad; you can tell a tree by its fruit. You vipers' brood! How can your words be good 34 when you yourselves are evil? For the words that the mouth utters come from the overflowing of the heart. A good 35 man produces good from the store of good within himself; and an evil man from evil within produces evil.

'I tell you this: there is not a thoughtless word that 36 comes from men's lips but they will have to account for it on the day of judgement. For out of your own mouth 37 you will be acquitted; out of your own mouth you will be condemned.'

* The controversy sharpens: the reader must be sure who gave Jesus his power. In his own day some said it was the devil.

22–4. Both Matthew and Luke substitute this for Mark 3: 20–1 (the family of Jesus seeking to take charge of him) to form a fitting introduction to the Beelzebub controversy.

23. *the Son of David*, i.e. the Messiah, who was expected to work miracles.

24. *Beelzebub*. The true reading found in nearly all the Greek MSS is Beelzebul. Jerome adopted the form Beelzebub for the Vulgate New Testament from which it has come into the English versions. The god of Ekron (2 Kings 1: 2)

must have been called *Baal zebul*, meaning 'exalted Lord', but the biblical writers call him *Baalzebub*, 'lord of flies' to show their contempt. The Jews, as the context here shows, regarded Beelzebul as the prince of demons (= Satan, the devil). If Satan, or one of the demons, casts out demons, his house or kingdom is divided against itself and will be brought to an end by civil war.

27. The Pharisees also apparently had their exorcists who cast out demons.

28. Jesus claims that he casts out demons by the *Spirit of God* (Luke 11: 20 has 'the finger of God'), and this is a sign that in some sense the Reign of God has already broken in upon the world, for the power of the demons is destined to be broken in the messianic age.

29. How can Satan be supposed to ruin himself? How can he be ruined without first being defeated by another who ransacks his house and makes off with his goods? So Jesus tied up and despoiled Satan in his temptations in the wilderness, throughout his ministry, and in his death and resurrection.

30. Jesus declares that neutrality towards his work is as bad as hostility.

31. *slander...against the Spirit*. This is to call white black and black white, and so to sin against the light, to attribute good works to an evil power instead of to a good one. So long as a man does this, repentance, and therefore forgiveness, are impossible.

33–7. These verses have parallels in 7: 16–20, and Luke 6: 43–4.

33–4. One must either declare the exorcist good and his works good, or declare that both are bad. Good actions can be done only by good people. Evil people can produce only evil whether in deeds or in words.

36. The *thoughtless word* is the one that especially gives the speaker away because it reveals his true character. The eschatological emphasis on *the day of judgement* is particularly characteristic of Matthew, though it is found in all the Gospels. *

AGAINST SEEKING FOR SIGNS; A SAYING ON
DEMON POSSESSION; JESUS' TRUE FAMILY

At this some of the doctors of the law and the Pharisees 38
said, 'Master, we should like you to show us a sign.' He 39
answered: 'It is a wicked, godless generation that asks for
a sign; and the only sign that will be given it is the sign
of the prophet Jonah. Jonah was in the sea-monster's 40
belly for three days and three nights, and in the same way
the Son of Man will be three days and three nights in the
bowels of the earth. At the Judgement, when this genera- 41
tion is on trial, the men of Nineveh will appear against it
and ensure its condemnation, for they repented at the
preaching of Jonah; and what is here is greater than Jonah.
The Queen of the South will appear at the Judgement 42
when this generation is on trial, and ensure its condemnation, for she came from the ends of the earth to hear the
wisdom of Solomon; and what is here is greater than
Solomon.

'When an unclean spirit comes out of a man it wanders 43
over the deserts seeking a resting-place; and finding none,
it says, "I will go back to the home I left." So it returns 44
and finds the house unoccupied, swept clean, and tidy.
Off it goes and collects seven other spirits more wicked 45
than itself, and they all come in and settle down; and in
the end the man's plight is worse than before. That is
how it will be with this wicked generation.'

He was still speaking to the crowd when his mother 46
and brothers appeared; they stood outside, wanting to
speak to him. Someone said, 'Your mother and your 47
brothers are here outside; they want to speak to you.'

48 Jesus turned to the man who brought the message, and
49 said, 'Who is my mother? Who are my brothers?'; and
pointing to the disciples, he said, 'Here are my mother and
50 my brothers. Whoever does the will of my heavenly
Father is my brother, my sister, my mother.'

* 38. In Matthew the request for a sign comes from certain
of the doctors of the law (Scribes). In Luke the Scribes and
Pharisees are not mentioned and Jesus addresses his words to
the crowds. The request is for some stupendous demonstration
of supernatural power.

39–40. *godless*. The Greek word means literally 'adulterous';
i.e. 'unfaithful to God', God being thought of in Old Testament fashion as the husband of his people. The sign offered is
that of *Jonah*. In Matthew the analogy between Jonah and the
Son of Man is that Jonah *in the sea-monster's belly* and returning
from it prefigures the descent of Christ to Hades *in the bowels
of the earth*, and his return from that abode of the dead. In
Luke the preaching of Jonah is the point, in Matthew his
adventures, of which the Ninevites presumably knew nothing.
Jesus was only *two* nights in the grave, not three. Probably
Luke's interpretation is nearer to what Jesus meant. Jonah's
preaching spoke for itself, and was its own sign of the truth of
God's judgement, and his invitation to repentance and salvation. So the ministry of Jesus, both preaching and action,
shows the Reign of God, and so speaks for itself. This interpretation is confirmed by verses 41 and 42, where it is *the
preaching of Jonah* to the Ninevites that matters.

42. *The Queen of the South* (1 Kings 10: 1–13) is the
Queen of Sheba. The *South* means 'the southern land' =
S. Arabia. Jesus says that in the coming Judgement the fact
that the Queen of the South responded to such revelation as
was available in her day, in Solomon's wisdom, will be con-
demning evidence against those who fail to respond to the
fuller revelation given by Jesus himself.

what is here is the Kingdom of God manifested in Jesus.

43. *unclean spirit* is one of the Jewish synonyms for 'demon' whose natural home is the desert.

44. But the exorcised demon wants to be back in the man from whom he was ejected ('the home I left'). On inspection he finds it clean and decorated and *unoccupied* (this last point is not in Luke).

45. Then the demon collects seven others, worse than himself, and together they take possession. The point is that eight will be better able to resist exorcism than one. Jesus teaches that exorcism by itself is not enough. When Jesus casts out devils, it is more than exorcism. It is the positive entry of the Reign of God which expels the demon. The former house of the demon must become God's dwelling, a temple of God.

46-50. Matthew does not say why the mother and brothers of Jesus came; but clearly they are not as yet followers of Jesus. His true family are his disciples who do the will of God. *

WHY IN PARABLES? THE SOWER

That same day Jesus went out and sat beside the lake, **13** where so many people gathered round him that he had 2 to get into a boat. He sat there, and all the people stood on the shore. He spoke to them in parables, at some length. 3

He said: 'A sower went out to sow. And as he sowed, 4 some seed fell along the footpath; and the birds came and ate it up. Some seed fell on rocky ground, where it had 5 little soil; it sprouted quickly because it had no depth of earth, but when the sun rose the young corn was scorched, 6 and as it had no root it withered away. Some seed fell 7 among thistles; and the thistles shot up, and choked the corn. And some of the seed fell into good soil, where it 8 bore fruit, yielding a hundredfold or, it might be, sixty-fold or thirtyfold. If you have ears, then hear.' 9

10   The disciples went up to him and asked, 'Why do you
11 speak to them in parables?' He replied, 'It has been
granted to you to know the secrets of the kingdom of
12 Heaven; but to those others it has not been granted. For
the man who has will be given more, till he has enough and
to spare; and the man who has not will forfeit even what
13 he has. That is why I speak to them in parables; for they
look without seeing, and listen without hearing or under-
14 standing. There is a prophecy of Isaiah which is being fulfilled for them: "You will hear and hear, but never under-
15 stand; you will look and look, but never see. For this
people has grown gross at heart; their ears are dull, and
their eyes are closed. Otherwise, their eyes might see,
their ears hear, and their heart understand, and then they
might turn again, and I would heal them."

16   'But happy are your eyes because they see, and your
17 ears because they hear! Many prophets and saints, I tell
you, desired to see what you now see, yet never saw it;
to hear what you hear, yet never heard it.

18, 19   'You, then, may hear the parable of the sower. When
a man hears the word that tells of the Kingdom but fails
to understand it, the evil one comes and carries off what
has been sown in his heart. There you have the seed sown
20 along the footpath. The seed sown on rocky ground stands
for the man who, on hearing the word, accepts it at once
21 with joy; but as it strikes no root in him he has no staying-
power, and when there is trouble or persecution on ac-
22 count of the word he falls away at once. The seed sown
among thistles represents the man who hears the word,
but worldly cares and the false glamour of wealth choke
23 it, and it proves barren. But the seed that fell into good

soil is the man who hears the word and understands it, who accordingly bears fruit, and yields a hundredfold or, it may be, sixtyfold or thirtyfold.'

✻ 13: 1–52 consists of parables addressed to the crowds for the most part. Matthew here follows Mark's framework, adopting and expanding the collection of parables in Mark 4, and so makes his third large discourse.

A parable is designed to illustrate a single point of teaching. It can be either a story or a brief metaphor or a proverb. If the story is designed to illustrate more than one point, and each item of the story corresponds to something it is meant to typify, it is better to call it an allegory. The parable was a favourite device of Jewish teachers.

2. Jesus uses the boat as a pulpit.

4–5. This story is drawn from real life. Jesus describes a man who broadcasts seed. It falls on various sorts of ground, and much of it is lost, but enough falls on fertile ground to yield a good crop. So it is with the work of Jesus and his disciples who proclaim the kingdom of Heaven by word and by deed. God will bless their labour, and they need not be discouraged.

footpath. Some seed accidentally fell on the path that went round or through the field.

5. *rocky ground.* Not the bare rock, but parts of the field where the soil was thin on rock. There is a good deal of this sort of land in Palestine, and the seed that falls on it soon perishes, though it sprouts quickly because the soil is warmed by the rock.

7. The *thistles* are the result of bad farming. They should have been dug out, but were just cut down or burnt, so that the roots remain in the earth and spring up afresh, choking the wheat. But the enormous yield of the seed that fell into good soil (verse 8) more than compensated for the loss. There is oriental exaggeration in the language used to describe the yield, though Josephus tells us that the plain of Gennesaret was unusually fertile (*Jewish War*, III, 10, 8).

10. In verse 2 Jesus was teaching in a boat. Matthew now forgets this. In Mark 4: 10–11 the disciples ask about the meaning of the parables, not as in Matthew about the purpose for which they were spoken. Yet it is this latter question which in Mark first receives an answer, which is here reproduced in Matthew. The reason which Jesus is represented as giving for speaking in parables is surprising. The parables were surely intended to make his teaching clearer, not more obscure. But by the time the Gospels were written the original context in which they were uttered had been lost, so that many of them did appear obscure to the evangelists. Perhaps also the doctrine that the parables were intended to conceal the Gospel was suggested by the knowledge that Jesus kept his Messiahship concealed, and by the knowledge that Jesus did not win universal acceptance although sent by God.

12. This verse occurs in a different context in Mark 4: 25 (=Luke 8: 18). It sounds like a proverb. In this context it probably means that the disciples, having faith, and being therefore spiritually receptive, will receive more and more revelation, while others, lacking faith, will become more and more blind to God's truth.

13. The meaning of this verse is expanded in the quotation from Isa. 6: 9–10 which follows.

14. Isaiah meant that though the people will have repeated opportunities of learning God's will, they will not heed. He did not mean necessarily that it was God's will that the people should be unheeding, but this is how the Gospel writers understood the passage. The quotation in Matthew follows the LXX.

16. Another beatitude: the disciples are blest in seeing the realization of God's promised kingdom which prophets and saints desired in vain to witness.

18–19. Whereas in the intention of Jesus the parable had one point and one only, the early Church tended to turn the parables into allegories. So here, the parable of the sower is changed into an allegory about different kinds of soil. The forced nature of the interpretation is shown by the fact that what is sown is made to indicate the kind of hearer, whereas it should represent 'the word', i.e. the Gospel. There are four classes of hearers: (1) the unresponsive hearer. The evil one (Satan), represented here by the birds, comes and carries off the seed and gives the man no chance to respond. (2) The shallow hearer, who lacks deep roots. He makes a start in receiving the word and entering upon the life of faith, but he lacks depth and persistence. (3) The worldly hearer who lets the seductions of this world choke the word. (4) The successful hearer, who hears, understands and bears abundant fruit in the life of faith and obedience, the amount of fruit varying with the individual disciple. ✻

PARABLES OF THE KINGDOM

Here is another parable that he put before them: 'The 24 kingdom of Heaven is like this. A man sowed his field with good seed; but while everyone was asleep his enemy 25 came, sowed darnel among the wheat, and made off. When the corn sprouted and began to fill out, the darnel 26 could be seen among it. The farmer's men went to their 27 master and said, "Sir, was it not good seed that you sowed in your field? Then where has the darnel come from?" "This is an enemy's doing", he replied. "Well then," 28 they said, "shall we go and gather the darnel?" "No," 29 he answered; "in gathering it you might pull up the wheat at the same time. Let them both grow together 30 till harvest; and at harvest-time I will tell the reapers, 'Gather the darnel first, and tie it in bundles for burning; then collect the wheat into my barn.'"'

And this is another parable that he put before them: 31 'The kingdom of Heaven is like mustard-seed, which a

32 man took and sowed in his field. As a seed, mustard is smaller than any other; but when it has grown it is bigger than any garden-plant; it becomes a tree, big enough for the birds to come and roost among its branches.'

33 He told them also this parable: 'The kingdom of Heaven is like yeast, which a woman took and mixed with half a hundredweight of flour till it was all leavened.'

34 In all this teaching to the crowds Jesus spoke in parables;
35 in fact he never spoke to them without a parable; thus making good the prophecy of Isaiah:

'I will open my mouth in parables;
I will utter things kept secret since the world was made.'

36 He then dismissed the people, and went into the house, where his disciples came to him and said, 'Explain to us
37 the parable of the darnel in the field.' And this was his answer: 'The sower of the good seed is the Son of Man.
38 The field is the world; the good seed stands for the children of the Kingdom, the darnel for the children of the evil one.
39 The enemy who sowed the darnel is the devil. The harvest
40 is the end of time. The reapers are angels. As the darnel,
41 then, is gathered up and burnt, so at the end of time the Son of Man will send out his angels, who will gather out of his kingdom everything that causes offence, and all
42 whose deeds are evil, and these will be thrown into the blazing furnace, the place of wailing and grinding of
43 teeth. And then the righteous will shine as brightly as the sun in the kingdom of their Father. If you have ears, then hear.

✻ 24–5. This parable is peculiar to Matthew. It concerns not the soil, but the kind of seed sown. Good seed was sown by the farmer, weeds by his enemy. The weed mentioned is the poisonous, bearded *darnel (lolium temulentum)* which grows to about the same height as wheat.

29–30. Pulling up *the darnel* will uproot *the wheat* also because their roots are intertwined. It is best to *let . . . both grow together till harvest.* Similarly it would spell disaster to attempt to achieve a pure church in which there are no sinners before the final judgement, for the judgement and the sorting out are God's work which he alone can do, and will do in his own time. The parable envisages a situation in the early Church in which it might be tempting but unwise to resort to excommunication. Fallible human judgement might make a serious mistake. In any case it is wrong for man to usurp the divine right of ultimate judgement. Jesus himself tolerated the presence of Judas among the twelve till the divine purpose was accomplished. On the Kingdom see pp. 10–11.

31–2. Mustard was cultivated in the days of Jesus for its seed and also as a vegetable. The *mustard-seed* was the smallest seed, but produced a remarkably large plant. The reference to birds roosting in the branches recalls Dan. 4: 21. Nebuchadnezzar in a dream saw a tree which reached to heaven and could be seen to the end of the earth, 'under which the beasts of the field dwelt, and upon whose branches the fowls of the heaven had their habitation'. The parable stresses huge growth from small beginnings. So the kingdom of Heaven has small beginnings in the ministry of Jesus, but will attain vast growth.

33. The parable of the *yeast* is found also in Luke 13: 20–1, in language largely identical. Like the former parable it illustrates extensive development from small beginnings, but the kind of development stressed is here one of permeation through the mass. Yeast in the Bible usually signifies an evil permeating force, but here a good one.

half a hundredweight of flour. Greek: 'three measures'. The measure is $1\frac{1}{2}$ Roman modius (about a peck and a half). Three measures (=one ephah) was about 50 lb. and was a usual quantity for household purposes, as Abraham seems to have known (Gen. 18: 6).

34. The statement that Jesus never spoke without a parable is clearly an exaggeration, unless it refers only to one stage of his ministry. Again the explanation may be that Matthew wants his readers to understand why so great a teacher was not always accepted.

35. The quotation is not from Isaiah (some MSS omit 'Isaiah'), but from Psalm 78: 2, following the Hebrew. Matthew has found an Old Testament text to explain why the Messiah's teaching was not believed by everyone.

36–43. Matthew interprets the parable as an allegory.

37. *the Son of Man.* Jesus himself, now the humble and suffering servant, destined to come again in glory and judgement.

38. *The field is the world.* For Matthew and the Church, for which he wrote, the missionary field is the whole world.

the children of the Kingdom...the children of the evil one. Hebraic expressions meaning 'those fitted by character for the Kingdom'...'those whose character is wicked'. These are identified with the good and bad seed respectively, because they are produced by it.

39. *The harvest* is here an eschatological metaphor of the last judgement, derived from the Old Testament, e.g. Joel 3: 13, 'Put ye in the sickle, for the harvest is ripe'.

40. *the end of time.* The Greek means literally 'the end of the age', i.e. the end of this present evil age which the Jews contrasted with the blessed messianic age to come. This is a phrase used repeatedly by Matthew and confined to him in the New Testament.

41. *his kingdom.* The kingdom of the Son of Man, later (in verse 43) called the kingdom of the Father, is the eschatological kingdom, the consummation of the Reign of God already begun in the ministry of Jesus on earth. 'Son of Man' here is the heavenly Messiah.

everything that causes offence. lit. the Greek means 'all the stumbling-blocks'.

42. *the blazing furnace,* i.e. the fires of Gehenna.

the place of wailing and grinding of teeth. See on 8: 12.

43. These words recall Daniel 12: 3, 'And they that be wise shall shine as the brightness of the firmament'. *

THE TREASURE; THE PEARL; THE DRAG-NET; THE HOUSEHOLDER

'The kingdom of Heaven is like treasure lying buried 44 in a field. The man who found it, buried it again; and for sheer joy went and sold everything he had, and bought that field.

'Here is another picture of the kingdom of Heaven. 45 A merchant looking out for fine pearls found one of very special value; so he went and sold everything he had, and 46 bought it.

'Again the kingdom of Heaven is like a net let down 47 into the sea, where fish of every kind were caught in it. When it was full, it was dragged ashore. Then the men 48 sat down and collected the good fish into pails and threw the worthless away. That is how it will be at the end 49 of time. The angels will go forth, and they will separate the wicked from the good, and throw them into the 50 blazing furnace, the place of wailing and grinding of teeth.

'Have you understood all this?' he asked; and they 51 answered, 'Yes.' He said to them, 'When, therefore, a 52 teacher of the law has become a learner in the kingdom of Heaven, he is like a householder who can produce from his store both the new and the old.'

✶ 44–6. The parables of the treasure and the pearl illustrate the immense worth of the Kingdom, for which the utmost sacrifice should be made. It is not the intention to commend the dishonesty of concealing the true value of the field in which the treasure was found. That has nothing to do with the point of the parable.

45. *A merchant looking out for fine pearls* would travel to distant lands, for instance Persia or even India. Both these parables are peculiar to Matthew. So is that of the net.

47. The *net* is a drag-net, one end of which can be fastened to the shore and the other to a boat; or it may be stretched from one boat to another. It is weighted to hold it down. Those of the disciples who were fishermen must often have used one. The point of this parable is similar to that of the wheat and the darnel.

52. The ideal disciple is a rabbi with understanding of the Kingdom, who can therefore bring forth from a well-stored mind *the old*, i.e. the riches of Old Testament truth, and the *new*, i.e. the riches of the new teaching of Jesus. ✶

THE VISIT TO NAZARETH;
JOHN THE BAPTIST

53 When he had finished these parables Jesus left that place,
54 and came to his home town, where he taught the people in their synagogue. In amazement they asked, 'Where does he get this wisdom from, and these miraculous powers?
55 Is he not the carpenter's son? Is not his mother called
56 Mary, his brothers James, Joseph, Simon, and Judas? And are not all his sisters here with us? Where then has he got
57 all this from?' So they fell foul of him, and this led him to say, 'A prophet will always be held in honour, except
58 in his home town, and in his own family.' And he did not work many miracles there: such was their want of faith.

It was at that time that reports about Jesus reached the **14**
ears of Prince Herod. 'This is John the Baptist,' he said 2
to his attendants; 'John has been raised to life, and that is
why these miraculous powers are at work in him.'

For Herod had arrested John, put him in chains, and 3
thrown him into prison, on account of Herodias, his
brother Philip's wife; for John had told him: 'You have 4
no right to her.' Herod would have liked to put him to 5
death, but he was afraid of the people, in whose eyes
John was a prophet. But at his birthday celebrations the 6
daughter of Herodias danced before the guests, and Herod
was so delighted that he took an oath to give her anything 7
she cared to ask. Prompted by her mother, she said, 'Give 8
me here on a dish the head of John the Baptist.' The king 9
was deeply distressed when he heard it; but out of regard
for his oath and for his guests, he ordered the request to
be granted, and had John beheaded in prison. The head 10,11
was brought in on a dish and given to the girl; and she
carried it to her mother. Then John's disciples came and 12
took away the body, and buried it; and they went and
told Jesus.

✵ Matthew now takes up his Marcan source again for the
visit to Nazareth: Mark 6: 1–6 (Luke 4: 16–30).

53. *When he had finished.* Matthew's usual formula at the
end of a section of discourse.

54. *his home town.* Nazareth.

55. *the carpenter's son.* Mark has 'the carpenter, the son of
Mary'. It was an insult for a man to be called the son of his
mother instead of his father. Hence Matthew's alteration
which he did not feel to be in conflict with the story of the
Virgin Birth. The word translated 'carpenter' could mean

'builder'. If Joseph was a carpenter or builder, Jesus the eldest son would be too.

his brothers. The natural meaning is that they were younger brothers of Jesus born by Mary to Joseph. The theory that they were foster-brothers, sons of Joseph by a former marriage, and the theory that they were really cousins, have no evidence to support them.

56. *his sisters* are not referred to elsewhere than here and Mark 6: 3 in the New Testament.

57. *fell foul of him*. It hurt the villagers' pride to think that he who had grown up as one of themselves had so far out-stripped them.

A prophet, etc. Cf. John 6: 42, 'we know his father and mother. How can he now say, "I have come down from heaven"?' The first of the Oxyrhynchus papyri gives Jesus' saying as follows: 'A prophet is not acceptable in his own country, nor does a physician cure those who know him.' Cf. John 4: 44, 'Jesus himself declared that a prophet is without honour in his own country'.

58. *And he did not work many miracles*. Matthew softens Mark's statement, 'he could work no miracle there, except that he put his hands on a few sick people and healed them' (p. 13).

14: 1. *Prince Herod*. Greek: Herod the tetrarch (ruler of the fourth part of a province). He ruled Galilee and Peraea, having been appointed soon after the death of Herod the Great (2: 1) in 4 B.C. He was the son of Herod the Great by his Samaritan wife Malthace, and thus full brother of Archelaus (2: 22). He governed until A.D. 39, when he was banished to Lyons in Gaul, where he died. He married first the daughter of Aretas, king of Arabia, and second the wife of his brother Herod Boethus, Herodias, whom he met on a visit to Rome. It was Herodias' daughter by Herod Boethus, Salome, who was later married to Philip, a half-brother of Antipas. In verse 3, therefore, there seems to be a confusion between Herodias and her daughter Salome. It was the latter who afterwards became Philip's wife. The Western Text (D, *Codex Bezae*) and some

Latin MSS omit 'Philip' in verse 3. The arrest of John has already been mentioned in 4: 12.

4. Herod divorced his first wife. Josephus, the Jewish historian, writing about A.D. 94, tells us that he did this in accordance with a secret agreement made between him and Herodias as a preliminary to their marriage. While the Law allowed the divorce, it was contrary to the Law for him to marry his brother's wife, while that brother was still living (Lev. 18: 16; 20: 21, 'if a man shall take his brother's wife, it is impurity'). In the case of a brother who has died, the Law commands such a marriage in a case where no son has been born (Deut. 25: 5). Herod Antipas claimed to be a Jew who conformed to the Law. John the Baptist therefore was right to rebuke him.

5. Josephus says that Herod arrested John because he was jealous of his influence over *the people*. Mark (6: 19) says that it was Herodias who was John's enemy, and that Herod liked to converse with John. Matthew's account disagrees with this, and ascribes the enmity to Herod.

6. *the daughter of Herodias*. Probably Salome, daughter of Herodias by her first marriage. She seems to have been married to Philip, her uncle, soon after this incident. The Dead Sea Scrolls condemn marriage with a niece. Apparently the *birthday celebrations* were held in the neighbourhood of Machaerus, where John was imprisoned. Josephus (*Jewish War*, VII, 6, 2) says that Herod had built a fortress and a palace close to the town of Machaerus.

8. *dish*. The Greek word means writing-tablet or any flat plate. Originally it meant a wooden board.

10. It was a violation of the Jewish Law to execute a man without trial, and execution by beheading was not allowed. But it was in accordance with Roman and Greek custom.

12. It seems that the disciples of John were allowed to visit the prison. Special permission for the burial was doubtless given, as in the case of Jesus.

went and told Jesus. These words are added by Matthew. ✳

THE FEEDING OF THE FIVE THOUSAND

13 When he heard what had happened Jesus withdrew privately by boat to a lonely place; but people heard of it,
and came after him in crowds by land from the towns.
14 When he came ashore, he saw a great crowd; his heart
went out to them, and he cured those of them who were
15 sick. When it grew late the disciples came up to him and
said, 'This is a lonely place, and the day has gone; send
16 the people off to the villages to buy themselves food.' He
answered, 'There is no need for them to go; give them
17 something to eat yourselves.' 'All we have here', they
18 said, 'is five loaves and two fishes.' 'Let me have them',
19 he replied. So he told the people to sit down on the grass;
then, taking the five loaves and the two fishes, he looked
up to heaven, said the blessing, broke the loaves, and gave
them to the disciples; and the disciples gave them to the
20 people. They all ate to their hearts' content; and the scraps
left over, which they picked up, were enough to fill
21 twelve great baskets. Some five thousand men shared in
this meal, to say nothing of women and children.

* 13. Matthew has considerably abridged Mark's account.
Matthew attributes the withdrawal of Jesus to the death of
John, just as in 4: 12 he attributes our Lord's withdrawal from
Judaea to Galilee to the arrest of John (cf. Mark 1: 14). Jesus
regarded John's fate as a warning of his own. In Mark the
withdrawal to a lonely place is not attributed to the death of
John, but to the need of the disciples for a rest after their
missionary tour.

15. *the day has gone.* lit. 'the hour has gone by', i.e. the hour
for the evening meal has passed. If this incident took place in
spring about Passover time, as is stated in John 6: 1–14, and

implied by Mark's reference to the green grass (Mark 6: 39), sunset would be about 6 p.m.

16. Cf. 2 Kings 4: 42–3, 'Give unto the people, that they may eat' (the miraculous feeding of a hundred prophets by Elisha).

18. *Let me have them.* These words are peculiar to Matthew.

19. *the grass.* Mark 'the green grass'. This indicates spring-time. See on verse 15. In Mark the people are arranged in groups and rows.

said the blessing, broke. The language is suggestive of the communion service, the Lord's supper. In the Fourth Gospel the teaching about the communion service is closely associated with the feeding of the five thousand; *said the blessing* means 'spoke a prayer of praise and thanksgiving'. The usual prayer at the beginning of a Jewish meal is 'Blessed art thou, O Lord our God, king of the world, who bringest forth bread from the earth'. The disciples, like the deacons at the com-munion service in the early Church, gave the bread to the crowds.

20. *twelve great baskets.* The word translated 'baskets' means food baskets, wicker baskets. The number twelve suggests not only the large number of the fragments, but also that each of the twelve disciples carried one to collect the broken pieces.

21. *to say nothing of women and children.* Matthew's ad-dition, which has the effect of increasing the number and so magnifying the miracle. This is the best-attested miracle in the Gospels, the only one recorded in all four. Some scholars interpret the miracle typologically, i.e. as symbolic (to-gether with the later feeding of the four thousand) of the preaching of the Gospel, the bread of life, to the twelve tribes of Israel. Five loaves were used for the feeding of the five thousand, seven for the feeding of the four thousand. $5+7=12$. Such an interpretation need not cast doubt on the historicity of a miracle so well attested. *

THE WALKING ON THE WATER;
HEALING IN GENNESARET

22 Then he made the disciples embark and go on ahead to the
23 other side, while he sent the people away; after doing that,
he went up the hill-side to pray alone. It grew late, and
24 he was there by himself. The boat was already some furlongs from the shore, battling with a head-wind and a
25 rough sea. Between three and six in the morning he came
26 to them, walking over the lake. When the disciples saw
him walking on the lake they were so shaken that they
27 cried out in terror: 'It is a ghost!' But at once he spoke
to them: 'Take heart! It is I; do not be afraid.'

28   Peter called to him: 'Lord, if it is you, tell me to come
29 to you over the water.' 'Come', said Jesus. Peter stepped
down from the boat, and walked over the water towards
30 Jesus. But when he saw the strength of the gale he was
seized with fear; and beginning to sink, he cried, 'Save
31 me, Lord.' Jesus at once reached out and caught hold of
him, and said, 'Why did you hesitate? How little faith
32 you have!' They then climbed into the boat; and the
33 wind dropped. And the men in the boat fell at his feet,
exclaiming, 'Truly you are the Son of God.'

34   So they finished the crossing and came to land at
35 Gennesaret. There Jesus was recognized by the people of
the place, who sent out word to all the country round.
36 And all who were ill were brought to him, and he was
begged to allow them simply to touch the edge of his
cloak. And everyone who touched it was completely
cured.

✻ **22.** *the other side.* Mark 6: 45 says 'to Bethsaida', i.e. Bethsaida Julias on the north-east shore of the lake.

23. *to pray alone.* The secret of Jesus' power lay not only in the fact that he was the Son of God, but in his constant fellowship with his Father in prayer. This was the essence of his inward life, of which his ministry was the outflowing. 'The right relation between prayer and conduct is not that conduct is supremely important and prayer may help it, but that prayer is supremely important and conduct tests it' (Archbishop William Temple).

24. *some furlongs from the shore.* The word translated 'furlongs' means lit. 'stades'. A stade was a Greek measure equal to 606 ft. 9 in. According to Josephus the lake was 40 stades (nearly $4\frac{1}{2}$ miles) wide. Another reading found in some MSS is 'already well out on the water', 'in the midst of the sea'.

battling. Mark says Jesus saw the disciples 'labouring at the oars against a head-wind' (6: 48). Matthew applies the same Greek verb to the boat.

25. *Between three and six.* Greek: 'in the fourth watch of the night'. This was by the Roman reckoning of four watches in the night. The Jews reckoned three.

27. *It is I.* The Greek means lit. 'I am'. These words are often used in the Old Testament to mark a self-revelation of Yahweh (e.g. Exod. 3: 14). 'And God said unto Moses, I AM THAT I AM: and he said, Thus shalt thou say unto the children of Israel, I AM hath sent me unto you'. Jesus uses the words in the Fourth Gospel, e.g. John 6: 35, 'I am the bread of life'; 8: 12, 'I am the light of the world'; 8: 58, 'Before Abraham was born, I am', etc.

28-31. This episode is peculiar to Matthew. It is in keeping with Peter's impulsive character. His decision to come to Jesus over the water required great courage. But his faith wavered, and Jesus saved him. The appropriateness of the episode for preaching purposes when the early Church was beset by storm and danger is obvious. The story may have taken its origin from such preaching. It is significant that

Mark appears to know nothing of this adventure. This is all the more surprising if, as Papias says, Mark derived his information from Peter himself.

33. The disciples acknowledge the divine sonship of Jesus. In the parallel passage, Mark 6: 52, 'their minds were closed', i.e. they were not yet clear in their minds as to who this wonderful Person was.

34. *Gennesaret* is a very fertile plain on the north-western side of the Sea of Galilee, lying between Capernaum and Tiberias.

36. *the edge of his cloak.* See on 9: 20. ✻

DISCOURSE ON THE
JEWISH LAW OF PURIFICATION

15 Then Jesus was approached by a group of Pharisees and
2 lawyers from Jerusalem, with the question: 'Why do your disciples break the old-established tradition? They
3 do not wash their hands before meals.' He answered them: 'And what of you? Why do you break God's
4 commandment in the interest of your tradition? For God said, "Honour your father and mother", and, "The man who curses his father or mother must suffer death."
5 But you say, "If a man says to his father or mother, 'Anything of mine which might have been used for your
6 benefit is set apart for God', then he must not honour his father or his mother." You have made God's law null and
7 void out of respect for your tradition. What hypocrisy!
8 Isaiah was right when he prophesied about you: "This people pays me lip-service, but their heart is far from me;
9 their worship of me is in vain, for they teach as doctrines the commandments of men."'
10   He called the crowd and said to them, 'Listen to me,

and understand this: a man is not defiled by what goes 11
into his mouth, but by what comes out of it.'

Then the disciples came to him and said, 'Do you know 12
that the Pharisees have taken great offence at what you
have been saying?' His answer was: 'Any plant that is 13
not of my heavenly Father's planting will be rooted up.
Leave them alone; they are blind guides, and if one blind 14
man guides another they will both fall into the ditch.'

Then Peter said, 'Tell us what that parable means.' 15
Jesus answered, 'Are you still as dull as the rest? Do you 16,17
not see that whatever goes in by the mouth passes into
the stomach and so is discharged into the drain? But 18
what comes out of the mouth has its origins in the heart;
and that is what defiles a man. Wicked thoughts, murder, 19
adultery, fornication, theft, perjury, slander—these all
proceed from the heart; and these are the things that 20
defile a man; but to eat without first washing his hands,
that cannot defile him.'

✶ This discourse falls into three parts: (a) 1-9, addressed to
the Pharisees and lawyers; (b) 10-11, addressed to the people;
(c) 12-20, addressed to the disciples. The interest of this discourse to the early Church would be in its showing Jesus as
championing in advance, so to speak, the freedom of Gentile
Christians to dispense with the restrictions of the Jewish Law.
Jesus regarded the Law itself as binding, being given by God,
but he rejected the traditions which the lawyers had added to
the Law. Even within the Law itself, he regarded the spirit
as more important than the letter, and some matters as more
important than others.

2. *the old-established tradition.* lit. 'the tradition of the elders',
i.e. the interpretation of the Law which in the time of Jesus
was passed on from rabbi to pupil in oral form. The Pharisees

regarded it as equally binding with the Law. The Sadducees rejected it. Ritual hand-washing (i.e. hand-washing for religious purposes) was not required by the Law in the Old Testament. It was part of the 'hedge about the Law' created by the tradition of the lawyers.

3–6. Jesus rebukes the Pharisees for setting their *tradition* above the Law, as in their ruling about the treatment of father and mother. '*If a man says to his father or mother, "Anything of mine which might have been used for your benefit is set apart for God"* [Greek 'gift', translating Aramaic *Corban*], *then he must not honour his father or his mother.*' The legal ruling thus allowed a man to escape looking after his parents.

8–9. The quotation comes from Isa. 29: 13 and follows the LXX against the Hebrew.

11. Matthew, unlike Mark, specifies the *mouth*, thus limiting the application of the saying to foods.

13. *plant.* Israel is described in Ps. 80: 8 as a vine which God planted.

14. Some MSS have 'blind guides of blind men'. But there is strong authority for omitting 'of blind men'.

15. *Peter said.* Mark has 'his disciples questioned him'. Peter is given special prominence in Matthew. The *parable* is the saying in verse 11, which Matthew by inserting 'mouth' has already interpreted by anticipation.

19. Matthew has a list of six vices, which follow (except for *slander*) the order in the Decalogue. Mark has a list of twelve vices.

20. *but to eat without first washing his hands,* etc. This is added by Matthew to the Marcan account to make it clear that it is the lawyers' tradition, not the Mosaic law, that Jesus attacked. ✳

Jesus and his Disciples

THE CANAANITE WOMAN

JESUS THEN LEFT that place and withdrew to the region 21 of Tyre and Sidon. And a Canaanite woman from those 22 parts came crying out, 'Sir! have pity on me, Son of David; my daughter is tormented by a devil.' But he 23 said not a word in reply. His disciples came and urged him: 'Send her away; see how she comes shouting after us.' Jesus replied, 'I was sent to the lost sheep of the house 24 of Israel, and to them alone.' But the woman came and 25 fell at his feet and cried, 'Help me, sir.' To this Jesus 26 replied, 'It is not right to take the children's bread and throw it to the dogs.' 'True, sir,' she answered; 'and yet 27 the dogs eat the scraps that fall from their masters' table.' Hearing this Jesus replied, 'Woman, what faith you have! 28 Be it as you wish!' And from that moment her daughter was restored to health.

* Matthew here uses Mark 7: 24–30 with some freedom.

21. *that place*, Gennesaret. Jesus withdrew to the region of Tyre and Sidon, i.e. Phoenicia. By withdrawing thus, Jesus was avoiding the territory ruled over by Herod Antipas.

22. Mark calls the woman 'a Phoenician of Syria by nationality'. Matthew calls her a Canaanite, perhaps regarding Phoenicians of Syria as descendants of the Canaanites, who in the Old Testament are often referred to in a derogatory manner.

Son of David is a messianic title.

23-4. Peculiar to Matthew who emphasizes the limitation of Jesus' ministry primarily to Jews (cf. 10: 5, 23); but Matthew draws out correctly what Mark implies: Jesus believes he is entrusted with powers for his own people (the children's bread) who must be fed (taught) first. Then they will teach others.

26. Mark prefaces this saying with the words, 'let the children be satisfied first'.

dogs. A term often applied by Jews to Gentiles (cf. 7: 6). Jesus is probably quoting a proverb, and testing the woman's faith.

28. As in the only other recorded cure of a Gentile—the centurion's boy at Capernaum (8: 13)—the cure is effected by a word spoken from a distance. ✳

HEALING GENTILES; FEEDING THE FOUR THOUSAND;
THE DEMAND FOR A SIGN

29 After leaving that region Jesus took the road by the Sea of Galilee and went up to the hills. When he was seated
30 there, crowds flocked to him, bringing with them the lame, blind, dumb, and crippled, and many other sufferers; they flung them down at his feet, and he healed
31 them. Great was the amazement of the people when they saw the dumb speaking, the crippled strong, the lame walking, and sight restored to the blind; and they gave praise to the God of Israel.

32 Jesus called his disciples and said to them, 'I feel sorry for all these people; they have been with me now for three days and have nothing to eat. I do not want to send
33 them away unfed; they might turn faint on the way.' The disciples replied, 'Where in this lonely place can we find
34 bread enough to feed such a crowd?' 'How many loaves have you?' Jesus asked. 'Seven,' they replied; 'and there
35 are a few small fishes.' So he ordered the people to sit down
36 on the ground; then he took the seven loaves and the fishes, and after giving thanks to God he broke them and

gave to the disciples, and the disciples gave to the people.
They all ate to their hearts' content; and the scraps left over, 37
which they picked up, were enough to fill seven baskets.
Four thousand men shared in this meal, to say nothing of 38
women and children. He then dismissed the crowds, got 39
into a boat, and went to the neighbourhood of Magadan.

The Pharisees and Sadducees came, and to test him they **16**
asked him to show them a sign from heaven. His answer 2
was: 'It is a wicked generation that asks for a sign; and 4
the only sign that will be given it is the sign of Jonah.' So
he went off and left them.

In crossing to the other side the disciples had forgotten 5
to take bread with them. So, when Jesus said to them, 6
'Beware, be on your guard against the leaven of the
Pharisees and Sadducees', they began to say among them- 7
selves, 'It is because we have brought no bread!' Knowing 8
what was in their minds, Jesus said to them: 'Why do you
talk about bringing no bread? Where is your faith? Do 9
you not understand even yet? Do you not remember the
five loaves for the five thousand, and how many basketfuls you picked up? Or the seven loaves for the four 10
thousand, and how many basketfuls you picked up? How 11
can you fail to see that I was not speaking about bread?
Be on your guard, I said, against the leaven of the Pharisees
and Sadducees.' Then they understood: they were to be 12
on their guard, not against the baker's leaven of the
Pharisees and Sadducees, but against their teaching.

✻ Matthew passes over the healing of the deaf and dumb man
in Mark 7: 31–7 (probably because Jesus is represented as using
saliva in effecting the cure and so looking like a magician), and
inserts a general account of healings.

30. What was done among Jews (9: 1–8, 27–33) is now repeated among the Gentiles.

31. *they gave praise to the God of Israel.* This implies that the crowd was mainly Gentile, drawn from the Hellenized district of Gaulonitis east of the lake.

The feeding of the four thousand (from Mark 8: 1–10) is a miracle among the Gentiles parallel to the feeding of the five thousand among the Jews, with which it has many features in common. In fact it is a doublet of that miracle. Hence Luke's omission, but Mark and Matthew evidently believed both feedings really happened.

32. *Jesus called*, etc. In 14: 15 the disciples took the first step; here Jesus takes the initiative.

three days. This is a feature not in the feeding of the five thousand.

faint on the way. Mark adds, 'some of them have come from a distance'.

36. *after giving thanks to God he broke them.* See on 14: 19.

37. *seven baskets.* A different Greek word is used here for basket (*sphuris*) from that used in 14: 20 (*kophinos*). The *sphuris* was a reed basket, often used for carrying fish and fruit.

38. *to say nothing of women and children.* Matthew's addition, as in 14: 21.

39. According to Mark 8: 10, Jesus crossed to Dalmanutha, a place which cannot now be identified. Matthew seems to have substituted *Magadan*, though late MSS read 'Magdala' which was on the west side of the lake. The name 'Magadan' or 'Mageda' suggests Megiddo, which is more than 20 miles from the lake. Some MSS give Magadan, others Magdala, at Mark 8: 10.

16: 1–4. A similar incident was recorded by Matthew in 12: 38–42, where there was no parallel in Mark, but one in Luke. Here Matthew is following Mark.

1. *The Pharisees and Sadducees.* Mark has 'the Pharisees' alone. In 12: 38 it is the doctors of the law and the Pharisees who ask for a sign and as here are promised only *the sign of Jonah* (verse 4).

2. *His answer was.* Some MSS insert here 'In the evening

you say, "It will be fine weather, for the sky is red"; (3) and in the morning you say, "It will be stormy today; the sky is red and lowering". You know how to interpret the appearance of the sky; can you not interpret the signs of the times?' But the most important MSS omit this passage. It was inserted in the Western Text at an early time, apparently in imitation of Luke 12: 54-6.

4. See on 12: 38-42. *he went off.* The direction he took (verse 5) was to avoid once more the dominion of Herod Antipas, as well as to get away from the Pharisees and Sadducees.

6. *leaven* is yeast. Mark has, 'the leaven of the Pharisees and the leaven of Herod'. Matthew (as we see from verse 12) understands the leaven to mean 'false teaching'.

7. Apparently they suppose that because in their hurry to depart from the hostility of their opponents they had brought no bread, Jesus is warning them against eating the bread of their opponents.

8-10. The thought is: 'The feedings of the five thousand and four thousand are symbolic of my teaching which is all-sufficient for you. You do not need the teaching of my enemies, and you must beware of it.'

11. Mark has, 'He said, "Do you still not understand?"' and with these words concludes the incident. The rest is added by Matthew.

Looking back over 14: 13 — 16: 12 we can see that there have been a number of doublets, which are best set out as follows:

(a) 14: 13-21; 15: 32-8. Miraculous feeding on east of the lake.

(b) 14: 22-33; 15: 39a. Crossing the lake.

(c) 14: 34-6; 15: 39b. Arrival west of the lake.

(d) 15: 1-20; 16: 1-4a. Conflict with authorities.

(e) 15: 21-8; 16: 4b-12. Avoidance of the dominion of Herod Antipas.

The duplication is already present in Mark. Luke omits the whole section Mark 6: 45 — 8: 26, thus avoiding the duplication. ✻

PETER'S CONFESSION AT CAESAREA PHILIPPI

13 When he came to the territory of Caesarea Philippi, Jesus asked his disciples, 'Who do men say that the Son of Man
14 is?' They answered, 'Some say John the Baptist, others
15 Elijah, others Jeremiah, or one of the prophets.' 'And
16 you,' he asked, 'who do you say I am?' Simon Peter answered: 'You are the Messiah, the Son of the living
17 God.' Then Jesus said: 'Simon son of Jonah, you are favoured indeed! You did not learn that from mortal man;
18 it was revealed to you by my heavenly Father. And I say this to you: You are Peter, the Rock; and on this rock I will build my church, and the forces of death shall never
19 overpower it. I will give you the keys of the kingdom of Heaven; what you forbid on earth shall be forbidden in heaven, and what you allow on earth shall be allowed in
20 heaven.' He then gave his disciples strict orders not to tell anyone that he was the Messiah.

* This section marks a crisis in the Gospel story. In Mark's Gospel (8: 27-30) Peter's confession is a point of crucial importance. From then on Jesus speaks openly to the disciples about his coming Passion (i.e. his suffering and death). His public ministry in Galilee was finished. The last journey to Jerusalem was soon to begin. In Matthew the importance of the event is even more emphasized by the addition of the section (verses 17-20) in which Jesus highly commends Peter and assigns to him a leading place in the Church.

13. *Caesarea Philippi.* This was the ancient town Paneas (modern Bânyâs), which the tetrarch Philip refounded and named Caesarea in honour of Caesar Augustus. It was called Caesarea Philippi (after Philip) to distinguish it from the many other cities which had this name. It lay at the foot of Mount

Hermon, close to the sources of the Jordan, and about 23 miles north of Bethsaida. This was the northernmost place that Jesus reached. He retired to this place of seclusion to prepare for the strenuous journey and ordeal that lay before him and his disciples.

Who do men say that the Son of Man is? Mark, 'Who do men say I am?' Matthew's insertion of the 'Son of Man' here is surprising and puzzling. He cannot have understood the term to mean 'Messiah' here, for this would anticipate Peter's confession: the answer would be given in the question. Some MSS read: 'Who do men say that I the Son of Man am?' but 'I' has probably crept into the text from Mark's account. The text that we have is therefore probably correct. In that case 'Son of Man' may simply represent the Aramaic equivalent which can mean simply 'I'.

14. *John the Baptist.* Herod thought this (14: 2).

Elijah. He was expected to return before the final Day of Judgement. Cf. Mal. 4: 5, 'Behold, I will send you Elijah the prophet before the great and terrible day of the Lord come'. Evidently the people did not identify John the Baptist with Elijah, as Jesus did (Matt. 11: 14; 17: 10–13).

Jeremiah. Matthew's addition. Matthew is the only Gospel that alludes to Jeremiah by name (cf. 2: 17; 27: 9).

one of the prophets. Jesus accepted the title of prophet (13: 57), i.e. a fearless spokesman of God.

16. *Messiah.* Greek *Christos*, i.e. anointed one (see p. 7). Matthew alone adds *the Son of the living God.* This may simply be equivalent to Messiah, but for Matthew it means more: one who alone knows God like a son (cf. 11: 27).

17–19. Peculiar to Matthew. Its absence from Mark is difficult to explain if it is a genuine saying of Jesus, especially if we believe that Mark derived his information from Peter. On the other hand, modesty may have prevented Peter from disclosing this saying to Mark.

17. *Simon.* Jesus always uses 'Simon' in addressing this disciple.

son of Jonah (Aramaic: *Bar-Jonas*). In John 1: 42 this is altered to 'son of John'.

favoured. The Greek word used here is the same as that translated 'blest' in the Beatitudes (5: 3–11). It means 'happy', but with the additional sense of having God's favour.

mortal man. Greek: 'flesh and blood'. 'Flesh' signified humanity in its frailty and fallibility. 'Blood' signified the human life (Lev. 17: 11, 'the life of the flesh is in the blood'). 'Flesh and blood' is a frequent expression in rabbinic writings for humanity in contrast with God.

18. *Peter.* Greek *Petros*, 'a stone'. The Aramaic form 'Cephas' occurs in John 1: 42 and Gal. 2: 9, 11. Both the Greek *petra* (feminine) and the Aramaic *Kepha* mean 'Rock'. *Petros*, the masculine form of the Greek word, is used here as more suitable for a man's name.

on this rock (Greek *petra*). It does not follow from the pun that 'this rock' must be Peter himself. It may be; but it could also be the faith that he has expressed. Even if it refers to Peter, it refers to him as the spokesman of this faith, not in his personal character, which at this time was impetuous and unsteady. As tradition says that Peter became the first bishop of Rome, the Roman Catholics have used this text to support their claim that the bishops of Rome, who later became Popes, have a position of supreme authority in the Church. Peter did indeed become the foundation of the Church in the sense that he preached the first Christian sermon on the day of Pentecost (Acts 2), but the privileges here assigned to Peter in verse 19 are assigned to all the apostles in 18: 18. Paul says that Christ is the Church's only foundation (1 Cor. 3: 11).

church (Greek *ecclesia*). This word occurs only here and in 18: 17 in the Gospels. Synonyms, however, like 'flock', 'sheep', occur in all the Gospels. The reference here is to the universal Church. In 18: 17 it refers to the local community and is translated 'congregation'. The word *ecclesia* in the New Testament is the equivalent of the Hebrew *qahal* in the Old Testament, which means the gathering or congregation of

Israel, the people of God. The Christian Church is the new
Israel, the people gathered and called by God out of the world.

forces of death. Greek: 'gates of Hades'. Jesus is here using Old
Testament language. 'The gates of death' (= Sheol = Hades)
is a phrase used in Ps. 9: 13; 107: 18. The metaphor of the
gates likens the abode of the dead to a city. Death will never
be able to hold the Church a prisoner within its gates, just as
it was unable to hold Christ himself, for he rose from the dead.
The Church, like its Lord, is immortal. Compare the saying of
Theodore Beza, the great reformer (1519–1605): 'The Church
is an anvil which has worn out many hammers.'

19. *the keys,* etc. These symbolize rule and authority.
Cf. Isa. 22: 22 (referring to Shebna), 'And the key of the
house of David will I lay upon his shoulder; and he shall open,
and none shall shut; and he shall shut, and none shall open.'
This is echoed in Rev. 3: 7, 'the holy one, the true one, who
holds the key of David; when he opens none may shut, when
he shuts none may open', where the reference is to the risen
Christ. He who holds the keys is the steward of the house,
invested with authority. Peter is given authority in the sphere
of the Reign of God.

The kingdom of Heaven here denotes the realm in which
God's Reign operates; it does not exactly mean the Church,
but it implies it as the community over which God reigns, as
in the parables of the Kingdom in 13: 24–43.

forbid. Greek: 'bind', a rabbinic term meaning 'to forbid'.

allow. Greek: 'loose', a rabbinic term meaning 'to allow'.
Peter's decisions in the Church on earth will be ratified in
Heaven (i.e. by God). The same authority is given to all the
disciples in 18: 18. Although Peter was the acknowledged
spokesman and leader of the apostles at the beginning of the
Church's life, the leadership afterwards passed to James the
Lord's brother (Acts 15: 13 f.). Paul was prepared to challenge
Peter's authority (Gal. 2: 11, 'when Cephas came to Antioch,
I opposed him to his face, because he was clearly in the
wrong').

20. Although Peter and the disciples now know the fact of Jesus' Messiahship, they do not yet understand all that it involves in suffering and death. Jesus' conception of Messiahship was entirely different from the popular one. To avoid misconception the disciples must keep it secret. *

JESUS' PREDICTION OF HIS SUFFERING AND FUTURE GLORY

21 From that time Jesus began to make it clear to his disciples that he had to go to Jerusalem, and there to suffer much from the elders, chief priests, and lawyers; to be put to
22 death and to be raised again on the third day. At this Peter took him by the arm and began to rebuke him: 'Heaven forbid!' he said. 'No, Lord, this shall never
23 happen to you.' Then Jesus turned and said to Peter, 'Away with you, Satan; you are a stumbling-block to me. You think as men think, not as God thinks.'

24   Jesus then said to his disciples, 'If anyone wishes to be a follower of mine, he must leave self behind; he must
25 take up his cross and come with me. Whoever cares for his own safety is lost; but if a man will let himself be lost
26 for my sake, he will find his true self. What will a man gain by winning the whole world, at the cost of his true self? Or what can he give that will buy that self back?
27 For the Son of Man is to come in the glory of his Father with his angels, and then he will give each man the due
28 reward for what he has done. I tell you this: there are some standing here who will not taste death before they have seen the Son of Man coming in his kingdom.'

* 21. *From that time.* Matthew stresses that this marks an important turning-point in the narrative.

elders, chief priests, and lawyers together make up the Sanhedrin.

on the third day means the same as Mark's 'three days afterwards'. There is possibly an echo of Hos. 6: 2, 'After two days
will he revive us: on the third day he will raise us up, and we
shall live before him'.

22. The actual words of rebuke are peculiar to Matthew.

Heaven forbid. The Greek literally means '(God be) gracious
to thee, Lord'. This phrase is the Hebrew way of saying 'God
forbid.'

23. Jesus recognizes in what Peter has said a real temptation
from Satan (cf. 4: 10). He says to Peter in effect: Get out of
my sight.

stumbling-block, hindrance. 'You are a stumbling-block to
me' is not in Mark. Peter, meant to be a foundation-stone,
threatens to be a stone which trips people up.

24. Matthew, unlike Mark 8: 34, makes the words an
address to the disciples only. The disciple must be prepared
for self-denial and must 'take up his cross'. This refers to
public humiliation, suffering, persecution and perhaps crucifixion itself.

25. This saying occurs in several places in the Gospels
(cf. 10: 38–9). Matthew here takes it over from Mark. It
would have special force in the days of the Neronian persecution in Rome where Mark wrote his Gospel.

26. Compare the *Apocalypse of Baruch* (c. A.D. 50-100),
LI, 15: 'For what, then, have men lost their life, and for what
have those who were on earth exchanged their souls?'

27. Mark 8: 38 speaks of the necessity of not being ashamed
to acknowledge the Son of Man, i.e. Jesus. Matthew alters
the saying to make it a general prediction of the last judgement, thus again bringing out what is implicit in Mark.

28. Mark 9: 1 has 'there are some of those standing here
who will not taste death before they have seen the kingdom
of God already come in power'. Matthew has *the Son of Man
coming in his kingdom*, thus interpreting the saying in Mark as

a reference to the *parousia*, the second coming. If Jesus did predict that his *parousia* would take place in the lifetime of some of his contemporaries, he was mistaken. But elsewhere Jesus says that he does not know when his *parousia* will take place (Matt. 24: 36 = Mark 13: 32). It is possible that the original saying on this occasion was uttered in a different context from that in which Mark has placed it at 9: 1, and did not refer to the *parousia*, but to some signal manifestation of the kingdom in power such as took place at his resurrection or at Pentecost.   *

THE TRANSFIGURATION; THE CURE OF THE EPILEPTIC BOY

17 Six days later Jesus took Peter and James and John the brother of James, and led them up a high mountain where
2 they were alone; and in their presence he was transfigured; his face shone like the sun, and his clothes became white
3 as the light. And they saw Moses and Elijah appear, con-
4 versing with him. Then Peter spoke: 'Lord,' he said, 'how good it is that we are here! If you wish it, I will make three shelters here, one for you, one for Moses, and one
5 for Elijah.' While he was still speaking, a bright cloud suddenly overshadowed them, and a voice called from the cloud: 'This is my Son, my Beloved, on whom my
6 favour rests; listen to him.' At the sound of the voice the
7 disciples fell on their faces in terror. Jesus then came up to them, touched them, and said, 'Stand up; do not be
8 afraid.' And when they raised their eyes they saw no one, but only Jesus.

9 On their way down the mountain Jesus enjoined them not to tell anyone of the vision until the Son of Man had
10 been raised from the dead. The disciples put a question to him: 'Why then do our teachers say that Elijah must come

first?' He replied, 'Yes, Elijah will come and set every- 11
thing right. But I tell you that Elijah has already come, 12
and they failed to recognize him, and worked their will
upon him; and in the same way the Son of Man is to
suffer at their hands.' Then the disciples understood that 13
he meant John the Baptist.

When they returned to the crowd, a man came up to 14
Jesus, fell on his knees before him, and said, 'Have pity, 15
sir, on my son: he is an epileptic and has bad fits, and he
keeps falling about, often into the fire, often into water.
I brought him to your disciples, but they could not cure 16
him.' Jesus answered, 'What an unbelieving and perverse 17
generation! How long shall I be with you? How much
longer must I endure you? Bring him here to me.' Jesus 18
then spoke sternly to the boy; the devil left him, and from
that moment he was cured.

Afterwards the disciples came to Jesus and asked him 19
privately, 'Why could not we cast it out?' He answered, 20
'Your faith is too weak. I tell you this: if you have faith
no bigger even than a mustard-seed, you will say to this
mountain, "Move from here to there!", and it will
move; nothing will prove impossible for you.'

* 1. *Six days later.* A curiously exact indication of time,
which Matthew takes from Mark. Luke has 'about eight days
after this conversation'.

Peter and James and John. These three were the 'inner circle'
of the disciples. They were chosen to be with Jesus on several
occasions, e.g. in the house of Jairus (Mark 5: 37), when Jesus
gave his eschatological discourse (i.e. his talk on the last things)
in Jerusalem (Mark 13: 3), and in Gethsemane (Matt. 26: 37;
Mark 14: 33).

a high mountain. Perhaps Mount Hermon, which was near Caesarea Philippi, about 14 miles to the north.

2. The disciples now saw in Jesus the heavenly glory that was really his.

his face shone like the sun. Peculiar to Matthew. Moses' face also shone after he had conversed with God (Exod. 34: 29–35). Cf. also 2 Esdras in the Apocrypha (*c.* A.D. 100), 7: 97, referring to the righteous after death: 'Their face shall shine as the sun.'

3. *Moses,* the representative of the Law, had, according to tradition, not died but had been taken up into Heaven (cf. *The Assumption of Moses,* an apocalyptic work written in the reign of Herod the Great).

Elijah, the representative of the prophets, had also been taken up into heaven (2 Kings 2: 11). These two visitants from Heaven accompany Jesus who will himself ascend into heaven.

conversing. Luke says that the subject of their conversation was 'his departure, the destiny he was to fulfil in Jerusalem', i.e. his death, resurrection and ascension.

4. The word translated 'shelters' means 'tents'. The Arabs erect tents to show respect to distinguished visitors.

5. *a bright cloud.* An allusion to the Shekinah, the bright cloud which marked God's visible presence or manifestation of glory.

overshadowed. The same Greek verb as is used of the cloud which rested on the Tabernacle when it was filled with the glory of God (Exod. 40: 34–8).

voice. God's voice, the voice of the Shekinah, similar to the voice at the Baptism (3: 17).

This is my Son, my Beloved. Another possible translation is 'This is my only Son', as at the Baptism. The human confession of Jesus' Messiahship at Caesarea Philippi now receives divine confirmation, on an occasion which has foretold the glory of his ascension and *parousia.*

on whom my favour rests. Matthew alone adds these words.

132

6-7. These verses are peculiar to Matthew, being his editorial expansion of the words in Mark: 'they were terrified'.

8. *only Jesus*. The representatives of the Law and the prophets have vanished. The revelation of God's will in Jesus, in fulfilling the Law and the prophets (5: 17), has superseded them.

9. The command of Jesus to his disciples to keep silent about what they had seen until after his resurrection is in accord with his whole policy of keeping his Messiahship secret until his triumphal entry into Jerusalem. There is no need to explain it as Mark's invention to account for the fact that Jesus was not widely acknowledged to be Messiah before his resurrection. After the resurrection the Messiahship of Jesus was openly proclaimed. Mark 9: 10 adds, 'They seized upon those words, and discussed among themselves what this "rising from the dead" could mean'. Matthew omits this exposure of the disciples' lack of understanding.

10. Jesus had spoken about his death and resurrection. Will there be time, then, for the fulfilment of the prophecy in Mal. 4: 5-6 that Elijah would come before the Day of Judgement to reconcile children and fathers? The teachers (i.e. doctors of the law) interpreted this to mean that Elijah must return to prepare the way for the Messiah. Jesus has been revealed to the disciples as Messiah. What of Elijah?

11. Jesus in reply first quotes the expectation of the teachers that *Elijah will come and set everything right*.

12. Then Jesus identifies John the Baptist with *Elijah*, as he did in 11: 14. In John *Elijah has...come*, but he was prevented from setting everything right by the failure of men *to recognize him*, which made it possible for Herod Antipas to arrest him and put him to death.

13. An editorial comment typical of Matthew's concern to bring out what is implicit in Mark.

14-17. Both Matthew and Luke considerably abridge Mark's account (Mark 9: 14-29). Raphael in a great picture portrayed the contrast between the heavenly beauty of the bright and holy vision granted to the three disciples on the mountain and the dark and piteous scene below of the epileptic boy, the sorrow of the father, and the helplessness of the crowd and the remaining disciples.

14. Matthew alone states that the father came up to Jesus and knelt before him.

15. *he is an epileptic.* A correct translation of the same Greek verb as occurs at 4: 24. It does not occur in Mark's account; but the symptoms which Mark describes suggest epilepsy.

17. *What an unbelieving and perverse generation!* Cf. Deut. 32: 5, 'they are a perverse and crooked generation'.

18. Matthew omits Mark's description of the boy's convulsions when the devil came out.

20. Matthew combines a saying from Mark 11: 23 about faith with another found in Luke 17: 6. To 'uproot the mountain' was a proverbial expression for doing something difficult. In Mark Jesus gives the answer: 'There is no means of casting out this sort but prayer.' Some MSS add that here in verse 21, with the addition 'and fasting'. But the best MSS omit it. ✳

THE SECOND PREDICTION OF THE PASSION;
THE COIN IN THE MOUTH OF THE FISH

22 They were going about together in Galilee when Jesus said to them, 'The Son of Man is to be given up into the
23 power of men, and they will kill him; then on the third day he will be raised again.' And they were filled with grief.

24 On their arrival at Capernaum the collectors of the temple-tax came up to Peter and asked, 'Does your master
25 not pay temple-tax?' 'He does', said Peter. When he went indoors Jesus forestalled him by asking, 'What do you think about this, Simon? From whom do earthly

monarchs collect tax or toll? From their own citizens, or
from aliens?' 'From aliens', said Peter. 'Why then,' 26
said Jesus, 'the citizens are exempt! But as we do not 27
want to cause difficulty for these people, go and cast a
line in the lake; take the first fish that comes to the hook,
open its mouth, and you will find a silver coin; take that
and pay it in; it will meet the tax for us both.'

＊ 22. *were going about together*. This is probably the meaning
of the Greek; but it could mean 'abode' as in R.V.

23. After the second prediction of the Passion, Matthew says
they were filled with grief. They took no heed of the promise of
the resurrection.

24. Mark relates the *arrival at Capernaum*; but the rest of
the story is peculiar to Matthew. Like much of such material
it gives prominence to Peter.

temple-tax. Greek: *didrachma*, a coin equal to two Attic
drachmae and equivalent to the Jewish half-shekel (value about
one and 7/10ths of a day's wages). The half-shekel (originally
⅓ shekel, Neh. 10: 32) was the amount of the contribution paid
annually by every male Jew above the age of 19 for the upkeep
of the temple services. The didrachma was seldom coined in the
time of Jesus, so that two persons must usually have combined
to pay a tetradrachma (= four drachmae) or stater (= Hebrew
shekel).

25. *tax*, i.e. local tax or customs, indirect taxation.

toll. Capitation tax, i.e. tax levied on each head, direct
taxation.

earthly monarchs refers to the Roman power.

citizens. The Greek word means 'sons', but not just members
of the royal family. The word means, in Hebraic metaphor,
all Roman citizens.

26. The argument is that if earthly kings do not tax their
own families and people, the same is also true of God. The
Jews, as aliens, pay taxes to the Lord of the temple, but the

Son of God and his followers are exempt. Jesus here once
again claims a unique relationship to God which confers upon
him and his disciples unusual privileges. But he decides to
forego these privileges. A Christian must not cause difficulty
for others.

27. It has been said that this miracle-story is similar to those
told in the apocryphal Gospels, and like them bears the mark
of legend. But in the apocryphal Gospels stress is laid on the
actual occurrence of the miracle. That is not so here. It is not
stated that the coin was found in the fish's mouth. It may be
implied. On the other hand, there may be a hidden meaning
in the story to which the clue has been lost.

a silver coin. Greek *stater.* ✶

THE IMPORTANCE OF LITTLE ONES

18 At that time the disciples came to Jesus and asked, 'Who
2   is the greatest in the kingdom of Heaven?' He called a
3   child, set him in front of them, and said, 'I tell you this:
unless you turn round and become like children, you will
4   never enter the kingdom of Heaven. Let a man humble
himself till he is like this child, and he will be the greatest
5   in the kingdom of Heaven. Whoever receives one such
6   child in my name receives me. But if a man is a cause of
stumbling to one of these little ones who have faith in me,
it would be better for him to have a millstone hung round
7   his neck and be drowned in the depths of the sea. Alas
for the world that such causes of stumbling arise! Come
they must, but woe betide the man through whom
they come!

8   'If your hand or your foot is your undoing, cut it off
and fling it away; it is better for you to enter into life
maimed or lame, than to keep two hands or two feet and

be thrown into the eternal fire. If it is your eye that is 9 your undoing, tear it out and fling it away; it is better to enter into life with one eye than to keep both eyes and be thrown into the fires of hell.

'Never despise one of these little ones; I tell you, they 10 have their guardian angels in heaven, who look continually on the face of my heavenly Father.

'What do you think? Suppose a man has a hundred 12 sheep. If one of them strays, does he not leave the other ninety-nine on the hill-side and go in search of the one that strayed? And if he should find it, I tell you this: he is 13 more delighted over that sheep than over the ninety-nine that never strayed. In the same way, it is not your heavenly 14 Father's will that one of these little ones should be lost.

✲ 1. The connexion with the previous incident appears to be this: Peter is treated as the chief disciple. Then, *who is the greatest in the kingdom of Heaven?*

2. Mark 9: 36 has: 'Then he took a child, set him in front of them, and put his arm round him.' This last detail is omitted by Matthew and Luke. Did they think that it stressed too much the human emotions of Jesus?

3–4. These verses are given here by Matthew only. Verse 3 = Mark 10: 15 = Luke 18: 17.

3. *turn round*, i.e. change your disposition and habits. The phrase signifies repentance, a rightabout face and a conversion.

4. The humility of little children lies in their utter dependence upon their parents. So Christians must be humble in acknowledging their utter dependence upon their heavenly Father.

5. This verse = Mark 9: 37. *in my name* means 'at my command' or 'for my sake'. Kindness to little children was urged by the rabbis also. But the pagan world was more callous. Girl babies or weaklings were often exposed to die.

6. *faith.* These *little ones* are old enough to be believers.

millstone, i.e. a large millstone driven by an ass, as distinct from the small handmill. Such a stone hung around the neck would of course ensure that the man thrown into the sea would sink to the bottom and be drowned.

7. Cf. Luke 17: 1. *Come they must.* Christ foresees that, human nature being what it is, causes of stumbling will inevitably be occasioned by the sinfulness of men. He does not say that God has foreordained that this must be so.

8. This saying is a good example of the oriental love of exaggeration. Cf. 5: 29, note.

life, i.e. eternal life.

eternal fire, i.e. Gehenna (see p. 50). In the early Church, which was looked upon as a body with limbs (members), the teaching of these verses would be used to justify excommunication of unworthy members of the Christian body.

9. The eye might be used to express scorn (see next verse) or lustful desire.

hell. Greek: 'Gehenna of fire'.

10. This verse is peculiar to Matthew.

little ones. The context suggests that here not children but disciples of Jesus are meant.

guardian angels. During the period following the exile of the Jews in Babylon (586–538 B.C.) a belief in angels grew up among them, derived to a large extent from Persian sources. In Daniel the idea that nations have guardian angels is already developed, Michael being Israel's guardian angel. In Jewish belief each child (in the original context of the saying this may have been the meaning of 'little one') had a guardian angel. Here the meaning is: 'However lowly and insignificant a believer may be in the eyes of men, in the eyes of God he is so important as to have a guardian angel in the presence of God.' The popular Jewish belief was that not only children, but all men had guardian angels, which were sometimes identified with stars.

11. This verse is omitted by the best MSS. It runs: 'For

the Son of Man came to save the lost.' It was introduced into
the text from Luke 19: 10.

12–14. In Matthew the parable of the lost sheep is addressed
to the disciples and urges the recovery of lapsed disciples. In
Luke 15: 3–7 it is addressed by Jesus to his enemies and critics
(the Pharisees and the doctors of the law) and justifies the
evangelistic mission to the unconverted (see p. 4).

12. *strayed* translates a Greek verb frequently used in early
Christian literature for lapsed church members.

14. In Luke's version a sinner has been converted and won
for Christ in an evangelistic mission. In Matthew a lapsed
member has been recovered for the Church and saved from
destruction. *

THE DISCIPLINE OF AN ERRING BROTHER;
THE DUTY OF FORGIVENESS

'If your brother commits a sin, go and take the matter up 15
with him, strictly between yourselves, and if he listens to
you, you have won your brother over. If he will not 16
listen, take one or two others with you, so that all facts
may be duly established on the evidence of two or three
witnesses. If he refuses to listen to them, report the matter 17
to the congregation; and if he will not listen even to the
congregation, you must then treat him as you would a
pagan or a tax-gatherer.

'I tell you this: whatever you forbid on earth shall be 18
forbidden in heaven, and whatever you allow on earth
shall be allowed in heaven.

'Again I tell you this: if two of you agree on earth about 19
any request you have to make, that request will be granted
by my heavenly Father. For where two or three have 20
met together in my name, I am there among them.'

21 Then Peter came up and asked him, 'Lord, how often am I to forgive my brother if he goes on wronging me?
22 As many as seven times?' Jesus replied, 'I do not say seven times; I say seventy times seven.

23 'The kingdom of Heaven, therefore, should be thought of in this way: There was once a king who decided to
24 settle accounts with the men who served him. At the outset there appeared before him a man whose debt ran
25 into millions. Since he had no means of paying, his master ordered him to be sold to meet the debt, with his
26 wife, his children, and everything he had. The man fell prostrate at his master's feet. "Be patient with me," he
27 said, "and I will pay in full"; and the master was so moved with pity that he let the man go and remitted the debt.
28 But no sooner had the man gone out than he met a fellow-servant who owed him a few pounds; and catching hold of him he gripped him by the throat and said, "Pay me
29 what you owe." The man fell at his fellow-servant's feet, and begged him, "Be patient with me, and I will pay
30 you"; but he refused, and had him jailed until he should
31 pay the debt. The other servants were deeply distressed when they saw what had happened, and they went to
32 their master and told him the whole story. He accordingly sent for the man. "You scoundrel!" he said to him; "I remitted the whole of your debt when you appealed to
33 me; were you not bound to show your fellow-servant the
34 same pity as I showed to you?" And so angry was the master that he condemned the man to torture until he
35 should pay the debt in full. And that is how my heavenly Father will deal with you, unless you each forgive your brother from your hearts.'

✣ 15. *brother*. In Jewish usage this means a co-religionist, a fellow member of the Jewish community as a religious group.

commits a sin. Some MSS add 'against you', but the best MSS omit the words.

16–17. If the offender will not receive friendly reproof, the official discipline of the Church must be brought to bear, taking account of the Law in Deut. 19: 15, 'One witness shall not rise up against a man for any iniquity, or for any sin, in any sin that he sinneth: at the mouth of two witnesses, or at the mouth of three witnesses, shall a matter be established'. No church member is to be condemned by the Church on the evidence of one witness. He must take one or two other witnesses with him. If the offender still refuses to repent and mend his ways, the matter must be laid before the congregation (Greek *ecclesia*, the same word that was translated 'Church' in 16: 18), i.e. the individual Church, the local community. (In 16: 18 *ecclesia* meant the universal Church; here it means the local congregation, and could perhaps even be translated 'Synagogue'.) If the Church cannot obtain satisfaction, the offender can no longer be regarded as a true brother. He is as a pagan, a Gentile, i.e. outside the true spiritual Israel, or an outcast like a tax-gatherer, who, being in the service of the hated Roman empire, was regarded practically as a Gentile traitor. Such a description of the unrepentant offender shows that the saying belongs to a Jewish–Christian tradition. It represents a development of church discipline in an early Jewish–Christian community.

18. Here the authority that had been granted to Peter (16: 19) is given to all the disciples.

forbid: Greek: 'bind'.

allow: Greek: 'loose'. Some commentators think that the binding and loosing in this context refer rather to excommunication and absolution. They quote John 20: 23, 'If you forgive any man's sins, they stand forgiven; if you pronounce them unforgiven, unforgiven they remain.' But it is best to take the Greek verbs here in the same sense which they have in 16: 19. The object is in the neuter which could hardly apply to people excommunicated or forgiven.

19. *Again I tell you.* This introduces a fresh saying, only loosely connected with what has gone before. As the corporate decision is valid in God's sight, so corporate prayer is powerful with him.

20. In a book of rabbinic tradition, *Aboth* III, 2, there is a saying of the early part of the second century A.D., 'If two sit together and the words of the Law are spoken between them, the Divine Presence rests between them'. Jesus in this saying is claiming to be the Divine Presence amongst those assembled in his name.

21–2. This is a dialogue on the forgiveness of wrongs done by one member of the Church to another. It is the Jewish teaching that the offender must repent, apologize, and make reparation for the wrong done. It is then the duty of the injured party to forgive him. In his teaching Jesus is reversing the old law of vengeance which finds expression in Gen. 4: 24, where the song of Lamech runs, 'If Cain shall be avenged sevenfold, truly Lamech seventy and sevenfold', i.e. the old blood feud was carried on without mercy and without limit. Jesus says: Just as in those old days there was no limit to hatred and vengeance, so among Christians there is to be no limit to mercy and forgiveness. The vengeance of Lamech in Gen. 4: 24 was 70 + 7 = seventy seven fold. Later, owing to the LXX rendering 70 × 7, it became four hundred and ninety fold. That is the version we have here. The R.V. margin suggests seventy times and seven, but the Greek cannot bear that meaning. D (*Codex Bezae*, the Western Text) has 'seventy times seven times', an alteration designed to make the meaning quite clear.

23–35. This parable emphasizes a characteristic feature of the teaching of Jesus, that only a forgiving spirit can receive forgiveness.

23. *a king.* The phrase in the Greek means 'a human king' as distinct from the Divine King with whom he is compared in verse 35.

24. *millions.* lit. 'who owed 10,000 talents', an immense sum. A talent was 6000 denarii. Note again the oriental love of exaggeration.

25. *ordered him to be sold.* Cf. 2 Kings 4: 1, where the widow with the pot of oil cries 'the creditor is come to take unto him my two children to be bondmen'.

27. *remitted the debt.* The Greek word translated 'debt', which occurs only here in the New Testament, means 'loan'. It is a case of money lent, and so the debt is greatly increased by the oriental scale of usury.

28. *a few pounds.* lit. 'a hundred denarii'. A deliberate contrast between the huge amount of his own remitted debt and this comparatively trifling amount.

29. Very like verse 26. This emphasizes the callousness of the refusal.

32–5. The master is angry at his mercilessness and shows him no mercy. The punishment of torture is to continue until the debt is wiped out. Tortures were practised in Herodian times. Doubtless punishment after death in Gehenna is envisaged. *

DIVORCE, MARRIAGE AND CELIBACY

When Jesus had finished this discourse he left Galilee and came into the region of Judaea across Jordan. Great **19** crowds followed him, and he healed them there. 2

Some Pharisees came and tested him by asking, 'Is it lawful for a man to divorce his wife on any and every 3 ground?' He asked in return, 'Have you never read that the Creator made them from the beginning male and 4 female?'; and he added, 'For this reason a man shall leave his father and mother, and be made one with his wife; 5 and the two shall become one flesh. It follows that they are no longer two individuals: they are one flesh. What 6

God has joined together, man must not separate.' 'Why
7 then', they objected, 'did Moses lay it down that a man
might divorce his wife by note of dismissal?' He
8 answered, 'It was because you were so unteachable that
Moses gave you permission to divorce your wives; but it
was not like that when all began. I tell you, if a man
9 divorces his wife for any cause other than unchastity, and
marries another, he commits adultery.'

The disciples said to him, 'If that is the position with
10 husband and wife, it is better to refrain from marriage.'
To this he replied, 'That is something which not every-
11 one can accept, but only those for whom God has appointed it. For while some are incapable of marriage
12 because they were born so, or were made so by men, there
are others who have themselves renounced marriage for
the sake of the kingdom of Heaven. Let those accept it
who can.'

✻ 1. The discourse closes with the usual formula. We begin
now the fifth great section of the Gospel 'About the Judgement'. Jesus left Galilee and went south. The precise route
taken is uncertain. According to Luke 17: 11, Jesus passed
'through the borderlands of Samaria and Galilee'. This would
mean that Jesus avoided the route through Peraea, which
would be natural, as Peraea was part of the territory of Herod
Antipas. But the following words create a difficulty: *the region
of Judaea across Jordan*. Actually Jordan separated Judaea from
Peraea. Perhaps Matthew is using the term Judaea loosely to
include Peraea.

2. Matthew speaks of healings, Mark 10: 1 of teaching.

3. *on any and every ground*. This is peculiar to Matthew. In
Mark 10: 2 the question concerns divorce absolutely. Here it
is given a form familiar in the rabbinic Schools where a debate

between the School of Hillel and that of Shammai raged over the question. The School of Hillel took the view that a man might divorce his wife for any reason if she displeased him. The School of Shammai limited the exercise of the right to the case of unchastity. See the note on 5: 32.

4–5. The quotations are from Gen. 1: 27; 2: 24.

7. Against the Creation story in Genesis the questioners appeal to the authority of Moses (Deut. 24: 1). In Mark, on the other hand, Jesus appeals to the Creation story in Genesis against the command in Deuteronomy.

9. *other than unchastity*. Like the excepting clause in 5: 32 (see note there) this is peculiar to Matthew, and brings the teaching of Jesus into line with that of Shammai. But according to Mark 10: 2–12; Luke 16: 18 and 1 Cor. 7: 10–11, there is no excepting clause in the teaching of Jesus, who forbids divorce absolutely and remarriage after divorce. (Some MSS add: 'And the man who marries a woman so divorced commits adultery.' But the best MSS omit this.) In Mark Jesus gives this explicit application of the teaching in Genesis privately to the disciples 'indoors'.

10–12. Peculiar to Matthew. In reply to the disciples' objection, Jesus teaches that celibacy is for *those for whom God has appointed it*, but there are many who cannot remain celibate. There are some for whom celibacy is the natural inevitable thing, the sexually impotent (lit. eunuchs), some born so, some made so by physical operation. There are also those who need not have remained celibate but voluntarily chose to do so *for the sake of the kingdom of Heaven*, i.e. in order to devote all their time and energies to the service of God in the Church. Cf. Clement of Alexandria, *Paedagogus* III, 4, 26. 'The true eunuch is not he who cannot but he who will not indulge himself.' Jesus himself voluntarily renounced marriage. According to tradition the apostle John did also. ✻

JESUS BLESSES THE CHILDREN;
THE HINDRANCE OF RICHES

13 They brought children for him to lay his hands on them
14 with prayer. The disciples scolded them for it, but Jesus
said to them, 'Let the children come to me; do not try to
stop them; for the kingdom of Heaven belongs to such
15 as these.' And he laid his hands on the children, and went
his way.

16   And now a man came up and asked him, 'Master, what
17 good must I do to gain eternal life?' 'Good?' said Jesus.
'Why do you ask me about that? One alone is good.
But if you wish to enter into life, keep the command-
18 ments.' 'Which commandments?' he asked. Jesus answered, 'Do not murder; do not commit adultery; do
19 not steal; do not give false evidence; honour your
father and mother; and love your neighbour as yourself.'
20 The young man answered, 'I have kept all these. Where
21 do I still fall short?' Jesus said to him, 'If you wish to go
the whole way, go, sell your possessions, and give to the
poor, and then you will have riches in heaven; and come,
22 follow me.' When the young man heard this, he went
away with a heavy heart; for he was a man of great wealth.

23   Jesus said to his disciples, 'I tell you this: a rich man will
24 find it hard to enter the kingdom of Heaven. I repeat, it is
easier for a camel to pass through the eye of a needle than
25 for a rich man to enter the kingdom of God.' The disciples
were amazed to hear this. 'Then who can be saved?' they
26 asked. Jesus looked them in the face, and said, 'For men
this is impossible; but everything is possible for God.'

27   At this Peter said, 'Here are we who left everything to

become your followers. What will there be for us?' Jesus replied, 'I tell you this: in the world that is to be, 28 when the Son of Man is seated on his throne in heavenly splendour, you my followers will have thrones of your own, where you will sit as judges of the twelve tribes of Israel. And anyone who has left brothers or sisters, father, 29 mother, or children, land or houses for the sake of my name will be repaid many times over, and gain eternal life. But many who are first will be last, and the last first. 30

* 13-15. Matthew here, as elsewhere, abridges the Marcan material. It is a natural transition from the sanctity of marriage to the sanctity of children.

13. *to lay his hands on them*. This act of blessing was an old Jewish custom usually accompanied by prayer. Jewish children are still brought to famous rabbis to be blessed.

14. *scolded them*, i.e. scolded the parents.

do not try to stop them. The Greek verb for 'stop' here occurs elsewhere in contexts where baptism is concerned. It is used of John the Baptist trying to stop Jesus from being baptized; when the eunuch in Acts 8: 36 asks 'what is there to prevent my being baptized?'; and when Peter asks in Acts 10: 47 (in regard to the Gentile believers) 'Is anyone prepared to withhold the water for baptism from these persons, who have received the Holy Spirit just as we did ourselves?' But despite such occurrences of the verb elsewhere, it does not follow that there is any reference to baptism in this passage.

such as these, i.e. children and those who are child-like.

15. Once more Matthew omits the reference in Mark (10: 16) to our Lord's embracing of little children (cf. 18: 2).

16. *Master*. Greek: 'teacher'. Mark and Luke have 'good master'. Matthew transfers 'good' to the question *what good must I do to gain eternal life?* i.e. the life of the age to come, the life of the full rich quality of the blessed messianic age which abides for ever.

17. '*Good... Why do you ask me about that?*' Mark 10: 18 has 'Why do you call me good? No one is good except God alone'. So also Luke 18: 19. Matthew avoids a form of question which might be taken to imply (1) that Jesus was not good, (2) that a distinction exists between Jesus and God. Actually the saying in Mark should not be taken to imply either. Jesus was trying to make the questioner realize the full force of what he had just said.

18–19. The commandments are taken from Mark 10: 19, but 'do not defraud', which is not in the Old Testament, is omitted. The wording is changed to agree more closely with the Hebrew text of Exod. 20: 12–16. Jesus adds the saying from Lev. 19: 18 ('love your neighbour as yourself').

20. *Where do I still fall short?* Taken from Mark's 'one thing you lack' in Jesus' answer.

21. *to go the whole way.* Greek: 'to be perfect', i.e. reach the goal of full Christian development. This probably represents a distinction drawn in the early Church between the 'perfect' who had given up all for Christ, and those who had not. In 5: 48 'perfection' ('all goodness') is associated with love of one's enemies.

24. The *camel* was the largest beast of burden known in Palestine. This is no doubt a proverbial saying. Note again the oriental love of exaggeration. It must not be explained away by understanding the Greek 'camēlos' as a ship's cable (hence in some late MSS the spelling *camîlos*, which means 'a rope') or the Greek word for 'eye of a needle' as meaning a narrow gorge or gate.

25. *who...?* i.e. what rich man? 'Rich' often implied impiety, and 'poor' often implied piety, especially in the Psalms (cf. 5: 3).

26. Cf. Mark 9: 23. Many rich men did become disciples, e.g. Matthew (9: 9), Joseph of Arimathaea (27: 57), Zacchaeus (Luke 19: 9).

27. *we who left everything.* They left their nets as soon as Jesus called them (4: 20).

28. *in the world that is to be.* Greek: 'in the regeneration', i.e. 'new birth of the world'. The idea of a 'new world' is common in Jewish apocalyptic. It is sometimes thought of as a renovation of the present world order in a changed earth, sometimes as a new world order which replaces the present world after its destruction. Cf. Rev. 21: 1, 'Then I saw a new heaven and a new earth, for the first heaven and the first earth had vanished'.

the Son of Man is seated on his throne. In Jewish apocalyptic God alone sits on the throne in heavenly splendour.

judges. When sin has ceased, the task of the judges will be purely administrative.

the twelve tribes of Israel are Israel restored to its ideal state, which is part of the new world that is to be. They will be governed by the ideal body of twelve apostles. In Luke this promise stands between a rebuke to the disciples for their strife as to who was greatest and a warning to Peter.

29. *eternal life.* This section has shown that to receive such life is the equivalent of entering the Kingdom, which in turn is the equivalent of becoming a disciple. It is significant that in the Fourth Gospel the phrase 'eternal life' virtually replaces 'the kingdom of God'.

30. In the age to come conditions will be reversed. The disciples who are now last will be first. ✶

THE LABOURERS IN THE VINEYARD

'The kingdom of Heaven is like this. There was once a **20** landowner who went out early one morning to hire labourers for his vineyard; and after agreeing to pay them 2 the usual day's wage he sent them off to work. Going out 3 three hours later he saw some more men standing idle in the market-place. "Go and join the others in the vine- 4 yard," he said, "and I will pay you a fair wage"; so off they went. At noon he went out again, and at three in the 5

6 afternoon, and made the same arrangement as before. An hour before sunset he went out and found another group standing there; so he said to them, "Why are you standing
7 about like this all day with nothing to do?" "Because no one has hired us", they replied; so he told them, "Go
8 and join the others in the vineyard." When evening fell, the owner of the vineyard said to his steward, "Call the labourers and give them their pay, beginning with those
9 who came last and ending with the first." Those who had started work an hour before sunset came forward, and
10 were paid the full day's wage. When it was the turn of the men who had come first, they expected something
11 extra, but were paid the same amount as the others. As
12 they took it, they grumbled at their employer: "These late-comers have done only one hour's work, yet you have put them on a level with us, who have sweated the
13 whole day long in the blazing sun!" The owner turned to one of them and said, "My friend, I am not being unfair to you. You agreed on the usual wage for the day,
14 did you not? Take your pay and go home. I choose to pay
15 the last man the same as you. Surely I am free to do what I like with my own money. Why be jealous because I am
16 kind?" Thus will the last be first, and the first last.'

* This parable follows naturally upon the last saying in 19: 30, which is repeated at the end of the parable.

1. *vineyard.* This is often a symbol of Israel as the sphere of the activity of God's kingdom in Scripture. E.g. Isa. 5: 1, 'My well-beloved had a vineyard in a very fruitful hill'. Jer. 12: 10, 'Many shepherds have destroyed my vineyard.'

2. *the usual day's wage.* lit. 'one denarius for the day'.

3. *three hours later.* Greek: 'about the third hour'. The working day would be from sunrise, about 6 a.m., to sunset, about 6 p.m. The third hour would therefore be 9 a.m.

5. *At noon.* Greek: 'about the sixth hour'.
at three in the afternoon. Greek: 'about the ninth hour'.

6. *An hour before sunset.* Greek: 'about the eleventh hour'.

8. *When evening fell,* i.e. the twelfth hour, 6 p.m. Deut. 24: 15 commands that the worker be paid every day: 'in his day thou shalt give him his hire, neither shall the sun go down upon it'. Payment was made by the *steward* or bailiff.

9. *the full day's wage.* lit. 'one denarius each'.

13. *the usual wage for the day.* lit. 'you agreed on a denarius'.

14. *the last.* This text inspired Ruskin's Essay *Unto this last,* in which he argued that all workers should receive equal pay. But Jesus was not teaching a principle of economics.

15. *Why be jealous?* The Greek means literally 'Is your eye evil?' The 'evil eye' was often used as a term for grudging, envy and jealousy.

16. Cf. 19: 30. For Matthew the vineyard is the Christian community and those who join it late will be treated as equal in privilege with those who join it early. In the intention of Jesus the parable simply illustrated the teaching that the gift of eternal life is not the reward of human merit but the free gift of divine grace. ✶

Challenge to Jerusalem

THIRD PREDICTION OF THE PASSION; REQUEST OF THE SONS OF ZEBEDEE; TWO BLIND MEN HEALED

JESUS WAS journeying towards Jerusalem, and on the 17
way he took the Twelve aside, and said to them, 'We 18
are going to Jerusalem, and the Son of Man will be given

up to the chief priests and the doctors of the law; they
19 will condemn him to death and hand him over to the
foreign power, to be mocked and flogged and crucified,
and on the third day he will be raised to life again.'

20 The mother of Zebedee's sons then came before him,
with her sons. She bowed low and begged a favour.
21 'What is it you wish?' asked Jesus. 'I want you', she
said, 'to give orders that in your kingdom my two sons
here may sit next to you, one at your right, and the other
22 at your left.' Jesus turned to the brothers and said, 'You
do not understand what you are asking. Can you drink
23 the cup that I am to drink?' 'We can', they replied. Then
he said to them, 'You shall indeed share my cup; but to
sit at my right or left is not for me to grant; it is for those
to whom it has already been assigned by my Father.'

24 When the other ten heard this, they were indignant
25 with the two brothers. So Jesus called them to him and
said, 'You know that in the world, rulers lord it over their
subjects, and their great men make them feel the weight
26 of authority; but it shall not be so with you. Among you,
27 whoever wants to be great must be your servant, and
whoever would be first must be the willing slave of all—
28 like the Son of Man; he did not come to be served, but to
serve, and to surrender his life as a ransom for many.'

29 As they were leaving Jericho he was followed by a
30 great crowd of people. At the roadside sat two blind men.
When they heard it said that Jesus was passing they
31 shouted, 'Have pity on us, Son of David.' The people
rounded on them and told them to be quiet. But they
shouted all the more, 'Sir, have pity on us, have pity on
32 us, Son of David.' Jesus stopped and called the men.

'What do you want me to do for you?' he asked. 'Sir,' 33
they answered, 'we want our sight.' Jesus was deeply 34
moved, and touched their eyes. At once their sight came
back, and they went on after him.

✻ 17–19. A third prediction of the Passion (cf. Mark 10: 32–4;
Luke 18: 31–4).

17. Mark 10: 32 implies a visible struggle going on in
Jesus which made the observers full of awe. Matthew is more
reserved.

18–19. This is the most detailed of the predictions of the
Passion. There is no need to doubt that Jesus really did
predict his death and resurrection, though the precise details
here may have been filled in later.

19. *crucified.* Peculiar to Matthew, who continues the
'filling in' process already beginning in Mark.

20. In Mark 10: 35 it is James and John themselves who
make this request. Matthew, in order to spare the apostles,
shifts the responsibility to their mother. Luke omits the story
altogether, probably regarding it as a doublet of 18: 1–2. The
mother may have been named Salome. (Mark 15: 40–41,
'Salome, who had...followed him and waited on him when
he was in Galilee, and...had come up to Jerusalem with him'.)

21. *right...left.* The chief ministers of a king sat on his right
and left, the right hand being the place of highest honour.

22. *cup.* A frequent metaphor in the Old Testament for
suffering inflicted by the wrath of God: e.g. Isa. 51: 17,
'O Jerusalem, which hast drunk at the hand of the Lord the
cup of his fury'. Both cup and baptism refer to his coming
suffering and death. Only through sharing his suffering can
the disciples achieve exaltation.

23. James was the first of the twelve to suffer martyrdom;
he was killed in the persecution in Jerusalem under Herod
Agrippa, A.D. 44 (Acts 12: 2). According to a later tradition
sometimes claimed to be founded on Papias (early second
century) John also was martyred; but the more widely

accepted church tradition identifies him with the author of the Fourth Gospel, and says that he died a natural death in old age at Ephesus. (For Papias see p. 16.)

is not for me to grant. Note the humility of Jesus in relation to his Father, as when he said 'One alone is good' (19: 17). The subordination of Jesus to the Father is frequently stressed in the New Testament. For example, John 14: 28, 'the Father is greater than I'; 1 Cor. 11: 3, 'Christ's Head is God'; 1 Cor. 15: 24, 'Then comes the end, when he delivers up the kingdom to God the Father'.

25. *in the world, rulers*: the Greek means literally 'the rulers of the Gentiles'. The Romans are probably chiefly in mind.

28. *the Son of Man.* Jesus here uses the title of himself in his present humility as the suffering servant of the Lord.

ransom. Jesus here points forward to his self-sacrifice in death upon the cross. The word 'ransom' occurs only here (and in the parallel passage in Mark 10: 45) in the Gospels. Literally it means a money-equivalent for a person or thing. It was the sum paid for the release of a slave or a prisoner of war. Jesus is saying that he came to give his life as the costly equivalent for the many sinners whom he came to release from the bondage and condemnation of sin. 'Many' really means 'all' in accordance with a Hebrew idiom, as in Isa. 53: 12 (a passage probably alluded to here): 'he poured out his soul unto death, and was numbered with the transgressors: yet he bare the sin of many, and made intercession for the transgressors'. The words in the prophecy refer to the suffering servant of the Lord.

29–34. Matthew has recorded a similar incident in 9: 27–33, perhaps a doublet of the present passage.

30. *two blind men.* Mark and Luke mention only one. Mark 10: 46 tells us that his name was Bartimaeus. Matthew is fond of doubling. Cf. 8: 28 (the demonized at Gadara) and 9: 27 (again two blind men).

Son of David. Title of the Messiah, used as at 9: 27.

34. Matthew adds *touched their eyes.* Thus what in Mark

was a miracle-story leading up to an important saying (a pronouncement-story) has been changed by Matthew into an ordinary miracle-story. *

THE TRIUMPHAL ENTRY AND CLEANSING
OF THE TEMPLE

They were now nearing Jerusalem; and when they reached **21** Bethphage at the Mount of Olives, Jesus sent two disciples with these instructions: 'Go to the village opposite, where 2 you will at once find a donkey tethered with her foal beside her; untie them, and bring them to me. If anyone 3 speaks to you, say, "Our Master needs them"; and he will let you take them at once.' This was in fulfilment of 4 the prophecy which says, 'Tell the daughter of Zion, 5 "Here is your king, who comes to you in gentleness, riding on an ass, riding on the foal of a beast of burden."'

The disciples went and did as Jesus had directed, and 6,7 brought the donkey and her foal; they laid their cloaks on them and Jesus mounted. Crowds of people carpeted 8 the road with their cloaks, and some cut branches from the trees to spread in his path. Then the crowd that went 9 ahead and the others that came behind raised the shout: 'Hosanna to the Son of David! Blessings on him who comes in the name of the Lord! Hosanna in the heavens!'

When he entered Jerusalem the whole city went wild 10 with excitement. 'Who is this?' people asked, and the 11 crowd replied, 'This is the prophet Jesus, from Nazareth in Galilee.'

Jesus then went into the temple and drove out all who 12 were buying and selling in the temple precincts; he upset the tables of the money-changers and the seats of the

13 dealers in pigeons; and said to them, 'Scripture says, "My house shall be called a house of prayer"; but you are making it a robbers' cave.'

14 In the temple blind men and cripples came to him, and
15 he healed them. The chief priests and doctors of the law saw the wonderful things he did, and heard the boys in the temple shouting, 'Hosanna to the Son of David!', and
16 they asked him indignantly, 'Do you hear what they are saying?' Jesus answered, 'I do; have you never read that text, "Thou hast made children and babes at the breast
17 sound aloud thy praise"?' Then he left them and went out of the city to Bethany, where he spent the night.

* 1-11. In the triumphal entry, which is commemorated on Palm Sunday, Jesus deliberately claims to be Messiah. For he is fulfilling the messianic prophecy in Zech. 9: 9 (quoted in verse 5).

1. *Bethphage* ('house of young figs') is not mentioned before the Gospels, and its site is uncertain, but it was near Bethany, which was 15 stades (less than two miles) south-east of Jerusalem, on a south-east spur of Mount Olivet. According to John 12: 1, Jesus arrived at Bethany six days before the Passover, i.e. on Saturday, Nisan 8. He probably rested on the Sabbath, and the entry took place on the following day (our Palm Sunday).

2. *a donkey...with her foal.* Matthew mentions two animals, Mark and Luke only one. Matthew misunderstood the prophecy in Zechariah (quoted in verse 5) as referring to two beasts, whereas it refers only to one.

4. Note the usual formula prefixed to the Old Testament text or 'testimony' (see p. 3).

5. The opening line 'Tell the daughter of Zion', is from Isa. 62: 11. The rest of the quotation is from Zech 9: 9.

king, i.e. an ideal king, the Messiah.

7. *on them*, on the two animals. Mark rightly has 'on it'.

8. *Crowds of people*, who had come to Jerusalem for the Passover. These would include Galileans who had witnessed the ministry of Jesus and some of whom had become his followers.

9. *Hosanna to the Son of David.* 'Hosanna' means 'Save now'. It occurs in Ps. 118: 25, 'Save now, we beseech thee, O Lord'. In its original use this cry was addressed to God. It was used as a prayer for blessing; here blessing is invoked upon the Messiah ('Son of David'), or possibly the cry is addressed to the Messiah. The people recognize in Jesus the Messiah fulfilling a messianic prophecy.

Blessings on him who comes in the name of the Lord! From Ps. 118: 26. This verse was used as a greeting to pilgrims approaching the temple. It was not in itself messianic.

Hosanna in the heavens! This means either 'raise the cry of hosanna to the heavens' or 'God in heaven save'.

12–13. According to Mark, Jesus did not cleanse the temple until the next day (Monday). Both Matthew and Luke represent the cleansing as taking place on the day of the triumphal entry, probably influenced by the prophecy in Mal. 3: 1, 'the Lord, whom ye seek, shall suddenly come to his temple'. In the Fourth Gospel the cleansing of the temple takes place near the beginning of the ministry (John 2: 14–17).

12. *the temple.* Some inferior MSS add 'of God'. In the outer court of the temple, the court of the Gentiles, the things necessary for sacrifice were for sale, i.e. animals, birds, wine, salt, oil, etc. This prevented the Gentiles from worshipping there. No doubt also the din of the market penetrated the inner courts too and impeded worship there. The sellers charged exorbitant prices and made an unfair profit. (See plan, p. viii.)

money-changers. The pilgrims who had come to Jerusalem from various countries were compelled to change their Greek and Roman coins into the temple coinage both in order to pay the temple tax of half a shekel (cf. 17: 24) and in order to buy the necessities for sacrifice, e.g. the pigeons.

13. Mark gives the full quotation from Isa. 56: 7 (LXX),

including the words 'for all the nations'. Both Matthew and Luke omit these words despite their relevance to the court of the Gentiles which is the scene of action.

a robbers' cave is an allusion to Jer. 7: 11 (LXX), 'Is this house, which is called by my name, become a den of robbers in your eyes?'

14. This is a general description of healings such as Matthew has already given in 14: 14; 19: 2.

15. *shouting* in the temple precincts was a violation of its sanctity, and would have been promptly stopped by the temple police. The scene is probably Matthew's invention designed to echo the shouts at the triumphal entry. It is to be noted that the objectors do not denounce the shouting itself, but the words that are shouted.

16. *that text* is from Ps. 8: 2 (LXX).

17. The city was overcrowded at Passover time and accommodation was scarce. Besides, in the city Jesus' life was in danger. *

THE CURSING OF THE FIG-TREE; THE POWER OF FAITH; JESUS' AUTHORITY

18,19 Next morning on his way to the city he felt hungry; and seeing a fig-tree at the roadside he went up to it, but found nothing on it but leaves. He said to the tree, 'You shall never bear fruit any more!'; and the tree withered away

20 at once. The disciples were amazed at the sight. 'How is it', they asked, 'that the tree has withered so suddenly?'

21 Jesus answered them, 'I tell you this: if only you have faith and have no doubts, you will do what has been done to the fig-tree; and more than that, you need only say to this mountain, "Be lifted from your place and hurled into

22 the sea", and what you say will be done. And whatever you pray for in faith you will receive.'

He entered the temple, and the chief priests and elders 23
of the nation came to him with the question: 'By what
authority are you acting like this? Who gave you this
authority?' Jesus replied, 'I have a question to ask too; 24
answer it, and I will tell you by what authority I act. The 25
baptism of John: was it from God, or from men?' This
set them arguing among themselves: 'If we say, "from
God", he will say, "Then why did you not believe him?"
But if we say, "from men", we are afraid of the people, 26
for they all take John for a prophet.' So they answered, 27
'We do not know.' And Jesus said: 'Then neither will
I tell you by what authority I act.

✶ 18–22. In Mark the cursing of the fig-tree on the day after
the triumphal entry immediately precedes the cleansing of the
temple, and probably enforces the same lesson—the unfruit-
fulness and falsity of the Jewish religion despite its fair and
promising exterior. Early the following morning (Tuesday)
Jesus and his disciples saw that the fig-tree had withered from
the roots up. Matthew has compressed the two parts of the
incident into one act. It has been suggested that the incident
is really an instance of a parable, such as the parable of the
fruitless fig-tree in Luke 13: 6–9, being turned into a miracle.
The miracle is certainly different from those usually performed
by Jesus, which were designed to help, to heal and to save.
Even as placed by Matthew, its significance is probably the
same as in Mark, a symbolic condemnation of the Jewish
religion as perverted by the chief priests and lawyers. Luke
omits the incident, probably because he regarded it as un-
edifying and also because he had already recorded the parable
above-mentioned.

19. A leafy *fig-tree*, unless it was barren for the year, would
have green figs on it, but these would probably be unfit for
eating before June. Mark 11: 13 explicitly says 'it was not

the season for figs'. Jesus experienced real human hunger and real human disappointment, but neither justifies the curse unless symbolism is intended.

21-2. The sayings about *faith* and prayer do not really fit here. The curse was neither an act of faith nor a prayer. These must be sayings of Jesus uttered on another occasion. Note the characteristic oriental love of exaggeration already mentioned. For the saying about the mountain cf. 17: 20. For the power of prayer cf. 7: 7-11; 18: 19.

23. *the chief priests*. Those who had control in the temple. These chief priests within the temple were drawn mostly from the Sadducees. It was they who were principally responsible for the crucifixion of Jesus.

acting like this. The reference is not to the cursing of the fig-tree but to the cleansing of the temple.

25. *'from God'*. Greek: 'from heaven', a reverent Jewish way of referring to God. The work of John the Baptist and the work of Jesus were intimately connected. The source of the one was the source of the other, i.e. the power of God.

26. *a prophet*. In the eyes of the Jews this was the highest ministry next to that of Messiah, who was also a prophet. John had claimed to be a prophet and the people had recognized him as such. The authority of Jesus was also prophetic.

27. If the critics of Jesus in their dilemma could not make up their minds about the source of John's authority, they were clearly incompetent to determine the source of that of Jesus, and Jesus did not propose to enlighten them, though the implication of his question was clear. ✳

THE TWO SONS AND THE WICKED VINE-GROWERS

28 'But what do you think about this? A man had two sons. He went to the first, and said, "My boy, go and work 29 today in the vineyard." "I will, sir", the boy replied; but 30 he never went. The father came to the second and said

the same. "I will not", he replied, but afterwards he changed his mind and went. Which of these two did as 31 his father wished?' 'The second', they said. Then Jesus answered, 'I tell you this: tax-gatherers and prostitutes are entering the kingdom of God ahead of you. For when 32 John came to show you the right way to live, you did not believe him, but the tax-gatherers and prostitutes did; and even when you had seen that, you did not change your minds and believe him.

'Listen to another parable. There was a landowner who 33 planted a vineyard: he put a wall round it, hewed out a winepress, and built a watch-tower; then he let it out to vine-growers and went abroad. When the vintage season 34 approached, he sent his servants to the tenants to collect the produce due to him. But they took his servants and 35 thrashed one, murdered another, and stoned a third. Again, he sent other servants, this time a larger number; 36 and they did the same to them. At last he sent to them 37 his son. "They will respect my son", he said. But when 38 they saw the son the tenants said to one another, "This is the heir; come on, let us kill him, and get his inheritance." And they took him, flung him out of the vineyard, 39 and murdered him. When the owner of the vineyard 40 comes, how do you think he will deal with those tenants?' 'He will bring those bad men to a bad end', they answered, 41 'and hand the vineyard over to other tenants, who will let him have his share of the crop when the season comes.' Then Jesus said to them, 'Have you never read in the 42 scriptures: "The stone which the builders rejected has become the main corner-stone. This is the Lord's doing, and it is wonderful in our eyes"? Therefore, I tell you, 43

the kingdom of God will be taken away from you, and
given to a nation that yields the proper fruit.'

45   When the chief priests and Pharisees heard his parables,
46 they saw that he was referring to them; they wanted to
arrest him, but they were afraid of the people, who looked
on Jesus as a prophet.

✽ 28-32. This passage falls into two parts: the parable proper
and its meaning (28-31), and an explanation (32). The explanation does not fit the parable very well. The point of the
parable is that the leaders of the Jews who have promised to
work for God, but have failed to do so, will be rejected.
Others who have said 'No' to God at first, but have afterwards repented and done his will, are received into God's
kingdom.

28-31. These verses present a very complicated textual
problem, for they have come down to us in three forms, each
form supported by important MSS or versions.

(1) The first son says 'No' and repents. The second son says
'Yes' and does nothing. Who did the will of his father? The
first.

(2) The first son says 'No' and repents. The second son
says 'Yes' and does nothing. Who did the will of his father?
The second.

(3) The first son says 'Yes' and does nothing. The second says
'No' and repents. Who did the will of his father? The second.

(1) is adopted by the A.V., R.V., and R.S.V. (2) does not
make sense. (3) This is our text, which has the support of the
oldest uncial (MS in capital letters), B (*Codex Vaticanus*). The
son who said 'Yes' and did not go is the type of those priests
and lawyers whose actions did not accord with their professions
of piety (cf. 7: 21). The son who said 'No' and then repented
stands for the tax-gatherers and sinners.

31. *I tell you this.* The idea in this saying is found also in the
parable of the Pharisee and tax-gatherer in Luke 18: 9-14.

32. This further application is obscure. Perhaps the point is that the tax-gatherers and harlots, by believing John's message while the priests and lawyers rejected it, entered into the Kingdom while the religious leaders did not. But Jesus in another saying (11: 11) placed John outside the Kingdom, at any rate as far as its manifestation in the ministry of Jesus was concerned.

33-46. This parable is an allegory. The landowner is God. The vineyard is Israel. The wicked vine-growers are the religious leaders in Israel. The servants are the prophets. The son is Jesus. The son's death is the crucifixion outside Jerusalem.

33. The description of the vineyard is clearly based on Isa. 5: 1-7. The comparison of Israel to a vineyard is common in the Old Testament and would be familiar to the hearers.

wall, as a protection against wild beasts.

winepress. This was usually hollowed out of rock, with two compartments, the upper (Greek: *lēnos*) where the grapes were crushed, and the lower (Greek: *hypolēnion*) into which the grape-juice was allowed to run.

watch-tower. This had a flat roof on which watchmen could stand for the purpose of guarding the vineyard against beasts or thieves. It served also as a storeroom for the new-made wine.

vine-growers. These were tenants, who paid a fixed proportion of the produce as annual rent.

34. *the vintage season*. This would be in the fifth year. Cf. Lev. 19: 25, 'in the fifth year shall ye eat of the fruit thereof'.

35-6. The *servants* are successive prophets. This would be clear to the hearers.

38. *This is the heir*. Cf. Heb. 1: 2, 'in this the final age he has spoken to us in the Son whom he has made heir to the whole universe'.

39. Mark 12: 8 places the casting out after the killing, meaning that they cast out his corpse unburied. Matthew reverses the order, mindful that Jesus died 'outside the gate' (Heb. 13: 12).

40. In Mark and Luke Jesus answers his own question. In Matthew the hearers answer it.

41. The prophets had repeatedly foretold the destruction of the sinful nation. The readers of Matthew would naturally think of the destruction of Jerusalem in A.D. 70.

42. *the scriptures*, i.e. the Old Testament. The reference is to Ps. 118: 22–23, the same Psalm from which the cry 'Hosanna' was taken. In Acts 4: 11; 1 Pet. 2: 7, it is applied to Jesus as Messiah.

the main corner-stone. The most important place in the foundation. In the Psalm the reference is probably to Israel, despised among the nations, but nevertheless in the purpose of God destined to become supreme. The Christian Church, however, taught by Jesus himself, according to this passage, saw in the Old Testament passage a prediction of the rejection of the Messiah by the priests and his exaltation by God.

43. This verse is peculiar to Matthew. *a nation that yields the proper fruit* is the Christian Church.

44. Some MSS add: 'Any man who falls on this stone will be dashed to pieces; and if it falls on a man he will be crushed by it'; but the words are absent from many important MSS. They mean that to 'fall foul of' the Messiah will bring destruction.

45–6. The meaning of the allegory was transparently clear and the authorities were enraged, but they dare not publicly arrest Jesus because of the high regard in which the people held him. ✳

PARABLE OF THE WEDDING FEAST

22 1,2 Then Jesus spoke to them again in parables: 'The kingdom of Heaven is like this. There was a king who prepared a
3 feast for his son's wedding; but when he sent his servants to summon the guests he had invited, they would not
4 come. He sent others again, telling them to say to the

guests, "See now! I have prepared this feast for you. I have had my bullocks and fatted beasts slaughtered; everything is ready; come to the wedding at once." But 5 they took no notice; one went off to his farm, another to his business, and the others seized the servants, attacked 6 them brutally, and killed them. The king was furious; he 7 sent troops to kill those murderers and set their town on fire. Then he said to his servants, "The wedding-feast is 8 ready; but the guests I invited did not deserve the honour. Go out to the main thoroughfares, and invite everyone 9 you can find to the wedding." The servants went out into 10 the streets, and collected all they could find, good and bad alike. So the hall was packed with guests.

'When the king came in to see the company at table, 11 he observed one man who was not dressed for a wedding. "My friend," said the king, "how do you come to be 12 here without your wedding clothes?" He had nothing to say. The king then said to his attendants, "Bind him 13 hand and foot; turn him out into the dark, the place of wailing and grinding of teeth." For though many are 14 invited, few are chosen.'

✶ The first ten verses of this passage have a parallel in Luke 14: 16–24, but there is nothing in Luke corresponding to verses 11–14. The story is not a consistent one. In verse 4 the feast is ready, and in verse 8 it is still ready. But in the meantime a war has taken place (verse 7). In some ways the story resembles that of the wicked vine-growers in the vineyard. Those invited to the kingdom—righteous Jews—maltreat the messengers who bear the invitation; the invitation is therefore given to others—tax-gatherers, sinners, Gentiles—who accept. The message of the story is similar to John 1: 11–12, 'He entered his own realm, and his own would not receive him.

But to all who did receive him...he gave the right to become children of God.'

6–7. These verses are probably a later addition. They allude to the persecution of Christian witnesses after the death and resurrection of Jesus, and the destruction of Jerusalem by Roman armies in A.D. 70.

11–14. (Matthew only.) This is possibly a fragment of an independent parable, the beginning of which has been lost. It teaches that at the coming of the king (at the *parousia*) some of those who have been invited will be found spiritually unprepared and unworthy. This is what is meant by *not dressed for a wedding*. Of course Jesus would not condemn a man for not having the right clothes in a literal sense.

13. *the dark*, i.e. the place of punishment that awaits the wicked (cf. 8: 12).

14. Many Jews had been *invited*, but few had accepted the invitation. Those few were the 'chosen' or 'elect', the pious or righteous remnant spoken of by Isaiah (10: 22), 'only a remnant of them shall return', i.e. reverse the present distrustful attitude of the nation. ✳

TAXES; RESURRECTION; THE GREAT COMMANDMENT; DAVID'S SON

15 Then the Pharisees went and agreed on a plan to trap him
16 in his own words. Some of their followers were sent to him in company with men of Herod's party. They said, 'Master, you are an honest man, we know; you teach in all honesty the way of life that God requires, truckling to
17 no man, whoever he may be. Give us your ruling on this: are we or are we not permitted to pay taxes to the Roman
18 Emperor?' Jesus was aware of their malicious intention and said to them, 'You hypocrites! Why are you trying
19 to catch me out? Show me the money in which the tax

is paid.' They handed him a silver piece. Jesus asked, 20
'Whose head is this, and whose inscription?' 'Caesar's', 21
they replied. He said to them, 'Then pay Caesar what is due
to Caesar, and pay God what is due to God.' This answer 22
took them by surprise, and they went away and left him
alone.

The same day Sadducees came to him, maintaining that 23
there is no resurrection. Their question was this: 'Master, 24
Moses said, "If a man should die childless, his brother
shall marry the widow and carry on his brother's family."
Now we knew of seven brothers. The first married and 25
died, and as he was without issue his wife was left to his
brother. The same thing happened with the second, and 26
the third, and so on with all seven. Last of all the woman 27
died. At the resurrection, then, whose wife will she be, 28
for they had all married her?' Jesus answered: 'You are 29
mistaken, because you know neither the scriptures nor
the power of God. At the resurrection men and women 30
do not marry, but are like angels in heaven.

'But about the resurrection of the dead, have you never 31
read what God himself said to you: "I am the God of 32
Abraham, the God of Isaac, and the God of Jacob"? He
is not God of the dead but of the living.' The people heard 33
what he said, and were astounded at his teaching.

Hearing that he had silenced the Sadducees, the 34
Pharisees met together; and one of their number tested 35
him with this question: 'Master, which is the greatest 36
commandment in the Law?' He answered, '"Love the 37
Lord your God with all your heart, with all your soul,
with all your mind." That is the greatest commandment. 38
It comes first. The second is like it: "Love your neighbour 39

40 as yourself." Everything in the Law and the prophets hangs on these two commandments.'

41 Turning to the assembled Pharisees Jesus asked them,
42 'What is your opinion about the Messiah? Whose son is
43 he?' 'The son of David', they replied. 'How then is it', he asked, 'that David by inspiration calls him "Lord"?
44 For he says, "The Lord said to my Lord, 'Sit at my right
45 hand until I put your enemies under your feet.'" If David
46 calls him "Lord", how can he be David's son?' Not a man could say a word in reply; and from that day forward no one dared ask him another question.

✻ 15–16. In Mark 12: 13–17 a number of Pharisees and men of Herod's party were sent, probably by the temple authorities. In Matthew the Pharisees take the lead.

16. *Herod's party*. These adherents of Herod would support a tax, while the Pharisees hated it. The intention was to place Jesus in a dilemma. If he denounced the tax, he would get himself into trouble with the civil authorities. If he pronounced in favour of the tax, he would make himself unpopular with the people.

17. *taxes*. The poll-tax or capitation-tax (i.e. a tax levied on each 'head'); it was a direct tax levied in the provinces (of which Judaea was now one) upon all males over the age of fourteen, and all females over twelve, up to the age of sixty-five. This tax was paid through the tax-gatherers into the imperial exchequer, and for payment of it silver denarii were struck with an 'image' of Caesar and an inscription which gave his name and titles. It was this levy which the Zealot Judas of Galilee resisted, as mentioned in Acts 5: 37 (see p. 20).

18. *hypocrites*. This does not occur in Mark. Though their intention was crafty and malicious, their praise of Jesus' honesty may have been sincere.

19. *silver piece.* Greek: *denarius.*

20. The emperor at the time was Tiberius. The coin may have borne his image or that of his predecessor, Augustus.

21. The answer of Jesus was not simply a clever way out of the dilemma. Jesus recognized the claims of the civil government in so far as these did not conflict with the claims of God. Of course the latter must have priority.

23. *Sadducees.* See p. 19.

24. The quotation is from Deut. 25: 5. Though marriage with a dead brother's widow is forbidden in Lev. 18: 16; 20: 21, it is commanded in Deut. 25: 5–10, if the brother had died without a son. Even then it was limited to brothers who were neighbours, i.e. who lived on the same estate. The obligation could be repudiated. By the time of Jesus the law in question had probably become almost obsolete. The case propounded by the Sadducees was doubtless an imaginary one invented for the purpose of controversy.

26. All the marriages must have failed to produce a son. If one had been born, he would have been regarded as the son of the original husband.

28. The popular view of the resurrection was evidently that the physical body was raised. But some rabbis taught that the resurrection body would be spiritual.

29. *the power of God,* i.e. his power to overcome any difficulties. The *scriptures* may be those which refer to God as Almighty, or Exod. 3: 6 quoted below in verse 32.

30. *like angels.* Jesus teaches the spiritual nature of the resurrection. The angelic body would be a spiritual body, like that with which, according to Paul, the Christian dead are raised (1 Cor. 15: 35–44), 'flesh and blood can never possess the kingdom of God, and the perishable cannot possess immortality' (1 Cor. 15: 50).

32. The quotation is from Exod. 3: 6. At the time referred to in that quotation, Abraham, Isaac and Jacob were long dead, yet says Jesus, they were still living, for God is not the God of the dead, but of the living.

34. *one of their number.* Some MSS insert 'a lawyer'. Mark 12: 28 says 'one of the lawyers'.

37. The quotation is from Deut. 6: 5, which formed part of the *Shema* ('Hear, O Israel', etc.; see p. 10).

39. From Lev. 19: 18.

40. The combination of the two commandments is also found in the *Testaments of the Twelve Patriarchs, Test. Issachar,* v, 2. But many scholars deny that this work is pre-Christian. If it is not, then Jesus seems to have been the first to combine them to form a double injunction and set it forth as a summary of the ethical code, consistently with what he says at Matt. 5: 17 and 7: 12.

42. It was the commonly accepted belief, shared by the Pharisees, that the Messiah would be a 'son of David'. Another view was that the Messiah would be a priest-king of Levitical descent. This is found in *Test. Levi* xviii, 2–5.

43. *by inspiration.* Greek: 'in the Spirit'. The meaning is that David was inspired by the Holy Spirit when he wrote the Psalm. The Pharisees believed that David wrote the Psalm, and Jesus argues from this assumption.

44. The quotation is from Psalm 110: 1 (quoted also in Acts 2: 34–5).

my Lord. David is assumed in these words to be referring to the Messiah.

45. If David addressed the Messiah as '*Lord*', the Messiah must be something more than his son, namely, of divine origin. Jesus is not denying that he was descended from David, but he is claiming to be something more, the Son of God. *

ON LAWYERS AND PHARISEES

23 1,2 Jesus then addressed the people and his disciples in these words: 'The doctors of the law and the Pharisees sit in 3 the chair of Moses; therefore do what they tell you; pay attention to their words. But do not follow their practice;

for they say one thing and do another. They make up 4 heavy packs and pile them on men's shoulders, but will not raise a finger to lift the load themselves. Whatever 5 they do is done for show. They go about with broad phylacteries and wear deep fringes on their robes; they 6 like to have places of honour at feasts and the chief seats in synagogues, to be greeted respectfully in the street, and 7 to be addressed as "rabbi".

'But you must not be called "rabbi"; for you have one 8 Rabbi, and you are all brothers. Do not call any man on 9 earth "father"; for you have one Father, and he is in heaven. Nor must you be called "teacher"; you have one 10 Teacher, the Messiah. The greatest among you must be 11 your servant. For whoever exalts himself will be humbled; 12 and whoever humbles himself will be exalted.

* 2. *the chair of Moses*. This was an article of furniture in the synagogue, reserved for the lawyers and the Pharisees because they were the constitutional authorities for determining the Law.

3. Cf. Rom. 2: 21, 'You proclaim, "Do not steal"; but are you yourself a thief?' It was such inconsistency that justified the name 'hypocrites'.

5. *phylacteries*. The phylactery consisted of (*a*) a small leather box or case containing certain texts of the Old Testament written on parchment; (*b*) a leather strap to which this box was attached. Two phylacteries were worn, one on the head, the other on the left arm (see Deut. 6: 8–9; Exod. 13: 9). The Greek word 'phylactery' really means an 'amulet' or 'charm'. It does not occur in the LXX nor elsewhere in the New Testament. It here represents the late Hebrew *t*ᵉ*phillin* (lit. 'prayers'), small cases still worn by pious Jews at morning prayer.

broad. The Greek means literally 'they make broad'. If this is to be taken literally, it must mean broadening the strap. But not very much could be done in this way. Alternatively, the broadening of the phylacteries might mean wearing the phylacteries more frequently. Probably the time for wearing them was the time of morning and evening prayer, and the lawyers and Pharisees extended the wearing to the whole day.

deep fringes. These were the tassels ordained in Num. 15: 38–9 and Deut. 22: 12. These tassels were to be fixed at the four corners of the rectangular shawl used as an outer garment. As no maximum length was prescribed for these decorations, those who wished to make a display of piety might make the tassels as long as they pleased.

7. *rabbi.* A title of respect used by disciples in addressing their teachers.

8–12. These verses are addressed to the disciples. They enjoin brotherly equality.

8. There is no room in Christianity for the distinctions used in Judaism.

you must not be called. Note the passive voice. What is forbidden is not the desire to show respect to a brother, but the desire to have respect shown to oneself. It is pride which is forbidden. God is the teacher. The duty of the disciple is to learn from him and be humble before him.

10. The Greek word (*kathegetes*) here translated 'teacher' occurs only here in the New Testament. It means in the first instance 'guide' and then 'teacher'. In modern Greek it means 'professor'. It has a root similar to 'exegete' and a similar meaning, i.e. interpreter of the Law. Christ is the sole interpreter of the Law, as he claimed in the Sermon on the Mount.

11–12. These two verses have several parallels in the Gospels, cf. Matt. 18: 4; Luke 14: 11; 18: 14. Compare also Phil. 2: 8–9, 'he humbled himself.... Therefore God raised him to the heights', referring to Christ. There are also parallels in rabbinic literature. ✻

SEVEN LAMENTATIONS ADDRESSED TO THE
LAWYERS AND PHARISEES

'Alas, alas for you, lawyers and Pharisees, hypocrites 13
that you are! You shut the door of the kingdom of
Heaven in men's faces; you do not enter yourselves, and
when others are entering, you stop them.

'Alas for you, lawyers and Pharisees, hypocrites! You 15
travel over sea and land to win one convert; and when
you have won him you make him twice as fit for hell as
you are yourselves.

'Alas for you, blind guides! You say, "If a man swears 16
by the sanctuary, that is nothing; but if he swears by the
gold in the sanctuary, he is bound by his oath." Blind 17
fools! Which is the more important, the gold, or the
sanctuary which sanctifies the gold? Or you say, "If a 18
man swears by the altar, that is nothing; but if he swears
by the offering that lies on the altar, he is bound by his
oath." What blindness! Which is the more important, 19
the offering, or the altar which sanctifies it? To swear by 20
the altar, then, is to swear both by the altar and by whatever lies on it; to swear by the sanctuary is to swear both 21
by the sanctuary and by him who dwells there; and to 22
swear by heaven is to swear both by the throne of God and
by him who sits upon it.

'Alas for you, lawyers and Pharisees, hypocrites! You 23
pay tithes of mint and dill and cummin; but you have
overlooked the weightier demands of the Law, justice,
mercy, and good faith. It is these you should have
practised, without neglecting the others. Blind guides! 24
You strain off a midge, yet gulp down a camel!

25 'Alas for you, lawyers and Pharisees, hypocrites! You clean the outside of cup and dish, which you have filled
26 inside by robbery and self-indulgence! Blind Pharisee! Clean the inside of the cup first; then the outside will be clean also.

27 'Alas for you, lawyers and Pharisees, hypocrites! You are like tombs covered with whitewash; they look well from outside, but inside they are full of dead men's bones
28 and all kinds of filth. So it is with you: outside you look like honest men, but inside you are brim-full of hypocrisy and crime.

29 'Alas for you, lawyers and Pharisees, hypocrites! You build up the tombs of the prophets and embellish the
30 monuments of the saints, and you say, "If we had been alive in our fathers' time, we should never have taken
31 part with them in the murder of the prophets." So you acknowledge that you are the sons of the men who killed
32 the prophets. Go on then, finish off what your fathers began!

✻ 13. *Alas.* The Greek is a word of sorrow and lamentation rather than of threat or fury. 'Alas' is therefore a better translation than 'woe' (R.V.).

14. Some MSS insert either before or after verse 13 an additional lamentation based on Mark 12: 40, 'Alas for you, lawyers and Pharisees, hypocrites! You eat up the property of widows, while you say long prayers for appearance' sake. You will receive the severest sentence.' The uncertainty in the placing of the verse is a sign that it is a later insertion. The best MSS omit it.

15. The synagogues of the Dispersion, because of their strong monotheism and their high ethical standards, were effective centres of Jewish propaganda and gathered many

Gentile converts or God-fearers. These people were not proselytes in the full sense, but adherents who worshipped the God of the Jews. Full membership of the Jewish community required in addition (1) further instructions in the Torah (the Law); (2) that a male convert must be circumcised; (3) that all converts must submit to the proselyte bath; (4) that the convert must offer sacrifice in the temple.

twice as fit for hell. lit. 'double a son of Gehenna', i.e. twice as much one destined for hell-fire.

16. *swears.* Oaths, not vows, are meant. Here lawyers are being denounced, for such distinctions as these are purely legal.

17–19. That which *sanctifies* is obviously *more important* than that which is sanctified.

21–2. These verses are directed against the careless use of oaths, for in an oath it is really God himself who is called upon.

23–8. Cf. Luke 11: 39–44.

23. *dill.* Anise, an aromatic plant.

cummin, too, is an aromatic plant. The tithing (i.e. giving to God a tenth) of mint, dill and cummin was demanded by the Law. Cf. Lev. 27: 30, 'And all the tithe of the land, whether of the seed of the land, or of the fruit of the tree, is the Lord's'. Cf. Deut. 14: 22, 'Thou shalt surely tithe all the increase of thy seed, that which cometh forth of the field year by year'. But, says Jesus, justice, mercy and faith take precedence. Luke in place of 'dill' has 'rue' (11: 42). The Aramaic for 'dill' is very similar to that for 'rue'. This suggests that the saying goes back to an Aramaic source. The mention of these small herbs illustrates the excessive zeal of the Pharisees in tithing. Jesus says that the observance of these minute points of the law is good, provided that the more important matters are not neglected.

24. Peculiar to Matthew. The distinction is between that which is tiny and that which is large. It is foolish to make a fuss over the little things and neglect the big ones. Note once more the oriental love of exaggeration in proverbs. This one is not without humour.

25. The *cup and dish* seem to be used figuratively of the lawyers and Pharisees themselves, who were very particular about ritual purity (i.e. cleanness for purposes of worship) not only of vessels, but of their own persons. But just as a ritually clean vessel may be full of poison, so a ritually clean person may be full of *robbery and self-indulgence*.

26. *Clean the inside of the cup*. Some MSS add 'and of the dish', to make the saying correspond to the previous verse. Our text is probably the original. The point of the saying is: an effective cleaning must begin within. Luke 11: 41 has the difficult version: 'let what is in the cup be given in charity, and all is clean'. The Aramaic for 'cleanse' is very similar to that for 'give in charity'. This suggests that the saying has an Aramaic origin, of which Matthew, not Luke, has the correct translation.

27. The whitewashing of *tombs* took place in the spring to guard the people, especially the priests, against accidental defilement by contact with them. The coat of *whitewash* thus acted as a warning to passers-by to keep their distance. But incidentally it beautified the tombs, covering up their ugliness and corruption.

28. This verse makes the application to the lawyers and Pharisees from this latter point of view—the incidental effect of the whitewash, instead of its real purpose.

29. Veneration for the *tombs* and *monuments* of saints and heroes has always been practised in the east.

31. *sons:* and therefore inheritors of their character.

32. Another possible translation is—'You too must come up to your fathers' standards'. ✶

PUNISHMENT FOR LAWYERS AND PHARISEES; LAMENT OVER JERUSALEM

33 'You snakes, you vipers' brood, how can you escape being
34 condemned to hell? I send you therefore prophets, sages, and teachers; some of them you will kill and crucify,

others you will flog in your synagogues and hound from
city to city. And so, on you will fall the guilt of all the 35
innocent blood spilt on the ground, from innocent Abel
to Zechariah son of Berachiah, whom you murdered
between the sanctuary and the altar. Believe me, this 36
generation will bear the guilt of it all.

'O Jerusalem, Jerusalem, the city that murders the 37
prophets and stones the messengers sent to her! How
often have I longed to gather your children, as a hen
gathers her brood under her wings; but you would not
let me. Look, look! there is your temple, forsaken by 38
God. And I tell you, you shall never see me until the 39
time when you say, "Blessings on him who comes in the
name of the Lord."'

* 34. Cf. Luke 11: 49, 'This is why the Wisdom of God
said, "I will send them prophets and messengers"'. Matthew
interprets the Wisdom of God as Christ himself, and puts
'you' for 'them'. Luke does not necessarily mean that Jesus
is quoting a book called 'The Wisdom of God'. He may
mean by the Wisdom of God, God himself. There is an
allusion to 2 Chron. 24: 19, 'Yet he sent prophets to them'.
(This introduces the story of Zechariah's murder, referred to
in verse 35.)

kill and crucify seems to refer to the Lord's death. What
follows refers to the later persecutions of Christians.

35. *Abel.* The first martyr in the Bible, a righteous man
murdered by his brother Cain (Gen. 4: 8).

Zechariah. The last martyr mentioned in the Hebrew Bible,
2 Chron. 24: 20–2 (this was the last book in the Hebrew Bible
where the order of the books is different from our Old
Testament). But this priest was the son of Jehoiada. Matthew
(or his source) is probably confusing him with Zechariah the
prophet, the son of Berechiah (Zech. 1: 1). Luke 11: 51 omits

'son of Berachiah'. It has been suggested that the words in Matthew were added after A.D. 69 when a Zechariah, son of Baruch, was murdered in the temple during the siege. But this speculation is unnecessary.

37. *How often.* These words seem to suggest more frequent visits to Jerusalem than are allowed for in the Synoptic Gospels. In the Fourth Gospel a much greater part of the ministry of Jesus takes place in Jerusalem. The imagery of the hen gathering her brood under her wings is very beautiful. Cf. Isa. 31: 5, 'As birds flying, so will the Lord of hosts protect Jerusalem'. Ps. 36: 7, 'How precious is thy lovingkindness, O God! and the children of men take refuge under the shadow of thy wings'. There is implicit a claim to be divine in these words of Jesus.

38. 'The presence of God, which would have saved you in the coming Judgement through me, his representative and prophet, is now finally deserting you' (A. H. McNeile). The verse could be translated—'Look, your home is desolate'. In this case the people of Jerusalem are in mind, and their home is the city, including of course the temple, the centre of the nation. Cf. Jer. 12: 7, where God says 'I have forsaken my house, I have cast off my heritage'. Again, Ezekiel believed he had seen the glory (visible sign of the presence) of God leave the temple (Ezek. 11: 23). Some MSS add in Matthew 'and laid waste'. Cf. Jer. 22: 5, 'this house shall become a desolation'. This addition in Matthew is probably not original. It would express a different thought, the destruction of the city by the Romans.

39. The quotation from Ps. 118: 26 was shouted by the crowd at the triumphal entry into Jerusalem. It was not in itself messianic. Luke places the present passage *before* the entry, so that the words are a prediction of it. Luke, like Matthew, understands them as messianic. In Matthew the words are a prediction of the *parousia*, his return as the heavenly Messiah. *

Prophecies and Warnings

THE DESTRUCTION OF THE TEMPLE;
THE TIME OF TROUBLES

JESUS WAS leaving the temple when his disciples came **24** and pointed to the temple buildings. He answered, 2 'You see all these buildings? I tell you this: not one stone will be left upon another; all will be thrown down.'

When he was sitting on the Mount of Olives the 3 disciples came to speak to him privately. 'Tell us,' they said, 'when will this happen? And what will be the signal for your coming and the end of the age?'

Jesus replied: 'Take care that no one misleads you. For 4,5 many will come claiming my name and saying, "I am the Messiah"; and many will be misled by them. The 6 time is coming when you will hear the noise of battle near at hand and the news of battles far away; see that you are not alarmed. Such things are bound to happen; but the end is still to come. For nation will make war upon 7 nation, kingdom upon kingdom; there will be famines and earthquakes in many places. With all these things the 8 birth-pangs of the new age begin.

'You will then be handed over for punishment and 9 execution; and men of all nations will hate you for your allegiance to me. Many will lose their faith; they will 10 betray one another and hate one another. Many false 11 prophets will arise, and will mislead many; and as lawless- 12 ness spreads, men's love for one another will grow cold. But the man who holds out to the end will be saved. And 13,14

179

this gospel of the Kingdom will be proclaimed throughout the earth as a testimony to all nations; and then the end will come.

15 'So when you see "the abomination of desolation", of which the prophet Daniel spoke, standing in the holy
16 place (let the reader understand), then those who are in
17 Judaea must take to the hills. If a man is on the roof, he
18 must not come down to fetch his goods from the house; if
19 in the field, he must not turn back for his coat. Alas for women with child in those days, and for those who have
20 children at the breast! Pray that it may not be winter
21 when you have to make your escape, or Sabbath. It will be a time of great distress, such as has never been from the beginning of the world until now, and will never be
22 again. If that time of troubles were not cut short, no living thing could survive; but for the sake of God's chosen it will be cut short.

23 'Then, if anyone says to you, "Look, here is the
24 Messiah", or, "There he is", do not believe it. Impostors will come claiming to be messiahs or prophets, and they will produce great signs and wonders to mislead even
25 God's chosen, if such a thing were possible. See, I have
26 forewarned you. If they tell you, "He is there in the wilderness", do not go out; or if they say, "He is there
27 in the inner room", do not believe it. Like lightning from the east, flashing as far as the west, will be the coming of the Son of Man.

28 'Wherever the corpse is, there the vultures will gather.

✻ 1. All the discourses since 21: 15 have been placed in the temple. Mark 12: 41–4 and Luke 21: 1–4 prefix to these verses the incident of the widow's mite; Matthew's omission of it brings these verses near to the saying 'there is your temple, forsaken by God' (23: 38).

the temple buildings. Herod's temple, begun in 20–19 B.C. and still unfinished in the time of Jesus, was truly magnificent. Josephus says its stones measured about $25 \times 8 \times 12$ cubits (a cubit = about 18 in.).

2. *I tell you this.* Greek: 'Amen (i.e. truly) I tell you'. Matthew alone has this formula here. The destruction is pictured in general terms. The actual destruction was by fire.

3. *privately.* Secret disclosure to a small inner circle of disciples is a regular feature of Jewish apocalyptic.

coming. Greek *parousia*, a word signifying 'presence' or 'arrival', sometimes of a king. Here it is used of Christ's final advent. Although it is frequent in the Epistles, this word is used only in this chapter in the Gospels. It occurs here four times (see verses 27, 37, 39).

4. *misleads.* At the time when the Gospels were written, it was very important that Christians should not be misled by false prophets like Simon Magus who pretended to be Messiah or the great power of God (Acts 8: 9–11).

5. False claimants to Messiahship are also referred to frequently by Josephus in connexion with the Jewish War (A.D. 66–70).

6–7. It was expected in Jewish apocalyptic that universal war would herald the End.

8. The rabbis described the time of trouble that was expected to precede the messianic age as 'birth-pangs of the Messiah'.

9–14. Persecution, false prophets and apostasy predicted. Most of Mark 13: 9–13 has been used by Matthew in 10: 17–22. Verse 9 gives a summary of it. Verses 10–12 are peculiar to Matthew.

9. *men of all nations will hate you.* Added by Matthew. It

reflects later development and expansion of the Christian Church.

10. *Many will lose their faith*; (Greek: 'be caused to stumble') because of suffering and disappointment.

11. *false prophets*, i.e. false Christian teachers, claiming to be prophets within the Church. Agabus (Acts 11: 27–8) was one of the true prophets. The work of the second century known as the *Didachē* tells Christians how to tell true from false Christian prophets (*Did.* 11: 7–12).

12. *love*. Greek: *agapē*, 'Christian love', 'pure good will'. This characteristically Christian word occurs only here and in Luke 11: 42 in the Synoptic Gospels. The love of Christians for one another will grow cold. Cf. Rev. 2: 4, 'you have lost your early love'.

14. *this gospel of the Kingdom*, i.e. the good news here being announced, that the messianic kingdom was at hand.

to all nations, i.e. all the nations then known, the civilized world, mostly embraced by the Roman empire. At the time when the Gospels were written, after the missionary enterprise of Paul, this must have seemed well within the bounds of possibility.

15. '*the abomination of desolation*'. This expression is found in Daniel 11: 31, 'they shall set up the abomination that maketh desolate' (cf. Dan. 12: 11). There it refers to the heathen altar with an image of Zeus Olympios which was set up on the altar in the temple by Antiochus Epiphanes, King of Syria, in 168 B.C. The prophecy was reinterpreted and applied to some act of desecration by the Romans, such as the plan of the Emperor Gaius Caligula (A.D. 37–41) to set up his image in the temple, or the erection of the statue of Titus on the site of the ruined temple in A.D. 70. Luke (21: 20) interprets the expression to mean 'when you see Jerusalem encircled by armies, then you may be sure that her destruction is near'.

16. The hill-country in Judaea contained many caves and hiding-places.

17. *on the roof.* The houses had flat roofs where people of leisure sat and rested. Such a man must come down the outside stairway and not even go into the house for his possessions.

18. Nor must the field labourer attempt to save his property. They must be ready to meet the Son of Man empty-handed.

20. The mention of the *Sabbath* is a Jewish touch peculiar to Matthew. The Sabbath was still observed by Jewish Christians when Matthew wrote.

21. Cf. Dan. 12: 1, 'there shall be a time of trouble, such as never was since there was a nation' and 1 Macc. 9: 27 (*c.* 125-100 B.C.), 'And there was great tribulation in Israel, such as was not since the time that no prophet appeared unto them'. Matthew is referring to the days of anti-Christ, the enemy of God's people who was expected to arise just before the end of the world, and the coming of the Son of Man.

24. *great signs and wonders* are associated with false prophets in Deut. 13: 1-5.

26-8. The *parousia* will be sudden and plain as in Luke 17: 23-4, 37. There is nothing corresponding in Mark, where the emphasis is throughout on warning signs of the coming End.

27. The sudden manifestation of the heavenly Messiah will be seen in every quarter of the world.

28. A proverbial saying. The Greek word can be translated either 'eagles' or 'vultures'. Vultures are more likely to be found around a carcase than eagles. Luke has this saying in 17: 37, and in that context it means 'wherever there is reason for judgement, judgement will take place'. In Matthew it simply expresses inevitability. *

THE COMING OF THE SON OF MAN

'As soon as the distress of those days has passed, the sun 29 will be darkened, the moon will not give her light, the stars will fall from the sky, the celestial powers will be

30 shaken. Then will appear in heaven the sign that heralds
the Son of Man. All the peoples of the world will make
lamentation, and they will see the Son of Man coming on
31 the clouds of heaven with great power and glory. With
a trumpet blast he will send out his angels, and they will
gather his chosen from the four winds, from the farthest
bounds of heaven on every side.

32 'Learn a lesson from the fig-tree. When its tender shoots
appear and are breaking into leaf, you know that summer
33 is near. In the same way, when you see all these things,
you may know that the end is near, at the very door.
34 I tell you this: the present generation will live to see it all.
35 Heaven and earth will pass away; my words will never
pass away.

36 'But about that day and hour no one knows, not even
the angels in heaven, not even the Son; only the Father.
37 'As things were in Noah's days, so will they be when
38 the Son of Man comes. In the days before the flood they
ate and drank and married, until the day that Noah went
39 into the ark, and they knew nothing until the flood came
and swept them all away. That is how it will be when the
40 Son of Man comes. Then there will be two men in the
41 field; one will be taken, the other left; two women
grinding at the mill; one will be taken, the other left.

⁎ 29. *the sun will be darkened.* Disturbance among the
heavenly bodies is a regular feature of Jewish apocalyptic
descriptions of the End. Cf. Isa. 13: 10, 'the stars of the heaven
and the constellations thereof shall not give their light: the
sun shall be darkened in his going forth, and the moon shall
not cause her light to shine'.

the celestial powers include all the heavenly bodies.

30. *the sign that heralds the Son of Man.* Greek: 'the sign of the Son of Man' (peculiar to Matthew). The N.E.B. has correctly interpreted the phrase. The sign is not the cross as some early Christian Fathers supposed. There may be a reference to Isa. 11: 12, 'And he shall set up an ensign for the nations'. (Whatever the sign in Matthew may be, it is more personally associated with the Messiah than the disturbances in the heavenly bodies.)

All...will make lamentation. The words appear to be based on Zech. 12: 10, but with a wider meaning since the prophet speaks only of the tribes of Israel and the land of Palestine.

the Son of Man. An allusion to Dan. 7: 13-14, the important passage for the interpretation of the term. In Daniel 'one like unto a son of man' stands for the community of the saints of the most High. Jesus took the title and applied it to himself as the inaugurator and leader of such a community (see pp. 8-9). Here he refers to himself as the future eschatological Son of Man coming in his glory.

with great power, may refer to an accompanying host of angels.

glory means the shining radiance of the presence of God.

31. *With a trumpet blast.* In Jewish apocalyptic the Day of Judgement is heralded by a trumpet call. Cf. Isa. 27: 13, 'And it shall come to pass in that day, that a great trumpet shall be blown'. Cf. 1 Cor. 15: 52, 'the trumpet will sound, and the dead will rise immortal'.

32-3. Parable of the fig-tree (Mark 13: 28-9; Luke 21: 29-31). It is not certain that Jesus originally uttered this parable in this context. It would apply well to the coming of the Kingdom in his own ministry.

33. *the end is near.* The Greek could also mean 'he is near' (i.e. the Son of Man). Cf. Rev. 3: 20, 'Here I stand knocking at the door', uttered by the risen Christ.

34. Note how imminent the *parousia* was believed to be.

36. Jesus is human as well as Divine. As human, he is limited in his knowledge. This must be a genuine utterance

of Jesus. The adoring early Church could not have invented it. Jesus did not know when the End would be. Yet in his discourse the End has been associated with the destruction of Jerusalem. Connecting the end of the world with that of Jerusalem must be due to the composition of the evangelists (especially Mark 13, the source passage). That is, in this discourse we have had some genuine utterances of Jesus, originally uttered at different times, brought together in the Gospel tradition and interspersed with later Christian additions.

37-9. A warning from the example of the Flood (Luke 17: 26-7). Luke adds the example of Sodom (Luke 17: 28-9).

37. As men were caught unprepared in the days of Noah at the time of the Flood, so will they be at the *parousia*. To those outside the Christian Church the *parousia* will come without warning. (For those inside, there will be the warning of the signs already mentioned.)

38. The conduct of men when the Son of Man comes will be like that of men who lived in the days before the *flood*. Their indifference to the seriousness of the situation proved their undoing. But Noah realized what was coming and took steps accordingly. The wise man will be alert to his danger and secure salvation.

39. In apocalyptic literature the Flood is often used to illustrate what the end of the world will be like. Cf. *Book of Enoch*, X, 2 (written *c.* 170 B.C.): 'the whole earth will be destroyed, and a deluge is about to come upon the whole earth, and will destroy all that is on it'.

41. *grinding* was the work of a slave-girl. Cf. Exod. 11: 5 'the maidservant that is behind the mill'. ✶

KEEP AWAKE

42 'Keep awake, then; for you do not know on what day
43 your Lord is to come. Remember, if the householder had known at what time of night the burglar was coming, he

would have kept awake and not have let his house be
broken into. Hold yourselves ready, therefore, because the 44
Son of Man will come at the time you least expect him.

'Who is the trusty servant, the sensible man charged by 45
his master to manage his household staff and issue their
rations at the proper time? Happy that servant who is 46
found at his task when his master comes! I tell you this: 47
he will be put in charge of all his master's property. But 48
if he is a bad servant and says to himself, "The master is
a long time coming", and begins to bully the other 49
servants and to eat and drink with his drunken friends,
then the master will arrive on a day that servant does not 50
expect, at a time he does not know, and will cut him in 51
pieces. Thus he will find his place among the hypocrites,
where there is wailing and grinding of teeth.

✻ 42–4. The householder and the burglar (Luke 12: 39–40;
cf. Mark 13: 33–7). There are considerable differences between
Matthew and Mark's version.

42. *your Lord* is a Christian title for Christ and can hardly have
been used by Jesus in reference to himself as Son of Man. Mark's
'when the moment comes' is more probable (Mark 13: 33).

43. *what time of night*. Greek: 'in what watch'. Cf.
1 Thess. 5: 2, 'the Day of the Lord comes like a thief in the
night'. The point is suddenness and unexpectedness.

45–51. The parable of the faithful and wise servant. Cf.
Luke 12: 42–6. The task of the disciple is not confined to
watchfulness. There is work to be done, which will be tested
in the *parousia*, and the evil-doer will be punished. If this is
a genuine utterance of Jesus, the trusty servant is the good
disciple, the bad one represents the Jewish religious leaders.
At a later time the story would suggest a distinction between
good and bad leaders in the Christian Church.

47. The reward for good service is higher responsibility,

the opportunity for greater service (i.e. in this context, in the Age to come).

49. He bullies those who oppose him and indulges himself with those who support him.

51. *will cut him in pieces.* This brutal form of punishment was sometimes actually used in ancient times. Cf. Heb. 11: 37, 'they were sawn in two'.

wailing and grinding of teeth. The usual Matthaean formula. See on 8: 12. *

PARABLE OF THE TEN GIRLS

25 'When that day comes, the kingdom of Heaven will be like this. There were ten girls, who took their lamps and
2 went out to meet the bridegroom. Five of them were
3 foolish, and five prudent; when the foolish ones took their
4 lamps, they took no oil with them, but the others took
5 flasks of oil with their lamps. As the bridegroom was late
6 in coming they all dozed off to sleep. But at midnight a cry was heard: "Here is the bridegroom! Come out to
7 meet him." With that the girls all got up and trimmed
8 their lamps. The foolish said to the prudent, "Our lamps
9 are going out; give us some of your oil." "No," they said; "there will never be enough for us both. You had better go to the shop and buy some for yourselves."
10 While they were away the bridegroom arrived; those who were ready went in with him to the wedding; and
11 the door was shut. And then the other five came back.
12 "Sir, sir," they cried, "open the door for us." But he
13 answered, "I declare, I do not know you." Keep awake then; for you never know the day or the hour.

* This is an eschatological parable (i.e. a story relating to the end of the world). The division of the girls into two classes,

the one destined for the blessing of the heavenly Kingdom, the other for the loss of that blessing, reflects the characteristic twofold division found in other parables peculiar to Matthew (e.g. the wheat and the darnel, the two sons, the marriage-feast) and in the saying about the broad road and the narrow road (7: 13–14). Such twofold division was also characteristic of the teaching of John the Baptist (e.g. the wheat and the chaff, 3: 12).

1. The **bride**, who is not mentioned in our text at all, awaits the coming of the bridegroom at her own home. The *girls* are her friends, the bridesmaids, who are to meet the bridegroom when he comes with *his* friends, and then join in escorting the couple back to the bridegroom's house, where the wedding-feast will take place.

to meet the bridegroom. Some MSS, led by the Western Text (D), add 'and the bride'; but this is not the true text. Whereas in other New Testament analogies the bride represents the Church (e.g. Eph. 5: 32; Rev. 22: 17, '"Come!" say the Spirit and the bride'), here it is the ten girls who represent the Church as a mixed community containing good and bad members.

2 ff. All the girls (the bridesmaids) have lamps and all the lamps have oil. But the wise ones have also flasks containing extra oil. The fault of the *foolish* ones is that they have no reserve of oil. The moral is perseverance in the faith and the consequent accumulation of reserves of spiritual resources.

5. *the bridegroom* delays: the *parousia* of Christ is deferred.

6–7. At midnight the coming of *the bridegroom* is announced and all prepare *to meet him.* That is a figure of the *parousia.*

8–10. *the prudent* have no oil to spare and advise the foolish to go and buy. There is an element of improbability here. One would not expect the shops to be open at midnight, but there is no suggestion that the foolish were unable to buy. The point of the story is that they return too late. Since they were not prepared to meet Christ whenever he came to them, *the door was shut.* ✻

PARABLE OF THE BAGS OF GOLD

14 'It is like a man going abroad, who called his servants and
15 put his capital in their hands; to one he gave five bags of
gold, to another two, to another one, each according to
16 his capacity. Then he left the country. The man who had
the five bags went at once and employed them in business,
17 and made a profit of five bags, and the man who had the
18 two bags made two. But the man who had been given
one bag of gold went off and dug a hole in the ground,
19 and hid his master's money. A long time afterwards their
master returned, and proceeded to settle accounts with
20 them. The man who had been given the five bags of gold
came and produced the five he had made: "Master," he
said, "you left five bags with me; look, I have made five
21 more." "Well done, my good and trusty servant!" said
the master. "You have proved trustworthy in a small way;
I will now put you in charge of something big. Come
22 and share your master's delight." The man with the two
bags then came and said, "Master, you left two bags with
23 me; look, I have made two more." "Well done, my good
and trusty servant!" said the master. "You have proved
trustworthy in a small way; I will now put you in charge
of something big. Come and share your master's delight."
24 Then the man who had been given one bag came and
said, "Master, I knew you to be a hard man: you reap
where you have not sown, you gather where you have
25 not scattered; so I was afraid, and I went and hid your
gold in the ground. Here it is—you have what belongs
26 to you." "You lazy rascal!" said the master. "You knew
that I reap where I have not sown, and gather where I have

not scattered? Then you ought to have put my money on 27
deposit, and on my return I should have got it back with
interest. Take the bag of gold from him, and give it to 28
the one with the ten bags. For the man who has will 29
always be given more, till he has enough and to spare;
and the man who has not will forfeit even what he has.
Fling the useless servant out into the dark, the place of 30
wailing and grinding of teeth!'"

✶ This too is an eschatological parable of judgement, like the
parable of the pounds (Luke 19: 11–27). Though the *parousia*
may be delayed, it will come and those who wish to share its
blessings must use the time wisely in serving God. Gifts
unused are lost, whereas the reward for service is further
service. The worst punishment for failure to serve is to be
deprived of the opportunity to serve.

14. *capital.* Greek: 'his possessions'.

15. *bags of gold.* Greek: 'talents'. A talent = 6000 denarii.
In Luke each servant is given a 'pound' (Greek *mina* = about
100 denarii). The sums allotted represent privileges and opportunities of service. These vary in extent with different individuals by divine ordinance.

18. Sums of money were often hidden in the earth (cf.
13: 44). In Luke the pound was put away in a handkerchief.

24. *a hard man.* This graphic touch forbids us to allegorize
the story and make the master represent God or Christ.

27. If too lazy to trade, he might at any rate have deposited
the money at the bank and have drawn interest.

30. Here the speaker is God as judge. It is an addition by
Matthew and has no counterpart in Luke (cf. Matt. 8: 12;
22: 13). ✶

THE LAST JUDGEMENT; THE SEPARATION OF
SHEEP FROM GOATS

31 'When the Son of Man comes in his glory and all the
32 angels with him, he will sit in state on his throne, with all
the nations gathered before him. He will separate men
into two groups, as a shepherd separates the sheep from
33 the goats, and he will place the sheep on his right hand
34 and the goats on his left. Then the king will say to those
on his right hand, "You have my Father's blessing; come,
enter and possess the kingdom that has been ready for you
35 since the world was made. For when I was hungry, you
gave me food; when thirsty, you gave me drink; when
36 I was a stranger you took me into your home, when
naked you clothed me; when I was ill you came to my
37 help, when in prison you visited me." Then the righteous
will reply, "Lord, when was it that we saw you hungry
38 and fed you, or thirsty and gave you drink, a stranger and
39 took you home, or naked and clothed you? When did
40 we see you ill or in prison, and come to visit you?" And
the king will answer, "I tell you this: anything you did
for one of my brothers here, however humble, you did
41 for me." Then he will say to those on his left hand, "The
curse is upon you; go from my sight to the eternal fire
42 that is ready for the devil and his angels. For when I was
hungry you gave me nothing to eat, when thirsty nothing
43 to drink; when I was a stranger you gave me no home,
when naked you did not clothe me; when I was ill and in
44 prison you did not come to my help." And they too will
reply, "Lord, when was it that we saw you hungry or
thirsty or a stranger or naked or ill or in prison, and did

nothing for you?" And he will answer, "I tell you this: 45
anything you did not do for one of these, however humble,
you did not do for me." And they will go away to eternal 46
punishment, but the righteous will enter eternal life.'

* This is not strictly a parable, but rather a picture which
forms a climax to the last of the five great discourses. It differs
from most Jewish apocalyptic in that the Judge is represented
to be not God but the Son of Man, who is also called 'the
king' which in the Old Testament is a title for God. The king
is the representative or spokesman of 'my brothers' (verse 40),
i.e. presumably the disciples. Note the favourite Matthaean
twofold division—the sheep and the goats.

31. Jesus refers to himself in the third person as the future
Son of Man who will come in glory (cf. 16: 27), attended by
angels (cf. 13: 41; 16: 27; 24: 31).

32. This verse implies the doctrine that all men will be
raised from the dead for the judgement. The right hand was
the place of honour.

34. *the king*, i.e. the Son of Man, the Messiah in his glory.

35-6. Service to Christ's disciples is service to Christ himself. The question whether this service has been rendered is
decisive in the final judgement. The kind of service specified
is that lovingkindness and compassion which are the will and
purpose of God himself.

41-3. Neglect of Christ's disciples is neglect of Christ himself. The sins condemned are sins of omission. Note how
closely Christ identifies himself with his people. The same
truth is implied in the words of the risen Christ to Saul of
Tarsus, who was persecuting the Christians: 'Saul, Saul, why
do you persecute me?' (Acts 9: 4).

41. *eternal fire*, i.e. the fire of Gehenna.

46. *eternal punishment*, i.e. punishment characteristic of the
Age to come, not meaning that it lasts for ever.

eternal life, i.e. the life that belongs to the Age to come, the
full abundant life which is fellowship with God. *

The Final Conflict

THE DECISION OF THE CHIEF PRIESTS;
THE ANOINTING AT BETHANY

26 W̲HEN JESUS had finished this discourse he said to his
2 disciples, 'You know that in two days' time it will
be Passover, and the Son of Man is to be handed over for
crucifixion.'

3 Then the chief priests and the elders of the nation met
4 in the palace of the High Priest, Caiaphas; and there they
conferred together on a scheme to have Jesus arrested by
5 some trick and put to death. 'It must not be during the
festival,' they said, 'or there may be rioting among the
people.'

6,7 Jesus was at Bethany in the house of Simon the leper, when
a woman came to him with a small bottle of fragrant oil,
very costly; and as he sat at table she began to pour it over
8 his head. The disciples were indignant when they saw it.
9 'Why this waste?' they said; 'it could have been sold for
10 a good sum and the money given to the poor.' Jesus was
aware of this, and said to them, 'Why must you make
trouble for the woman? It is a fine thing she has done for
11 me. You have the poor among you always; but you will
12 not always have me. When she poured this oil on
my body it was her way of preparing me for burial.
13 I tell you this: wherever in all the world this gospel
is proclaimed, what she has done will be told as her
memorial.'

194

✶ 1. Note the usual Matthaean formula at the end of a great discourse.

2. *in two days' time it will be Passover.* Matthew, like Mark and Luke, regards the Passover as falling on the day, 6 p.m. Thursday until 6 p.m. Friday, the day of the crucifixion. The day referred to in this verse is therefore the Wednesday of Holy Week (6 p.m. Tuesday until 6 p.m. Wednesday). The institution of the Passover is described in Exod. 12. It commemorated the safe departure of Israel from Egypt, the land of bondage. The Passover lambs were sacrificed in the temple in the late afternoon on the 14th day of the Jewish month Nisan, and the Passover meal was eaten the same evening between sundown and midnight, regarded as the beginning of the day 15th Nisan, the actual Passover day.

3. An informal meeting of the leading members of the Sanhedrin in the court of Joseph Caiaphas, the High Priest (c. A.D. 18–36). The Sadducean priests ('the chief priests') were the instigators in the movement to arrest Jesus.

6–13. Neither Mark nor Matthew give a connexion in time between this incident and what has gone before. In John 12: 1–8 the anointing is done by Mary in the house of Lazarus at Bethany six days before the Passover (i.e. the day before the triumphal entry), which may be right.

7. *a small bottle.* Greek: 'alabaster bottle'. Alabaster is a soft, semi-transparent, marble-like mineral. Such bottles were used for precious ointment. In Luke and John the feet of Jesus are anointed.

8. *the disciples.* John mentions only Judas; Mark, 'some' of the disciples.

9. *a good sum.* Mark and John have 'thirty pounds' (lit. 300 denarii).

poor. The giving of charity to the poor was expected of pilgrims to the feast of the Passover.

11. Cf. Deut. 15: 11, 'the poor shall never cease out of the land'.

you will not always have me, i.e. in the flesh, under the conditions of human life on earth. Spiritually Christ is always with his Church (18: 20; 28: 20).

12. The women on the first Easter morning were too late to anoint Jesus' body, since he had already been raised from dead. This woman's anointing was the only one his body received, and he received it before instead of after his death. If this is a genuine utterance of Jesus, it shows that he knew what the coming course of events would be. It was especially suitable that Jesus should be anointed, for he was the Messiah, which means 'anointed one'. Was the woman indicating that she wished Jesus to rule over the people as Messiah?

13. The woman's action was a fine one. It showed love, faith, courage, initiative and self-sacrifice, qualities required of all Christ's disciples. Hence Jesus' high commendation and his command that the woman's deed be commemorated wherever the Gospel is preached. ✳

THE TREACHERY OF JUDAS;
PREPARATION FOR THE PASSOVER

14 Then one of the Twelve, the man called Judas Iscariot,
15 went to the chief priests and said, 'What will you give me to betray him to you?' They weighed him out thirty
16 silver pieces. From that moment he began to look for a good opportunity to betray him.

17 On the first day of Unleavened Bread the disciples came to ask Jesus, 'Where would you like us to prepare
18 for your Passover supper?' He answered, 'Go to a certain man in the city, and tell him, "The Master says, 'My appointed time is near; I am to keep Passover with my
19 disciples at your house.'"' The disciples did as Jesus directed them and prepared for Passover.

✳ 14. *Judas Iscariot* (cf. on 10: 4). All the Gospels agree that Judas was responsible for Jesus' arrest. He probably betrayed to the chief priests the place where Jesus could be found.

15. The Greek could mean either *they weighed him out* or 'they agreed to pay'. Matthew alone mentions the thirty pieces of silver, i.e. thirty shekels = tetradrachms = staters. The thirty shekels were equivalent to 120 denarii. Matthew is thinking of Zech. 11: 12, 'they weighed for my hire thirty pieces of silver'.

16. The promise of so small a sum cannot in itself have been sufficient inducement to persuade Judas to betray Jesus. Why he turned traitor we do not know. He may have been disappointed by Jesus' refusal to be an earthly king.

17. *the first day of Unleavened Bread* strictly began after 6 p.m. on Nisan 14. In the late afternoon of that day the Passover lambs were sacrificed in the temple, and the Passover meal was eaten after sunset when the new day, the Passover day (Nisan 15) began. According to this chronology of the Synoptic Gospels the Last Supper was the Passover meal, and Jesus was crucified on the Passover day. But in the Fourth Gospel the Last Supper and crucifixion took place on the day before the Passover (i.e. on Nisan 14). All the Gospels agree that Jesus was crucified on Friday. It is the date that is in dispute. It is impossible to be sure which dating is right. To some scholars it seems unlikely that the Jews would have allowed the trial of Jesus and his crucifixion and all the details associated with it to take place on so holy a day as the Passover. On the other hand, it was permissible by Jewish Law to try and execute one deemed to be a false prophet on the feast day. The dating in the Fourth Gospel may be due to a doctrinal interest in making the death of Jesus synchronize with the slaying of the Passover lambs in the temple on the afternoon before the Passover. There are several features of the Last Supper which resemble those of the Passover meal. (1) The Last Supper took place in the evening and extended into the night. (2) Jesus and his disciples reclined at the meal instead of sitting. (3) A dish precedes the breaking of bread only at

the Passover. This preliminary dish is referred to in Mark 14:20 and Matt. 26: 23. (4) Wine was drunk at the Last Supper, and the drinking of wine was obligatory at the Passover. The wine moreover had to be red. The comparison of the wine at the Last Supper with the blood of the Lord suggests that the wine was red. (5) The Last Supper concluded with the singing of a hymn. This was most probably the second part (Psalms 114 or 115–18) of the Hallel (i.e. the 'Praise' Psalms) which closed the Passover meal. (6) After the meal Jesus did not return, as he was probably accustomed to do, to Bethany, but went to the Mount of Olives. This was in accordance with the Passover regulation that after the Passover had been eaten within the walls of Jerusalem, the rest of the night might be spent inside a larger area, which excluded Bethany but included Gethsemane. (7) At the Passover meal the person presiding explained the various elements in the meal. Jesus explained the meaning of the bread and the wine. This did not necessarily replace the customary Passover explanation, but may have been suggested by it (see further J. Jeremias, *The Eucharistic Words of Jesus*, and A. J. B. Higgins, *The Lord's Supper in the New Testament*).

18. It is clear that Jesus had friends in Jerusalem. It therefore seems unlikely that he had no ministry there until the last week. Matthew adds *My appointed time is near* as a prophecy of the crucifixion.

19. *prepared for Passover*, i.e. got the room ready, laid the table, and provided the lamb which had to be sacrificed in the temple by all who were to partake of the Supper. But no mention is made of the lamb in the Gospel accounts. ✻

THE LAST SUPPER; THE DESERTION OF THE DISCIPLES FORETOLD

20,21 In the evening he sat down with the twelve disciples; and during supper he said, 'I tell you this: one of you will
22 betray me.' In great distress they exclaimed one after the
23 other, 'Can you mean me, Lord?' He answered, 'One

who has dipped his hand into this bowl with me will betray me. The Son of Man is going the way appointed 24 for him in the scriptures; but alas for that man by whom the Son of Man is betrayed! It would be better for that man if he had never been born.' Then Judas spoke, the 25 one who was to betray him. 'Rabbi,' he said, 'can you mean me?' Jesus replied, 'The words are yours.'

During supper Jesus took bread, and having said the 26 blessing he broke it and gave it to the disciples with the words: 'Take this and eat; this is my body.' Then he 27 took a cup, and having offered thanks to God he gave it to them with the words: 'Drink from it, all of you. For 28 this is my blood, the blood of the covenant, shed for many for the forgiveness of sins. I tell you, never again 29 shall I drink from the fruit of the vine until that day when I drink it new with you in the kingdom of my Father.'

After singing the Passover Hymn, they went out to the 30 Mount of Olives. Then Jesus said to them, 'Tonight you 31 will all fall from your faith on my account; for it stands written: "I will strike the shepherd down and the sheep of his flock will be scattered." But after I am raised again, 32 I will go on before you into Galilee.' Peter replied, 33 'Everyone else may fall away on your account, but I never will.' Jesus said to him, 'I tell you, tonight before the cock 34 crows you will disown me three times.' Peter said, 'Even 35 if I must die with you, I will never disown you.' And all the disciples said the same.

✳ 20. *sat down.* The Greek word means 'reclined'. It was the custom to recline at the Passover meal.

21. Jesus could read the thoughts of all his disciples, including Judas.

23. If this was a Passover meal, this was the *bowl* containing a sauce composed of fruits, spices and vinegar, into which food (including bitter herbs) was dipped.

24. *the scriptures*. E.g. Ps. 22: 16, 'they pierced my hands and my feet', etc. Isa. 53: 3, 'he was despised and rejected of men', etc. A similar saying is found in 18: 7=Luke 17: 1.

25. *The words are yours*. Or 'it is as you say'.

26. *having said the blessing*, i.e. having given thanks to God, as every pious Jew did over bread and wine. Cf. the grace before partaking of bread in the Jewish Daily Prayer Book: 'Blessed art thou, O Lord our God, King of the Universe, who bringest forth bread from the earth', and before partaking of wine: 'Blessed...Universe, Creator of the fruit of the vine.'

he broke it: so that each disciple could have a portion of the loaf. But the action was also symbolic of the coming Passion and death.

and eat. Matthew's addition to Mark. Matthew rewrites Mark's account (Mark 14: 22–5) to make it more suitable for an order of service in the eucharistic worship of the Church.

this is my body, i.e. this represents my body.

27. *Drink from it, all of you*. Mark 14: 23 simply states 'they all drank from it'.

28. *this is my blood, the blood of the covenant*. 'This is' means 'this represents'. In *the blood of the covenant* there is a reference to Exod. 24: 8, 'Behold the blood of the covenant' spoken by Moses in connexion with the inauguration of God's covenant with Israel at Sinai. So Jesus inaugurates a covenant for those whom he has drawn from the new Israel. This includes the thought of sacrifice, i.e. the application of the victim's blood, which is its life, poured out and available for the use of others. Luke 22: 20 and 1 Cor. 11: 25 have 'the new covenant sealed by my blood' which implies a reference to Jer. 31: 31 ff., 'I will make a new covenant with the house of Israel, and with the house of Judah...I will put my law in their inward parts, and in their heart will I write it; and I will be their God, and

they shall be my people...I will forgive their iniquity, and their sin will I remember no more'. Jesus probably had this passage also in mind.

for many. The Greek phrase suggests sacrifice. 'Many' really means 'all' in accordance with Hebrew idiom, as in Isa. 53: 12, 'he bare the sins of many', cf. Matt. 20: 28.

for the forgiveness of sins. Matthew's addition to Mark 14: 24. On the other hand, Matthew took this detail away from the teaching of John the Baptist as given in Mark 1: 4 ('baptism in token of repentance, for the forgiveness of sins'). By introducing it here, Matthew echoes the prophecy of Jeremiah, cited above, and emphasizes the thought of sacrifice.

29. The cup not only points back to the covenant of old Israel, of which Jeremiah prophesied a new and more inward version, but looks forward to the perfection of new Israel, the Christian Church, in the new messianic age *the kingdom of my Father*. This forward-looking eschatological aspect is differently represented in Paul's account in 1 Cor. 11: 26, 'For every time you eat this bread and drink the cup, you proclaim the death of the Lord, until he comes'. In Mark and Matthew there is no command to repeat the rite, as there is in Paul's account and in Luke 22: 19 (in the longer text); but the disciples probably (on looking back) believed it to have been Jesus' intention.

30. *the Passover Hymn*, i.e. probably Psalms 114 or 115–18, the second half of 'Hallel' Psalms, the word 'Hallel' meaning 'praise', as in 'Hallelujah', 'Praise God'. See note on verse 17.

Mount of Olives. North-east of the city.

31. *it stands written*. The quotation is adapted from Zech. 13: 7, 'Smite the shepherd, and the sheep shall be scattered'.

32. Mark has this verse, which implies that if his Gospel had contained a record of a resurrection appearance of the Lord, it would have taken place in Galilee, like the last resurrection appearance in Matthew.

34. Cock-crowing marked the third Roman watch (12–3 a.m.). The disowning would take place before dawn. ✻

GETHSEMANE; THE ARREST

36 Jesus then came with his disciples to a place called
Gethsemane. He said to them, 'Sit here while I go over
37 there to pray.' He took with him Peter and the two
sons of Zebedee. Anguish and dismay came over him,
38 and he said to them, 'My heart is ready to break with
39 grief. Stop here, and stay awake with me.' He went on
a little, fell on his face in prayer, and said, 'My Father,
if it is possible, let this cup pass me by. Yet not as I will,
but as thou wilt.'

40 He came to the disciples and found them asleep; and he
said to Peter, 'What! Could none of you stay awake with
41 me one hour? Stay awake, and pray that you may be
spared the test. The spirit is willing, but the flesh is weak.'
42 He went away a second time, and prayed: 'My Father,
if it is not possible for this cup to pass me by without my
43 drinking it, thy will be done.' He came again and found
44 them asleep, for their eyes were heavy. So he left them
and went away again; and he prayed the third time, using
the same words as before.

45 Then he came to the disciples and said to them, 'Still
sleeping? Still taking your ease? The hour has come!
46 The Son of Man is betrayed to sinful men. Up, let us go
forward; the traitor is upon us.'

47 While he was still speaking, Judas, one of the Twelve,
appeared; with him was a great crowd armed with swords
and cudgels, sent by the chief priests and the elders of the
48 nation. The traitor gave them this sign: 'The one I kiss is
49 your man; seize him'; and stepping forward at once, he
50 said, 'Hail, Rabbi!', and kissed him. Jesus replied, 'Friend,

do what you are here to do.' They then came forward, seized Jesus, and held him fast.

At that moment one of those with Jesus reached for his 51 sword and drew it, and he struck at the High Priest's servant and cut off his ear. But Jesus said to him, 'Put up 52 your sword. All who take the sword die by the sword. Do you suppose that I cannot appeal to my Father, who 53 would at once send to my aid more than twelve legions of angels? But how then could the scriptures be fulfilled, 54 which say that this must be?'

At the same time Jesus spoke to the crowd. 'Do you 55 take me for a bandit,' he said, 'that you have come out with swords and cudgels to arrest me? Day after day I sat teaching in the temple, and you did not lay hands on me. But this has all happened to fulfil what the prophets wrote.' 56

Then the disciples all deserted him and ran away.

* 36. *place.* Greek: 'an enclosed piece of ground'.

Gethsemane means 'olive press'. Probably the place was a well-known olive orchard.

37. The chosen three, cf. 17: 1. Peter, as usual, is given prominence. He alone is mentioned by name.

38. Cf. Ps. 42: 6, 'O my God, my soul is cast down within me'.

39. Mark 14: 36 gives the Aramaic word Jesus used, *Abba,* Father. Jesus has a truly human shrinking from death; but he triumphed over it and dedicated himself perfectly to the doing of his Father's will. This dedication was part of his divine Sonship, nurtured by a lifetime of prayer like that which he taught his followers (6: 10).

40. Note Jesus' human longing for companionship.

41. Cf. 24: 42. The disciples have been warned beforehand to keep awake, and that involves prayer. Failure to do this will make them unfit for the test about to come.

45. *Still sleeping? Still taking your ease?* The Greek could mean 'Sleep on now, and take your rest'. But then the words in the next verse do not fit very well.

46. *go forward*, i.e. to meet them. In the light of the Passover moon Jesus would be able to see the party approaching.

47. The arrest was authorized by the Sanhedrin, who seem to have hired the crowd for the purpose.

48. *sign*. Necessary because Jesus was not known to the crowd. This was a different crowd from that which had welcomed him at his triumphal entry or had heard him teach in the temple.

I kiss. An ordinary salutation to a guest or a rabbi.

50. *do what you are here to do*. The Greek may mean—'what are you here for?' or 'Is it this for which you have come?'

52–4. Peculiar to Matthew.

52. Cf. John 18: 36: Jesus replied (to Pilate), 'My kingdom does not belong to this world. If it did, my followers would be fighting to save me from arrest by the Jews. My kingly authority comes from elsewhere.'

53. This saying hardly seems to agree with Jesus' own prayer in Gethsemane.

A legion was a Roman body of infantry consisting at different periods of from 3000 to above 6000.

54. *the scriptures*, e.g. Isa. 53: 5, 'he was wounded for our transgressions', etc.

55. *Day after day*. This seems to imply a longer period of teaching in Jerusalem than is allowed for in the Synoptic Gospels. It seems to confirm the Fourth Gospel in its representation of a longer period of ministry there.

56. Note the Matthaean formula. Mark 14: 49 has simply, 'But let the scriptures be fulfilled'. *

THE TRIAL BEFORE THE SANHEDRIN;
PETER'S DENIAL

Jesus was led off under arrest to the house of Caiaphas the 57
High Priest, where the lawyers and elders were assembled.
Peter followed him at a distance till he came to the High 58
Priest's courtyard, and going in he sat down there among
the attendants, meaning to see the end of it all.

The chief priests and the whole Council tried to find 59
some allegation against Jesus on which a death-sentence
could be based; but they failed to find one, though many 60
came forward with false evidence. Finally two men 61
alleged that he had said, 'I can pull down the temple of
God, and rebuild it in three days.' At this the High Priest 62
rose and said to him, 'Have you no answer to the charge
that these witnesses bring against you?' But Jesus kept 63
silence. The High Priest then said, 'By the living God
I charge you to tell us: Are you the Messiah, the Son of
God?' Jesus replied, 'The words are yours. But I tell 64
you this: from now on, you will see the Son of Man
seated at the right hand of God and coming on the clouds
of heaven.' At these words the High Priest tore his robes 65
and exclaimed, 'Blasphemy! Need we call further witnesses? You have heard the blasphemy. What is your 66
opinion?' 'He is guilty,' they answered; 'he should die.'

Then they spat in his face and beat him with their fists; 67
and others said, as they struck him, 'Now, Messiah, if you 68
are a prophet, tell us who hit you.'

Meanwhile Peter was sitting outside in the courtyard 69
when a serving-maid accosted him and said, 'You were
there too with Jesus the Galilean.' Peter denied it in face 70

of them all. 'I do not know what you mean', he said.
71 He then went out to the gateway, where another girl,
seeing him, said to the people there, 'This fellow was with
72 Jesus of Nazareth.' Once again he denied it, saying with
73 an oath, 'I do not know the man.' Shortly afterwards
the bystanders came up and said to Peter, 'Surely you are
74 another of them; your accent gives you away!' At this
he broke into curses and declared with an oath: 'I do
75 not know the man.' At that moment the cock crew. And
Peter remembered how Jesus had said, 'Before the cock
crows you will disown me three times.' He went outside,
and wept bitterly.

* Jesus is taken to the High Priest's house (57-8). Then takes
place a night-session of the Sanhedrin in the house of the High
Priest, including an examination of witnesses and the trial of
Jesus, ending in his being condemned to death for blasphemy
(59-66). The mocking of Jesus follows (67-8). Meanwhile
Peter disowns Jesus three times (69-75). In Mark (14: 53-72)
and Matthew, but not in Luke (22: 54-71) or John (18: 12-27)
there is a trial of Jesus before the Sanhedrin at night. This
seems improbable. Probably Mark confused preliminary
inquiries at night with the real trial in the morning.

58. Peter went right into the hall of the High Priest and sat
with the attendants, i.e. those attached to the High Priest's
household, not the men who had arrested Jesus; these remained
outside in the courtyard.

59. *the whole Council.* It is very improbable that the whole
Sanhedrin would be assembled in the middle of the night,
especially Passover night. According to rabbinic law, criminal
cases must be tried in the daytime and finished in the daytime.
What probably took place at night was an informal inquiry
by the Sadducean priests who would not feel bound by these
laws. In the Fourth Gospel the Jewish trial is omitted. Jesus

is sent to Caiaphas and by him to the Procurator, Pontius Pilate. The Jewish authorities could condemn, but not execute.

60. No two witnesses agreed. Two witnesses were required to sustain any charge.

61. Two were finally found who could agree on some point of evidence.

I can pull down the temple. Cf. John 2: 19 and 21, 'Destroy this temple...and in three days I will raise it again...the temple he was speaking of was his body'. It is possible that some such saying of Jesus was misinterpreted. Cf. Acts 6: 14, where false witnesses against Stephen say 'we have heard him say that Jesus of Nazareth will destroy this place'.

62. Jesus had the right by law to defend himself. The High Priest invites him to do so.

63. Cf. Isa. 53: 7, 'he opened not his mouth'.

Are you the Messiah, the Son of God? The High Priest had heard of Jesus' messianic claim. Was it the messianic secret, among other things, that Judas had betrayed? Not necessarily: for by the triumphal entry into Jerusalem Jesus had made his messianic claim public and no longer secret.

64. *The words are yours.* The Greek could mean 'It is as you say'. In what follows Jesus alludes to Dan. 7: 13, 'there came with the clouds of heaven one like unto a son of man, and he came even to the ancient of days', coupled with Ps. 110: 1, 'The Lord said unto my lord, Sit thou at my right hand'.

of God. The Greek means literally 'of the Power', a Jewish way of referring to God. The verse in Daniel appears to refer to an *ascent* of one like unto a son of man on the clouds up to God (the ancient of days). Some scholars, therefore, have argued that here Jesus prophesies his ascension into heaven; but the order of the words, first describing the sitting at the right hand of God, then the coming on the clouds, seems to indicate that the latter phrase is to be interpreted as referring to the *parousia*.

65. The blasphemy lay in the claim to sit at God's right hand.

66. The penalty for blasphemy was death.

67. *beat him.* Cf. Isa. 50: 6, 'I gave my back to the smiters...
I hid not my face from shame and spitting' (the Servant of
the Lord is speaking).

69–75. Peter's disowning of Jesus.

69. *the courtyard* was outside the palace and below the
council chamber.

72. *with an oath.* Peculiar to Matthew.

73. The oddities of Galilean pronunciation are ridiculed in
the Talmud.

75. *wept bitterly.* Repentance has already begun. ✳

JESUS SURRENDERED TO PILATE; DEATH OF JUDAS

27 When morning came, the chief priests and the elders of
the nation met in conference to plan the death of Jesus.

2 They then put him in chains and led him off, to hand him
over to Pilate, the Roman Governor.

3 When Judas the traitor saw that Jesus had been condemned, he was seized with remorse, and returned the

4 thirty silver pieces to the chief priests and elders. 'I have
sinned,' he said; 'I have brought an innocent man to his
death.' But they said, 'What is that to us? See to that

5 yourself.' So he threw the money down in the temple and
left them, and went and hanged himself.

6 Taking up the money, the chief priests argued: 'This
cannot be put into the temple fund; it is blood-money.'

7 So after conferring they used it to buy the Potter's Field,

8 as a burial-place for foreigners. This explains the name
'Blood Acre', by which that field has been known ever

9 since; and in this way fulfilment was given to the prophetic utterance of Jeremiah: 'They took the thirty silver
pieces, the price set on a man's head (for that was his price

among the Israelites), and gave the money for the potter's 10
field, as the Lord directed me.'

Jesus was now brought before the Governor; and as he 11
stood there the Governor asked him, 'Are you the king
of the Jews?' 'The words are yours', said Jesus; and to the 12
charges laid against him by the chief priests and elders he
made no reply. Then Pilate said to him, 'Do you not hear 13
all this evidence that is brought against you?'; but he still 14
refused to answer one word, to the Governor's great
astonishment.

At the festival season it was the Governor's custom to 15
release one prisoner chosen by the people. There was then 16
in custody a man of some notoriety, called Jesus Bar-
Abbas. When they were assembled Pilate said to them, 17
'Which would you like me to release to you—Jesus Bar-
Abbas, or Jesus called Messiah?' For he knew that it was 18
out of spite that they had brought Jesus before him.

While Pilate was sitting in court a message came to him 19
from his wife: 'Have nothing to do with that innocent
man; I was much troubled on his account in my dreams
last night.'

Meanwhile the chief priests and elders had persuaded 20
the crowd to ask for the release of Bar-Abbas and to have
Jesus put to death. So when the Governor asked, 'Which 21
of the two do you wish me to release to you?', they said,
'Bar-Abbas.' 'Then what am I to do with Jesus called 22
Messiah?' asked Pilate; and with one voice they answered,
'Crucify him!' 'Why, what harm has he done?' Pilate 23
asked; but they shouted all the louder, 'Crucify him!'

Pilate could see that nothing was being gained, and a 24
riot was starting; so he took water and washed his hands

in full view of the people, saying, 'My hands are clean of
25 this man's blood; see to that yourselves.' And with one
voice the people cried, 'His blood be on us, and on
26 our children.' He then released Bar-Abbas to them;
but he had Jesus flogged, and handed him over to be
crucified.

* 1. This assembly of the Sanhedrin is represented as a purely
formal one, a brief deliberation in the Sanhedrin council hall,
early in the morning after Jesus' arrest, resulting in the despatch
of Jesus to Pilate.

2. Pontius Pilate was appointed Procurator of the province
of Judaea in A.D. 26 by Tiberius, and was recalled in A.D. 36
(see p. 18).

3-4. How did information about this interview reach the
early Church? Judas never returned to tell what conversation
passed between him and the chief priests. Did some of the
priests themselves become Christians and disclose the information? See Acts 6: 7, 'very many of the priests adhered to the
Faith'.

A different account of the death of Judas in Acts 1: 18-19
says that Judas used the money to buy a plot of land, 'fell
forward on the ground, and burst open, so that his entrails
poured out'. The plot of land came to be known as Akeldama,
an Aramaic word meaning 'the field of blood' (N.E.B.
'*Blood Acre*').

3. *thirty silver pieces.* Cf. 26: 15 note.

5. i.e. he placed the money in the temple treasury.

hanged himself. As did Ahithophel, the treacherous friend of
David (2 Sam. 17: 23).

6. The price of blood would defile the treasury (cf. Deut.
23: 18: unworthy hire is 'an abomination unto the Lord thy
God'). The money was therefore taken out of the treasury and
used for secular purposes.

7-8. *the Potter's Field.* There was a cemetery near Jerusalem in which foreigners who died in the city were buried. Possibly its original name had been 'the Potter's Field', but it came to be known as 'the field of blood' ('Blood Acre'), and this story seeks to explain how the name arose. For a different explanation, see Acts 1: 18–19 (cited above).

9. The Old Testament passage said to have been fulfilled, in the usual Matthaean formula, is not from Jeremiah, but from Zech. 11: 13, 'And the Lord said unto me, Cast it unto the potter, the goodly price that I was prised at of them. And I took the thirty pieces of silver, and cast them unto the potter in the house of the Lord'. Matthew has adapted this prophecy, and has introduced the *Potter's Field* from the story about the field of blood. In the passage in Zechariah, the Syriac, instead of 'unto the potter', has 'into the treasury' on both occasions. Such an interpretation has coloured Matthew's narrative. The quotation is independent of the LXX and the Hebrew, and is probably a free rendering of Matthew's own. Some MSS omit the erroneous reference to Jeremiah. Some substitute Zechariah, others Isaiah. The reading 'Jeremiah' is genuine, but a mistaken reference.

They took. The Greek could be rendered 'I took'.

12. *The words are yours.* Or 'it is as you say'.

15. It was a widespread custom in the ancient world to release a prisoner at festival times.

16. *Jesus Bar-Abbas.* Some MSS omit 'Jesus', but the Sinaitic Syriac has it, and the reading 'Jesus Bar-Abbas' is almost certainly the right one. 'Jesus' was omitted to avoid associating the sacred name with a man of ill-repute.

18. It was not the crowd who had been responsible for Jesus' arrest, as seems to be implied here, but the Sadducean priests (as Mark 15: 11 makes clear).

19. This verse is peculiar to Matthew, and was probably derived from the same Palestinian source as verses 24–5 and 62–6 of this chapter, and 28: 11–15 (all about Pilate).

22. *Crucify.* This was the Roman (not Jewish) mode of execution.

24-5. Peculiar to Matthew. Ceremonial hand-washing was a Jewish, not Roman custom. This incident, therefore, may not be historical.

25. The Jewish nation invokes the guilt of the crucifixion upon itself, but as part of an incident which Matthew has added to the story. Much harm has been done by foolishly quoting this verse as though the whole Jewish nation were responsible for Jesus' death.

26. Flogging was a usual preliminary to execution in Roman practice. *

THE MOCKING BY THE SOLDIERS AND
THE CRUCIFIXION

27 Pilate's soldiers then took Jesus into the Governor's head-quarters, where they collected the whole company round
28 him. First they stripped him and dressed him in a scarlet
29 mantle; and plaiting a crown of thorns they placed it on his head, with a cane in his right hand. Falling on their knees before him they jeered at him: 'Hail, King of the
30 Jews!' They spat on him, and used the cane to beat him
31 about the head. Finally, when the mockery was over, they took off the mantle and dressed him in his own clothes.

32   Then they led him away to be crucified. On their way out they met a man from Cyrene, Simon by name, and pressed him into service to carry his cross.

33   So they came to a place called Golgotha (which means
34 'Place of a skull') and there they offered him a draught of wine mixed with gall; but when he had tasted it he would not drink.

35   After fastening him to the cross they divided his clothes
36 among them by casting lots, and then sat down there to

keep watch. Over his head was placed the inscription 37
giving the charge: 'This is Jesus the king of the Jews.'

Two bandits were crucified with him, one on his right 38
and the other on his left.

The passers-by hurled abuse at him: they wagged their 39
heads and cried, 'You would pull the temple down, would 40
you, and build it in three days? Come down from the
cross and save yourself, if you are indeed the Son of God.'
So too the chief priests with the lawyers and elders mocked 41
at him: 'He saved others,' they said, 'but he cannot save 42
himself. King of Israel, indeed! Let him come down now
from the cross, and then we will believe him. Did he 43
trust in God? Let God rescue him, if he wants him—for
he said he was God's Son.' Even the bandits who were 44
crucified with him taunted him in the same way.

Darkness fell over the whole land from midday until 45
three in the afternoon; and about three Jesus cried aloud, 46
'*Eli, Eli, lema sabachthani?*', which means, 'My God, my
God, why hast thou forsaken me?' Some of the by- 47
standers, on hearing this, said, 'He is calling Elijah.' One 48
of them ran at once and fetched a sponge, which he soaked
in sour wine, and held it to his lips on the end of a cane.
But the others said, 'Let us see if Elijah will come to save 49
him.'

Jesus again gave a loud cry, and breathed his last. At 50,51
that moment the curtain of the temple was torn in two
from top to bottom. There was an earthquake, the rocks
split and the graves opened, and many of God's people 52
arose from sleep; and coming out of their graves after his 53
resurrection they entered the Holy City, where many saw
them. And when the centurion and his men who were 54

keeping watch over Jesus saw the earthquake and all that was happening, they were filled with awe, and they said, 'Truly this man was a son of God.'

✶ 27. *Pilate's soldiers.* These had accompanied the Governor from Caesarea to Jerusalem. They assisted in keeping order during the feast.

the Governor's headquarters. Greek *praetorium*, i.e. the official residence of the Governor.

the whole company. The Greek means 'cohort'. This would strictly number from 500 to 600 men. But a smaller number is implied here.

28. *a scarlet mantle.* Probably a soldier's scarlet mantle, in imitation of an imperial robe.

29. *a crown of thorns.* lit. 'a garland' of thorns. The garland was awarded to the victor in battle or the games. It was used here in mockery for a royal diadem.

The *cane*, mentioned only by Matthew, corresponds to a sceptre.

32. John 19: 17 says that Jesus carried his own cross. He must have done so at least a short distance, until they came out of the city and met Simon of Cyrene. They *pressed him into service* (the same Greek word that is used in 5: 41) to carry the cross, doubtless because Jesus was staggering under the burden, having been weakened by the flogging. A condemned person did not usually carry the whole cross, but only the cross-beam. The upright beam was generally standing ready to receive it.

33. *'Place of a skull'.* Golgotha is the Hebrew and Aramaic equivalent of 'skull'. The place was so named because it was a skull-shaped mound.

34. *wine mixed with gall.* Mark 15: 23 has 'drugged wine' (lit. wine mingled with myrrh). Matthew has derived 'gall' from Ps. 69: 21, 'they gave me also gall for my meat; and in my thirst they gave me vinegar to drink'.

35. *fastening him to the cross.* Jesus was probably laid down

upon the cross-beam, his hands nailed to each end, and then the cross-beam with Jesus on it was lifted and fixed to the upright beam. Perhaps the feet were then nailed to the upright beam. John mentions the print of the nails in the hands (John 20: 25); Luke implies that there was the print of nails in the feet also (Luke 24: 39).

divided his clothes among them. Cf. Ps. 22: 18, 'They part my garments among them, and upon my vesture do they cast lots'. Some MSS quote this. The executioners were allowed to share the clothes of the victim.

36. Peculiar to Matthew. They kept watch to prevent his friends from rescuing him.

37. This charge was written on a placard affixed to the cross. John says that it was written in Hebrew (Aramaic), Latin and Greek. This would be for the benefit of the Passover pilgrims from many parts of the world. Jesus was executed on the charge of having claimed to be the Messiah, a king (John 19: 12–16).

39. Cf. Ps. 22: 7, 'All they that see me laugh me to scorn: they shoot out the lip'.

43. Cf. Ps. 22: 8, 'Commit thyself unto the Lord; let him deliver him: let him deliver him, seeing he delighteth in him'.

45. *from midday until three.* Greek: 'from the sixth to the ninth hour'.

46. A quotation from Ps. 22: 1, given in the Aramaic (though *Eli* is the Hebrew form). The cry reveals the true humanity of Jesus, his depression, his agony of mind and spirit. 'He bare the sins of many' (Isa. 53: 12). Actually never was God nearer to him than in that moment. 'God was in Christ reconciling the world to himself' (2 Cor. 5: 19). Yet in that work of reconciliation he experienced the real significance of sin which is separation from God.

47. A natural mistake, if the words were half-drowned in the hubbub of the crowd. The Jews believed that Elijah was the rescuer of the pious in their need.

48. The drink here offered on the sponge and cane is

probably the sour wine brought by the soldiers for their refreshment. If so, then presumably one of the soldiers offered it out of kindness.

50. *breathed his last.* Greek: 'yielded up the spirit'. Mark 15: 37 has literally 'breathed his last'. The phrase in Matthew perhaps has more the suggestion of voluntary action. The fact that Jesus gave a loud cry shows that he still had strength, and did not die from slow exhaustion of the physical powers.

51. *the curtain of the temple.* There were two beautiful curtains or veils in the temple. The outer one hung over the entrance to the Holy Place. The inner one hung over the entrance to the Holy of Holies, the most holy place (see plan p. viii). The inner veil is the curtain referred to here. The significance of the statement is symbolic. Jesus had opened the way to God.

52–3. Peculiar to Matthew. Jesus' death was pictured, like the Fall of Jerusalem, as accompanied by portents; it can hardly be literally true, but means that Jesus' resurrection is the beginning of the resurrection of all who belong to him (1 Cor. 15: 23).

53. *after his resurrection.* This looks like a later addition to safeguard the truth that Christ was the first to be raised (1 Cor. 15: 20).

54. *a son of God.* These words in the mouth of a heathen would mean a hero or demigod. *

THE WOMEN AND JOSEPH OF ARIMATHAEA; THE BURIAL OF JESUS; THE GUARD SET ON THE GRAVE

55 A number of women were also present, watching from a distance; they had followed Jesus from Galilee and waited
56 on him. Among them were Mary of Magdala, Mary the mother of James and Joseph, and the mother of the sons of Zebedee.
57 When evening fell, there came a man of Arimathaea,

Joseph by name, who was a man of means, and had himself become a disciple of Jesus. He approached Pilate, and 58 asked for the body of Jesus; and Pilate gave orders that he should have it. Joseph took the body, wrapped it in a 59 clean linen sheet, and laid it in his own unused tomb, 60 which he had cut out of the rock; he then rolled a large stone against the entrance, and went away. Mary of 61 Magdala was there, and the other Mary, sitting opposite the grave.

Next day, the morning after that Friday, the chief priests 62 and the Pharisees came in a body to Pilate. 'Your 63 Excellency,' they said, 'we recall how that impostor said while he was still alive, "I am to rise after three days." So will you give orders for the grave to be made secure 64 until the third day? Otherwise his disciples may come, steal the body, and then tell the people that he has been raised from the dead; and the final deception will be worse than the first.' 'You may have your guard,' said 65 Pilate; 'go and make it secure as best you can.' So they 66 went and made the grave secure; they sealed the stone, and left the guard in charge.

* 55. According to the Fourth Gospel, Jesus' mother, other women and the beloved disciple stood by the cross.

56. *Mary of Magdala* appears in the list of ministering women in Luke 8: 1–3. There it is said that seven devils had come out from her, that is, that she had been healed of a serious illness.

Joseph. Some MSS read 'Joses' here and in Mark 15: 40.

Mary the mother of James. This is probably James the son of Alphaeus. Alphaeus = Halpai = Clopas. In this case this Mary is 'Mary, wife of Clopas' (John 19: 25).

the mother of the sons of Zebedee. Salome, who may have been the sister of the Virgin Mary.

57. *When evening fell*, i.e. just before the Sabbath began, which it did at 6 p.m.

Arimathaea is often identified with Ramathaim-zophim (1 Sam. 1: 1) about 15 miles east of Joppa. Matthew and John (19: 38) call Joseph *a disciple of Jesus*; John adds 'but a secret disciple for fear of the Jews'.

58. Cf. 14: 12 and note.

59. It was usual to bury people on the day of death, and the body of an executed man was not allowed to remain hanging overnight. (Deut. 21: 23, 'his body shall not remain all night upon the tree, but thou shalt surely bury him the same day; for he that is hanged is accursed of God; that thou defile not thy land which the Lord thy God giveth thee for an inheritance'.)

clean linen sheet. This agrees with rabbinical custom.

60. The *tomb* was *cut out of the rock*, as many tombs are in and near Jerusalem. Joseph may have intended the new tomb for the use of his own family; but he would not be able to use it again after Jesus had lain there, because the rabbis forbade the burying of one's kin in the tomb where an executed man was laid.

61. Friends or relatives often watched at the tomb in case the person supposed to be dead should revive.

the other Mary, i.e. Mary the wife of Clopas. See verse 56 note.

62–6. This section may belong to the body of tradition connected with Pilate which Matthew probably derived from a Palestinian source, like verses 19, 24–5, and 28: 11–15.

62. *the chief priests and the Pharisees*. The rival parties, Sadducees and Pharisees, overcome their opposition to one another sufficiently to take common action on the Sabbath. This seems hardly probable.

63. It also seems improbable that the predictions of suffering and resurrection which Jesus made privately to his disciples (16: 21; 17: 23; 20: 19) were known to the chief priests and Pharisees (unless Judas had told them).

64. The whole of this section is probably due to a Christian attempt to refute the accusation of the Jews that the disciples had stolen the body of Jesus. Clearly the Jews had to explain the fact of the empty tomb somehow. The final deception would be belief in the resurrection of Jesus; the first would be belief in his Messiahship.

65. *guard*, i.e. from among the Roman soldiers. ✳

THE WOMEN AT THE TOMB; THEIR MEETING WITH JESUS; THE BRIBING OF THE GUARD; APPEARANCE TO THE ELEVEN AND FINAL COMMISSION

The Sabbath had passed, and it was about daybreak on **28** Sunday, when Mary of Magdala and the other Mary came to look at the grave. Suddenly there was a violent earth- 2 quake; an angel of the Lord descended from heaven; he came to the stone and rolled it away, and sat himself down on it. His face shone like lightning; his garments were 3 white as snow. At the sight of him the guards shook with 4 fear and lay like the dead.

The angel then addressed the women: 'You', he said, 5 'have nothing to fear. I know you are looking for Jesus who was crucified. He is not here; he has been raised 6 again, as he said he would be. Come and see the place where he was laid, and then go quickly and tell his 7 disciples: "He has been raised from the dead and is going on before you into Galilee; there you will see him." That is what I had to tell you.'

They hurried away from the tomb in awe and great 8 joy, and ran to tell the disciples. Suddenly Jesus was there 9 in their path. He gave them his greeting, and they came up and clasped his feet, falling prostrate before him. Then 10 Jesus said to them, 'Do not be afraid. Go and take word to my brothers that they are to leave for Galilee. They will see me there.'

11 The women had started on their way when some of the guard went into the city and reported to the chief priests
12 everything that had happened. After meeting with the elders and conferring together, the chief priests offered
13 the soldiers a substantial bribe and told them to say, 'His disciples came by night and stole the body while we were
14 asleep.' They added, 'If this should reach the Governor's ears, we will put matters right with him and see that you
15 do not suffer.' So they took the money and did as they were told. This story became widely known, and is current in Jewish circles to this day.

16 The eleven disciples made their way to Galilee, to the
17 mountain where Jesus had told them to meet him. When they saw him, they fell prostrate before him, though some
18 were doubtful. Jesus then came up and spoke to them. He said: 'Full authority in heaven and on earth has been
19 committed to me. Go forth therefore and make all nations my disciples; baptize men everywhere in the name of the
20 Father and the Son and the Holy Spirit, and teach them to observe all that I have commanded you. And be assured, I am with you always, to the end of time.'

* 1. *Sunday.* Greek: 'when it was dawning toward the first day of the week'. The reason why Matthew omits Mark's statement (16: 1) that the women intended to anoint the body, is probably because the guard would have prevented this.

2–4. Peculiar to Matthew. Cf. 27: 51 *b* for another earthquake introduced by Matthew.

6. *as he said.* Added by Matthew. Cf. 12: 40; 16: 21; 17: 9, 23; 26: 32.

7. *is going on before you into Galilee.* This refers to the prediction in 26: 32. Matthew has changed the words in Mark 16: 7 'as he told you' to 'that is what I had to tell you' (lit. 'I have told you'), because that prediction was not addressed to the women. The disciples are at present still in Jerusalem.

8. Here Matthew and Luke part company with Mark and go their separate ways. But both agree in omitting Mark's words 'they said nothing to anybody, for they were afraid', with which the genuine text of Mark's Gospel ends (Mark 16: 8). And both Matthew and Luke say that the women went to deliver the message to the disciples.

9. *He gave them his greeting.* Greek: 'saying "Hail"'. The Greek word is the regular greeting.

10. Jesus' message is the same as that of the angel.

11–15. This section is a continuation of 27: 62–6.

the guard of Roman soldiers whom Pilate placed at the disposal of the Sanhedrin take their report to the chief priests.

15. *to this day,* i.e. to the time when the Gospel was written. The same story was still current in A.D. 150 when Justin wrote his Dialogue with Trypho (CXVIII). In the apocryphal Gospel of Peter (*c.* A.D. 165), 11: 46–9, the soldiers and elders report directly to Pilate, and he advises them to keep silent lest the Jewish people stone them all.

16. In Luke and John, Jesus appears to the disciples in Jerusalem: in the last chapter of John (an appendix) in Galilee also.

17. *fell prostrate,* i.e. in worship. They had not done this before the crucifixion.

18–20. The command to baptize. Doubt has been expressed whether Jesus actually uttered these words. There can be no doubt that they stood in the original text of Matthew. The words are found in all the MSS and versions. But the saying may be a construction of the early Church.

18. Cf. 11: 27; and Phil. 2: 9, 'therefore God raised him to the heights and bestowed upon him the name above all names, that at the name of Jesus every knee should bow'.

19. Jesus must have given a command to *baptize*, otherwise we cannot account for the universal practice of baptism in the early Church from the beginning. There is therefore no need to doubt that a genuine utterance of Jesus underlies this passage, though the form it has taken may be due to later development within the Church. It is true there was at first a reluctance to baptize Gentiles (Acts 10 — 11: 18), which is difficult to explain if Jesus had commanded baptism for all the nations. But perhaps the apostles, while accepting the ideal of Jesus, were slow to understand its immediate practical possibility, as they were slow to understand much in Jesus' teaching. Although much in Matthew is Judaistic and anti-Gentile in tone, the Gospel begins and ends by giving prominence to the Gentiles in the world mission, as in chapter 2.

in the name of the Father and the Son and the Holy Spirit. Eusebius gives 'go and make disciples of all nations teaching them in my name', thus making no mention of the threefold Name. But Eusebius was probably not intending an exact quotation, but only a paraphrase. The threefold Name is the genuine text of Matthew, and is evidence that at the time of the writing of his Gospel the threefold Name was coming to be used in baptism in place of the earlier formula 'in the name of the Lord Jesus' (Acts 2: 38; 8: 16, etc.)

in the name. Greek lit. 'into the name'. To baptize into the name means to baptize into the possession, protection and blessing of the Godhead, and to establish a living union between the believer and the Father, the Son and the Holy Spirit.

20. At the beginning of the Gospel stress was laid upon the name of Jesus, 'Emmanuel', 'God with us' (1: 23). That note is taken up again at the end of the Gospel: *I am with you always.* These words express the experience of Christians through the ages. ✻

✻   ✻   ✻   ✻   ✻   ✻   ✻   ✻   ✻   ✻   ✻   ✻   ✻

INDEX AND GLOSSARY

The references are to pages.